Coaching Presence

Coaching Presence

Understanding the power of the non-verbal relationship

Tünde Erdös

 Open University Press

Open University Press
8th Floor, 338 Euston Road
London
England
NW1 3BH

email: enquiries@openup.co.uk
world wide web: www.openup.co.uk

First edition published 2021

Copyright © Open International Publishing Limited, 2021

All rights reserved. Except for the quotation of short passages for the purposes of criticism and review, no part of this publication may be reproduced, stored in a retrieval system, or transmitted, in any form or by any means, electronic, mechanical, photocopying, recording or otherwise, without the prior written permission of the publisher or a licence from the Copyright Licensing Agency Limited. Details of such licences (for reprographic reproduction) may be obtained from the Copyright Licensing Agency Ltd of Saffron House, 6–10 Kirby Street, London EC1N 8TS.

A catalogue record of this book is available from the British Library

ISBN-13: 9780335249657
ISBN-10: 0335249655
eISBN: 9780335249664

Library of Congress Cataloging-in-Publication Data
CIP data applied for

Typeset by Transforma Pvt. Ltd., Chennai, India

Fictitious names of companies, products, people, characters and/or data that may be used herein (in case studies or in examples) are not intended to represent any real individual, company, product or event.

Praise page

Coaching Presence is a remarkable work that reveals the extant literature on this topic and its relationship to Tünde's innovative research study on synchronicity between coaches and their clients. Extending this work further, she masterfully weaves the past and present into strategies and tips to enhance your coaching.
Joel A. DiGirolamo, International Coaching Federation Director of Coaching Science

WBECS is delighted to have been able to help support Tunde in her research to complete this valuable work on the importance of presence in the coaching experience. We honour the work that is being done to further the support of coaching as a highly ethical profession that continues to develop and promote standards of excellence in the field.
Marva Sadler, CEO, WBECS Group

In Coaching Presence: Understanding the power of the non-verbal relationship, Tünde Erdös takes the reader on an exciting journey of discovery. She examines the coaching presence from the coachee's perspective, whilst simultaneously encouraging the coach to learn more about presence. This insightful book will help coaches to reflect on and enhance their practice.
Prof Stephen Palmer, Wales Academy for Professional Practice and Applied Research, University of Wales Trinity Saint David, UK

At HEC Paris, after training Executive coaches for 20 years, we have observed that developing an effective coaching posture is more difficult than learning any tools. The participants of our Global Executive Coaching Program are lucky to have Tünde helping them work on coaching presence in class. Tünde knows how to facilitate an amazing learning experience that combines feelings, practice and structure, regardless of the participants' culture. This book includes many high-quality and universal components to help professional coaches to make valuable progress.
Patrick Delamaire, co-developer of the Global Executive Coaching Program at HEC Paris

To the beauty of the flow in life

Contents

Acknowledgements xi
Foreword xii

INTRODUCTION 1
    Finding the fit of this book 1

PART I – Laying the foundation 7

1 WHEN THE DOORBELL RINGS, IT'D BETTER RING A BELL –
FORMING THROUGH A CLIENT 9
    Introduction 9

2 WHAT DO WE MEAN BY PRESENCE ANYWAY? – FORMING THROUGH
SOME REALITIES AND MYTHS 13
    Introduction 13

3 HOW MOVEMENT SYNCHRONY EMBODIES YOUR PRESENCE – FORMING
THROUGH EVIDENCE BASE 27
    Introduction 27
    Formulating concepts and finding qualitative wisdom 28
    Fusing movement synchrony, self-regulation, and goal
    attainment in coaching presence 36
    Framing the quantitative results 47

PART II – Framing the findings in practice 55

4 INTEGRATIVE PRESENCE – FRAMING THE FINDINGS WITH
A METHODOLOGY AND PHILOSOPHY 57
    Introduction 57

5 SOMATIC THINKING – FRAMING THE FINDINGS WITH
DELIBERATE PRACTICE 71
    Introduction 71

PART III – Feeding the findings with participants' voices　　　83

6　FEEDING IN COACHES' VOICES　　　85

From masquerades to just be whatever comes to the surface　　　85
The journey of presence: From having to being　　　89
The dance of caring and daring　　　92

7　FEEDING IN CLIENTS' VOICES　　　97

What is life about, so to speak?　　　97
Permission to dream　　　101
Reborn through being　　　105

8　FEEDING IN THE RESEARCHER'S VOICE　　　109

Answering the door: My journey of meeting with
my mentor – serendipity　　　109

PART IV – Fusing Integrative Presence into wider fields of practice　　　115

9　FUTURE FLOWERING OF COACHING TRAINING PROGRAMMES　　　117

Introduction　　　117

10　FACETING LEADERSHIP – THE FOCUS OF INTEGRATIVE PRESENCE　　　124

Introduction　　　124

Forging final reflections　　　131

Introduction　　　131

Further Reading　　　141
References　　　143
Index　　　154

Acknowledgements

I feel deep gratitude to those who accompany me on my professional and personal journey. Their contributions are rich and I acknowledge these contributions as generous gifts on the path for us to travel. In particular, I would like to thank the following companions.

Professor Dr Erik de Haan, Professor Dr Joshua Wilt, and Professor Dr Svetlana N Khapova have shared their valuable experience and ethical approach to evidence-based practice with me. I appreciate the significant contribution that Professor Dr Fabian Ramseyer has made to expand my perspective of process research through the use of technology.

Professor Dr Stefan Heusinkveld, Professor Dr Maria Tims, Niki Konijn and Michael Tichelmann whose co-ordination support and technical consultations have been invaluable in keeping me on track and inspired me to finalize the research project, without which this book would not be possible.

Angelis Iglesias at Applied Sciences Publications, Fer van den Boomen at TvB, Liz Hall at Coaching@Work, David Brode at NOBCO (nederlandse orde van beropescoaches), Sijtze de Roos at ANSE (Association of National Organisations for Supervision in Europe), Joel DiGirolamo at ICF (International Coaching Federation), Marva Sadler at World Business and Executive Coach Summit (WBECS), Irene Sobolevska at EMCC (European Mentoring and Coaching Council), Jeffrey Hull at Institute of Coaching, Mclean Hospital, a Harvard Medical School Affiliate as well as representatives of LVSC (Landelijke Vereniging voor Supervisie en Coaching), and APAC (Asia Pacific Alliance of Coaches) who offered a professional platform and perspectives in our discipline that significantly influenced the direction of this book. I would also like to thank Vrije Universiteit Amsterdam (VU), Amsterdam Business Research Institute (ABRI), NL and Case Western Reserve University (CWRU), and the Department of Psychology, Cleveland, Ohio, USA.

Laura Pacey and Clara Heathcock at McGraw Hill whose trust in our collaboration and delightful clarity of purpose as well as gentleness gave this book a consistent drive and urged me forward.

Martin F. Tichelmann who supported my work in the pre-book phase, made space for me to create awareness for my passion and the theme of the book internationally, while putting up with having the project invade our life and home for longer than he ever imagined.

Claire Venetsanakou, whose sense of caring and depth challenged my sense of caring and depth, and all the coaches and clients who made the research project possible and buoyed me during the writing process.

My dear mother, father, and brother who have encouraged me in this and in all of my other major transitions in life.

Tünde Erdös
Eichgraben, Austria
October 2020

Foreword

A very 'present' book, bursting with energy

Here is a new writer bursting forth on the stage with energy, passion and commitment. The topic of the book is knowing yourself in the moment, knowing something about your own presence with your clients. 'Only when we know our limits, can we grow beyond them', the writer puts forward and then goes on to investigate those limits we may all experience, the limits to having a firm knowledge of our own presence. I think this is a bold and daring book that will help us to overcome those limitations, at least in part. It shows great courage to study the intensely subjective and co-created phenomenon of presence. It also shows an equal amount of tenacity to move slowly toward beginning an objective understanding of this presence. I think her presence as a writer is congruent with her discoveries around presence as a coach. She knows no limits. She moves on boldly in waves and waves of assertions, counter-assertions, different ways of describing the same topic, and dives deeply dive into the inspiration of popular culture and venerable theory, an unstoppable stream of consciousness that in the end gives us a new understanding of the phenomenon of our co-created presence as coaches.

I have had the privilege of working with Tünde from her first tentative steps in the coaching profession, or should I say her first stampedes: blasts of consummate activity and boundary testing, driven by a passion to understand, to know and to master. I am very proud to see her arriving at this stage, where she completes her PhD and manages her first book just in the same way as she managed her first coaching sessions and relationships with peer coaches: with unstoppable, raw, passionate energy and with an unmistakable, overwhelming, deliberate presence knocking loudly at the door of established knowledge and academia. Well done Tünde, for mustering and channelling so much energy, and for completing the ambitious project that you set out to do. Well done for bringing us this passionately disturbing, engaging, whirlwind of a text on the topic of coaching presence. You describe as well as demonstrate how our presence is always determined by what we receive back in relationship, and what we can read in the mirror of the other person with whom we are present.

Knowing Tünde, I am not in the least surprised she has written a book for 'you to know, push and grow beyond your limits when being present with your clients', because that is, in my experience, what Tünde does every day. The sheer urge to be present, to listen and speak, the push to be lively and present gushes from every page and sometimes leads to oxymorons that barely contain their meaning but pique one's interest, such as the 'solid glimpse', the 'walk away building up', the 'embodied cognition', or the 'steady dance'.

I really liked the free and open observation of the phenomena at stake, making use of excellent, revealing case studies, of sincere introspection, parables, scholarly thinking and empirical research to grow an ever-greater understanding in the minds of readers of this relational dance called presence. I wish the book a well-deserved, prominent presence in the minds of practising coaches so that they too can grow their presence with their clients, following its kind guidance.

Erik de Haan
London
August 2020

Introduction

Finding the fit of this book

Observing the professional business arena

Watching the tenth World Business and Executive Coach Summit (WBECS), which you can now access directly all year-round, through an interactive and digital learning experience delivered by coaching industry leaders, I am in awe at what coaches have been able to achieve over the past 25 years since coaching was first regarded as a potentially relevant field of practice in the mid-1990s. At the world's leading learning platform for business and executive coaches, professional coaches push the boundaries of the coaching business. Training and practising for many years, some even for decades, they have worked very hard to be at the peak of their abilities in the coaching industry. Indeed, progress in coaching as a business is incredible to witness beyond WBECS.

Observing the free-rider practitioner arena

While I immersed myself in the WBECS summit experience, I hear – mostly from life coaches – that doing a coach certification is not necessary to be successful and well paid. First, these coaches claim that you do not need a certifying body to give permission to support clients in achieving their goals and dreams. Second, these life coaches believe that what they refer to as the coaching industry – worth $1 billion, according to Forbes, and the second fastest growing industry behind IT, according to the *National Post* – is holding a lot of people back from making the impact they want to make in the world. Third, these life coaches suggest that most people become a coach because they have a big heart and a huge desire to help people. Therefore, you had better forget the idea that you need a special certification to become a coach.

These assumptions and statements contrast with more than two decades of coaching research (Turner and Passmore, 2018) indicating that coaching can involve complex conversations that go beyond reaching goals. In most cases, coaching includes successfully dealing with complex issues of:

- identity and morality
- personal, professional and ethical dilemmas
- intrapersonal and interpersonal conflicts
- enhanced performance in moments of crisis.

Coaching does not have an independent regulatory body that sets and monitors professional standards, therefore, some coaches see no value in assuming responsibility to serve their clients with solid training, continuous further development and evidence-based practice. It resembles the animated movie

Ratatouille, 2007[1] where the garbage boy is helped by the rat to prepare the award-winning dish; the common belief being '*anyone can cook*'.

Observing my professional practice through a client's lens

In late 2016, when I had reached a peak in my coaching career, a client asked me early on in our coaching engagement, 'When you say you understand me, how come your body goes backward?' My heart raced. Didn't I understand my clients well enough yet? What was my client showing me that I couldn't grasp? I am a Master Certified Coach (MCC).[2] Why was this happening to me?

I was reminded that when we believe we know what is 'good' coaching practice, then we are probably the wicked queen in Snow White and the Seven Dwarfs, the fairy tale of the Brothers Grimm,[3] who is obsessed with asking the mirror: 'Mirror, mirror on the wall, who is the fairest of them all?' What if the mirror told the queen that she was not gentle enough? Would the queen listen? If the queen refused to listen, she would be trapped in what I refer to as the Snow White Phenomenon© (Erdös and Angelis, 2020). It implies that it is difficult for the queen to be objective about her beauty or, for that matter, her own faults.

I did not want to be the queen in the fairy tale. My client's well-articulated question prompted me to become curious about an emerging phenomenon in my coaching relationships: presence. What followed was some deep relational feedback in our engagement, an extensive reflective enquiry into my practice, and some research on coaching presence through movement synchrony[4] as the 'unspoken' element in the coach–client relationship.

Three observations – One conclusion

On the one hand, we spend significant amounts of money on robust coaching training, which is completely necessary and valuable, unless the programme is delivered by pseudo-credentialling mills without professionalism featuring anywhere on their training agenda. On the other hand, many coaches hold the view that you do not need to be trained in coaching, least of all in coaching presence. After all, 'presence' is 'something you either have or you don't. It's not possible to research presence, and what for?' While it is certainly true that trained competences will not replace a coach's talent and that it does not take trained competences to be a talented coach, talent alone will not satisfy the

---

1 *Ratatouille* (2007) [DVD] Directed by Brad Bird. Burbank, CA: Walt Disney Home Entertainment.
2 For credentialling requirements, see also: https://coachfederation.org/icf-credential/mcc-path
3 Grimm, J. and Grimm, W. (1972) *Snow White and the Seven Dwarfs* (trans. from German by R. Jarrell), New York: Farrar, Straus, and Giroux.
4 The terms 'movement synchrony' and 'non-verbal behavioural exchanges' are used interchangeably for the purposes of this book. See Chapter 3 for a definition of the term 'movement synchrony'.

requirements of acquiring and working with professional competences. The issue is that while we have wisdom through individual experience, we do not really know what presence involves, nor do we have any understanding or evidence about how it impacts on our clients' learning and growth. What is our commitment to accountability in coaching?

In our quest to be at the peak of the coaching industry, we are pushing the boundaries of coaching as a business but what are we doing to push the boundaries of professional coaching performance? Being at the top in the coaching business and acting with professional maturity by applying a solid evidence base, practical wisdom and competence-based knowledge are two separate issues.

I believe that we can replicate high standards and achieve better consistency when serving our clients by:

- following up client feedback with research, and
- applying coaching practices based on a feedback-driven empirical evidence base.

We need to push the boundaries of our professional coaching performance and implement our learning when we return to our coaching room and are placed in the heat of the moment in our practice. In order to do this, we need to adopt:

- an experiential learning attitude with clients to replicate wisdom, and
- a conceptual, rational and intellectual attitude to generate knowledge.

The way forward

In this book I put forward the view that understanding the flaws in our attachment to and detachment from the concepts of presence that are not supported by research is the key to our individual and professional maturity. Neither infatuation with any specific presence model, nor a belligerent attitude that fights certification, training and an evidence base is particularly coach-like. Indeed, both approaches offer fundamentalist views. One of the major issues in coaching is that coaches have fundamentalist views about their practice. Being unaware of any extremism in their ideals is a danger to clients' development (Iordanou and Williams, 2017).

I contend that holding our wisdom and knowledge about coaching presence lightly and putting both on a solid evidence base, while exposing ourselves to client feedback, will free up enough space for coaches to become genuinely curious about how we can push the boundaries of professional coaching performance in a sustainable manner. Only when we know our limits can we grow beyond them. How can we 'know our limits' without being trained in coaching standards, evidence base and professional ethics?

Holding our practice lightly also means that we become aware that neither coaching nor presence is about the 'coach' but the partnering process and the impact presence has on clients' learning. In other words, the 'I' attitude of 'I do not need training to be a good coach' or 'my business is thriving so I am a good coach' implies, in my opinion, that we do not care about what our clients need.

This book is designed to give you a solid glimpse into what our clients, rather than coaches, need when it comes to coaching presence. Rolling out presence as a core competence as I uncovered it experientially with my client and investigated it to build an evidence base, this book invites you to know, push and grow beyond your limits when being present with your clients. While anyone can learn how to be present, it is hard work rather than a given and its impact on our clients is more complex than we think. Adopting this awareness for our scope of competences when practising coaching presence means that we are becoming individually and professionally mature. The aim is to avoid doing harm to anyone who has a stake in the coaching engagement. This is one of the core ethical principles all professional coaching bodies have agreed on (Iordanou and Williams, 2017).

The structure of this book

Part I of this book starts by describing how I first became interested in presence. The book moves on to consider a number of well-known concepts concerning presence. In doing so, it brings together the fields of knowledge that fill entire libraries, exploring presence-specific concepts discussed in this book. While I am aware that I might be going beyond my scope of competence in fields such as psychotherapy, neuroscience, behavioural and cognitive sciences, philosophy of the mind, social sciences, and spirituality, my intention is to highlight the complexity of presence as a phenomenological skill. Finally, Part I covers the unprecedented and truly unexpected outcomes of the research as well as the relevance of these outcomes for both our coaching practice and our clients.

Part II explores the research findings covered in Part I to produce learning that can be channelled back into practice. It is partly co-authored with Samer Hassan, a highly experienced executive coach and martial arts practitioner, who complements research findings with Somatic Thinking as a set of deliberate practices that you can use to develop and enhance your presence in coaching. It also rolls out a unique philosophical and methodological framework of presence that coaches can apply as a conceptual umbrella in their practice.

In Part III, we hear from three coaches and three clients about their experience of presence through a research project which aimed to look at how their experiential learning can enhance our understanding of presence, an area which has been poorly researched to date. Additionally, I relate how my own experiential journey transformed me as a practitioner through the lens of a researcher. The coaches and clients speak about the impact the research process has had on our coaching practice and the wider coaching community.

Part IV identifies ways in which findings can be passed on in training programmes and applied to leadership. It also generates new questions that can be further elaborated in practice and explored in research.

The matryoshka – The pivot of our progress as practitioners

The truth about presence, and coaching more generally, is concealed within many layers of meaning. Both are complex processes that unfold layer by layer, like the Russian Matryoshka doll.[5] Arguably the best-known symbol of Russia, it represents the manifold facets of coaching presence by integrating:

- *respect* for existing knowledge and wisdom as we stand on giants' shoulders
- *unity* of related concepts of presence
- *abundance* of concepts of presence
- *search for truth* and meaning of presence.

In fact, every client brings their micro-cosmos of interconnected issues and relationships into the coaching room. The same holds true for coaches. Both are embedded in an even larger complexity of global interconnectedness. Understanding the dynamics of presence in its complexity becomes a relevant skill to master presence in its integrity. This will increase our credibility with clients which is essential as it is our clients who pay our bills.

---

5   Roosevelt, P. (2004) 'Martyoshka doll', in J.R. Millar (ed.) *Encyclopedia of Russian History*, vol. 3. New York: Macmillan Reference USA.

Part I

Laying the foundation

Part I addresses the meaning of presence as a core coaching competence. As we have not yet explored how presence impacts on clients' learning and growth, coaches may have a flawed idea of what it is to be present and how it affects what clients want to achieve. Therefore, I examine the need to update our way of viewing presence if we are to advance our level of expertise. I will start by introducing my knowledge based on my experience, and I will close by putting forward some evidence investigating presence as expressive of body movement synchrony as a specific type of non-verbal synchrony.

My aim in Part I is that you gain an understanding that presence is not about the coach. This might not be obvious but it is one that appears to be the most relevant for clients and coaching effectiveness.

When the doorbell rings, it'd better ring a bell – Forming through a client

Introduction

The story of the story of doing research

This is not a case study. Rather, it is a true story about what happened to me as an experienced executive coach. How could a well-established and triple-credentialed executive coach with a Masters in Executive Coaching miss the point of a core competence that was the foundation of mastery in coaching? I remember feeling grateful to my client and genuinely inspired to find an answer to the question: What do I need to do to improve my understanding of coaching?

Hearing the doorbell ring

> One day in 2017 I had a female client. Let us call her Maria. Maria is a talented mechanical engineer. She has just been promoted to a senior sales position and put in charge of a major market in her industry. Maria signs herself up for coaching and her CEO supports her learning because he has high hopes for her in the company. Maria agrees to see me for 10 sessions, each lasting 2 hours. We clarify her goals and agree to have feedback sessions with her CEO, colleagues and customers. We set the boundaries, clarify the way she wishes to achieve her goals and engage in productive reflection on her challenging questions. We also use learning frames and pay attention to her progress. Long story short, the coaching engagement is set up according to plan, however, there is a problem.
>
> From time to time, still early on in the coaching engagement, Maria asks, 'Do you understand what I mean?' While I might nod my head to this question, it seems that it has not convinced her so I ask, 'Why do you ask this question?' Maria is surprised as she has not noticed herself asking that question and she cannot explain it either. We agree to consider it the next time that she asks the question.

> That is the moment when I start asking myself the question, 'Where am I with this client? Where is me *being* in this relationship? What is the unspoken text that seems to operate between Maria and me? What is the unspoken text that seems to leave us with such a big question mark?'
>
> Meanwhile, Maria makes huge progress with applying her learning and getting positive feedback from her CEO for being assertive in her new senior sales management position.
>
> Paradoxically, in the third session, Maria suggests that she would like to opt out of coaching despite being recognized for her achievements. I listen to her and say, 'Maria, do I understand you correctly? Are you missing me in this relationship?' Her eyes brighten and she replies, 'Tünde, you are doing such a fabulous job and I am so amazed at the progress we are making. I am getting what I want and what the company wants and yet I feel so alone.' I take that up and say, 'Do you want to dance with me?' at which she chuckles and I continue: 'Would you be willing to find out how we can *be* with each other for a change?' Maria replies, 'I think, yes. I appreciate you but I wonder who you are.' I note that she does not refer to my résumé. At that point I realize that she means I am not present for her.
>
> We agree to meet again and I suggest that we change tack. I ask her to think of a goal for next time and a question that she wants to explore. I also ask her to imagine the place where she would like to go to explore that question.

Before I disclose how the story ends, I would like to explore my experience of being with Maria. I reflect on Maria's comment, 'I feel so alone.' I wondered how it was that nodding my head did not resonate with her. Nodding my head was about signalling understanding, wasn't it? I was showing her that I was with her, wasn't I? I came to realize that while I might have been nodding my head, the nodding did not come spontaneously. Maria might have perceived a time lag which was too long for her to trust.

You may be familiar with this experience when you feel grateful to your partner but you do not express your gratitude at the time. You may think it is not necessary, or that you feel awkward for saying it. Later, when you say thank you, it somehow does not resonate with them. Perhaps a late expression of gratitude is not effective because it is not effortless: you might have considered your gratitude for some time, which is different to how you might spontaneously thank them in the moment. There is no effort, no contemplation involved. It is spontaneous. It is in the moment. It comes with ease.

Reflecting on my spontaneous responsiveness, it surprised me that the time lag could not have been very long but it still had a huge impact on how Maria felt about being with me. I asked myself, 'What is being present?'

I did not feel that it was the way we mimic each other or parrot the client either verbally or non-verbally. Would it not imply wanting to consciously imitate them to potentially 'manipulate' their thoughts or actions? As Maria became sensitive to some incongruence between my words and my physical responses,

When the doorbell rings, it'd better ring a bell – Forming through a client 11

I was hooked on the idea of exploring how we can become sensitive to our clients' needs as well as our responsiveness at the non-verbal level. I discovered my pet peeve: the unspoken text operating between coach and client, which I later dubbed 'the spontaneous non-verbal responsiveness and its potential effects on clients in the coaching relationship'. What was that? Presence? The International Coaching Federation (ICF) defines presence as 'The ability to be fully conscious and create a spontaneous relationship with the client, employing a style that is open, flexible and confident.'[1]

I was curious how my hunch about the essence of spontaneous responsiveness might unfold in my next session with Maria. Would I be open to the powerful energies dancing around us? Maria wanted our next session to take place on the shores of a lake outside the city where she works and lives. What happened next is described below.

> Maria wanted to explore why she might feel rejected by some figures of authority and how she could learn to cope with that. I ask her why she had chosen this particular location, and she says that 'she likes looking at the ripples of water from the shores and enjoys the trees around her'. We start investigating her sense of rejection and I ask her to look at the water to see how the ripples might affect her.
>
> So there we are standing on a slight hill some 50 metres away from the shore when two people walk past us from the right. Well, there is nothing unusual about that. Some other people had passed by us before. However, the special thing about this couple is that they are naked. Now this is a public place and not a nudist beach where you would expect people to be running around naked. I spot the couple, and I feel my head turn to the right – where Maria is standing next to me – and I see her turn her head to meet my eyes and we burst out laughing. In the moment. No premeditation, no thinking, no nothing. Just *being* there with her. That goes on for a while before Maria says to me, 'Tünde, thank you. This is so liberating to know that you respond the same way as I do.' We both know that we are not laughing at the people but that we are amused by the strangeness of the situation: it is so weird, so out of place that we cannot help ourselves but burst into hearty laughter. So, creating this spontaneous lightness in a moment without first checking 'will it be appropriate to laugh with Maria being in her centring exercise' turns out to be a pivotal moment that transforms our relationship. We manage to experience a wonderful dance in the moment.

In hindsight, the critical moment that I experienced in my coaching engagement with Maria was like a doorbell ringing, 'I want to investigate "presence".' I realized that I barely understood this key core competence despite my

---

1 https://coachfederation.org/blog/from-the-toolbox-the-challenge-of-coaching-presence

long-standing practice and business success. Arriving at a definition through reflective enquiry and experiential wisdom set the stage for the next question: how can I measure spontaneous non-verbal responsiveness?

To conclude, I have shared this story to illustrate that paying attention to our clients' coaching experiences and openly receiving relational feedback from them can help us know and grow beyond our limits. It will inspire us to engage in some sort of research towards enhancing our individual and professional maturity which is important because, after all, it is our clients who pay our bills.

2 What do we mean by presence anyway? – Forming through some realities and myths

Introduction

The need to reflect the way you think about presence

> **The man who loved dragons – A traditional Chinese parable**
>
> *(Adapted from Steve Chapman[1])*
>
> Once upon a time there was a man who loved dragons, had dragon curtains, pictures of dragons on every wall of his house. He wore a dragon tie and had a dragon screensaver on his computer next to his dragon mouse mat. He would even dream of dragons in his dragon pajamas.
>
> One day, the queen of the dragons thought she would say hi to this man who loved dragons. She flew to his village, landed outside his dragon-shaped house and knocked on the door. The man opened the door and, on seeing a *real* dragon standing right in front of him, screamed and ran for the hills. The queen was confused and a little upset. When she returned to her kingdom, she told her wise friend about the man. Her wise friend explained to her that this was a man who liked the *idea* of dragons but not dragons themselves!

The story addresses a root question: how do you know that your presence is not just a figment of your imagination? It is a question that you can neither prove nor disprove. It invites you to ask yourself: 'How do I know where my mind stops and the world begins out there?' Someone having a hallucination is as convinced about what they are experiencing as I am convinced about typing these letters here. So, ignoring what presence may be about in its various

---

1 https://canscorpionssmoke.com/2017/11/28/man-loved-dragons-rhetoric-meets-reality/

shapes and forms implies failing to make meaning of it or making meaning of something you ignore. Loving presence the way the man loved dragons does not mean you master presence. What are the consequences for your coach–client relationships?

The realities and myths around presence – Where two paths converge

Distinguishing between realities and myths in terms of presence is a matter of choice. As I value the quality of distinction, I choose these paths (adapted from Grant, 2017) to characterize presence as:

- an empirical body of knowledge referred to as realities (seven realities), and
- professional wisdom referred to as myths (eight myths).

Both realities and myths form one landscape for defining presence, and I fully acknowledge that both paths have a good place in our practice. The point of this landscape is not to be exhaustive and all-encompassing or reductionist but rather to serve as an anchor and inspire what I hope will be a rich and reasoned discourse about coaching presence. The concepts selected for either path might diverge or interrelate, and even overlap. In doing so, they invite us to develop a keen eye for identifying some subtle practices in presence. However, neither concept is better or worse, as I believe that this attitude has no place in our coaching practice. Instead, by pulling these concepts together, I aim to problematize presence in its richness to refine our understanding of its complexity: body-self, body-mind, cognitive processes, emotions, verbal and non-verbal responses, energy flow, and external influences.

As there is no theatre play without a theatre stage, we also need a definition of coaching in the context of presence to set the stage for a reasoned discourse about presence. The following definition appears suitable as it allows space to develop our understanding of presence based on subtle practices of felt experience (Gendlin, 2003a): 'Coaching is a human development process that involves structured, focused interaction, and the use of appropriate strategies, tools and techniques to promote desirable and sustainable change for the benefit of the coachee and potentially for other stakeholders' (Bachkirova, Cox, and Clutterbuck, 2014, p. 1).

The essence of realities – Vehicles of broader knowledge base

In coaching, formal research aims to produce a generalizable evidence base and build theory (Grant, 2017) for a broader empirical body of knowledge and reliable replicable realities.

Unlike in medical contexts where the evidence-base paradigm dictates that formal research should inform practice following prescribed regimes, some coaching scholars (Drake, 2009; Grant, 2017) argue that we need to flexibly translate the realities of formal research into coaching practice. This flexibility is best reflected in a recent definition of coaching evidence base as: 'An intelligent and conscientious use of relevant and best current knowledge integrated with professional practitioner expertise in making decisions about how to deliver coaching to coaching clients and in designing and delivering coach training programs' (Grant, 2017, p. 64).

While we need the convergence of both paths to ultimately build an evidence base in coaching presence, we need to keep in mind that, as Grant (2017) argues, each path pursues a different purpose and hence will produce different contributions to how we can understand presence.

The essence of myths – Containers of supreme truths

A quick search for a definition in the Merriam Webster dictionary reveals that a myth is a story '… that serves to unfold part of the world view of a people or explain a practice, belief, or natural phenomenon' or 'a popular belief or tradition that has grown up around something or someone'.[2] Essentially, myths fill the gap between what we experience as a narrative and the experience that we have no quantifiable evidence for. While the term is widely used with negative connotations to imply that a narrative is not objectively true, I view myths as 'storied vehicles of supreme truth, the most basic and important truths of all. By them people regulate and interpret their lives and find worth and purpose in their existence. Myths put one in touch with sacred realities, the fundamental sources of being, power, and truth' (Hyers, 1984, p. 107).

For the purpose of this book, myths comprise all the individual and group experiences we collect about what works and what does not work in coaching. They constitute professional wisdom from self-enquiry (Argyris, Putnam and Smith, 1985) and practitioner experience, all of which serves to improve our performance from a practical point of view.

Landscape of presence for a timeless practice

Each reality and myth laid out in the landscape of presence is accompanied by a reflective question to prompt a reality check: what can we potentially add to each concept to extend our thinking around presence? I hate to tell you but keeping the entire problem in mind while working on its individual parts is all that ever works.

Landscape of seven contemporary realities of presence

Reality #1 – Presence is about clients' embodied mind focusing

Literature on coaching is relatively devoid of any mention of the body. It is as if the body does not play a part in coaching practice (Jackson, 2017). However,

---

2 Merriam-Webster. (n.d.). Myth. In Merriam-Webster.com dictionary. Available at: https://www.merriam-webster.com/dictionary/myth (accessed 15 September 2020).

some coaching scientists (Silsbee, 2008) claim that experience is carried in the body and is expressed in the here and now of a situation (Whitworth et al., 2007). For instance, we might sense when we feel anger as our voice becomes tense or when our throat needs clearing in a discussion.

The past two decades have seen interesting developments. While emotional intelligence and social intelligence have been on the rise in business, the absence of the body in coaching literature is somewhat reminiscent of Descartes'[3] position that thinking is more important than feeling and that the requirement for rationality is still strong in our world (Hamill, 2013). Actually, we have support for the embodied mind perspective from some neuroscientists (Cockburn, 2001; Pert, 1997; Tallis, 2011) claiming that the body is inseparable from our thought processes. These scientists connect the concept of our embodied mind experiences of ourselves to our wider biological heritage, closer environment, wider community and even humanity. Even some supporters of embodied artificial intelligence (Pfeifer and Bongard, 2007) in robotics (IBM's Deep Blue, the chess supercomputer, against Gary Kasparov[4]) show that AI can only be achieved by machines that have sensory and motor skills and are connected to the world through the body.

The embodied mind focus approach to presence implies working with the whole self (Hamill, 2013), including the felt sense (Gendlin, 2003a; Madison, 2012). On experiencing some shift in the body, we bring about a change in how we understand ourselves and others: in detail, the body shapes our perception, which shapes our emotion, which shapes our thinking, which shapes our behaviour. Somatic awareness researchers in coaching (Hunt, 2009; Jackson, 2017; Kennedy, 2013; Stoneham, 2009) and coaching theorists (Silsbee, 2008; Strean and Strozzi-Heckler, 2009; Strozzi-Heckler, 2014) argue that this is possible because the self (mind) and the body are one and the same. So, presence is about supporting the client's process of becoming whole and developing self-cultivation.

Reality check:

> Where and how does the 'body-shapes-perception-shapes-emotion-shapes-thinking-shapes-behaviour' paradigm play out in the coach-client relationship? Where does my 'whole self' meet my client's 'whole self'?

---

3 Damasio, A. (1994). *Descartes' Error: Emotions, Reason, and the Human Brain.* Revised edition. London: Vintage Books.
4 IBM project Deep Blue (1997): Garry Kasparov and Deep Blue in two six-game human-computer chess matches.

Reality #2 – Presence is about working with energy flow

We know from Einstein[5] in physics that energy is matter and matter is energy and that matter consists of particles and energetic waves. Matter and energy are completely interchangeable. For instance, coaches often work with clients' moods as an expression of energy by inviting clients to notice what their mood is and where it is lodged in the body and how that particular mood shapes how they see the world and what they feel like doing and thinking as a result of that mood (see also Reality #1). This embodied-self approach involves the flow of emotional and psychological states either in the coach or in the client (Jackson, 2017).

Bioenergetics is a well-researched discipline and scientists are engaged in developing our understanding of how the body retains emotional and psychological traits (Cotter, 1996; Lowen, 1994). Using the language of the body to treat the problems of the mind can release tensions in the body. The energy flow can be deblocked in the body through some sort of physical exercise. Bioenergetically, lack of energy stems from chronic muscular tensions. Tensions are a condition that result from suppressed feelings and can be associated with either personality traits, behaviour patterns or emotional states. It is argued that identifying and working with how the body functions energetically and how it determines what we feel, think, and do has a liberating effect on emotional, physical, and psychic distress.

Reality check:

> How does my energy flow impact on how my client's energy flow can develop in the here and now of our coaching sessions?

Reality #3 – Presence as clients' attunement to their transpersonal system

In integral coaching (Hunt, 2009) as a methodology intended to be the most comprehensive response to human life, the central tenet is that in order to generate a lasting impact on another human being, we need to fully understand the forces that construct and course through a human being's life: the inward and outward manifestation of development beyond the individual's personal system.

Integral coaching is grounded in integral theory (Wilber, 2000, 2006), which describes three types of forces as part of a transpersonal system in which a human being develops:

- the gross realm: non-living forces, such as gravity, electromagnetic and nuclear forces
- the subtle realm: lived forces such as sexual, psychic and emotional forces

---

5 Calaprice, A. (2011) *The Ultimate Quotable Einstein*. Princeton, NJ: Princeton University Press, p. 366.

- the causal realm: forces that emerge in deep sleep as 'a vast, infinite almost over-mental consciousness' (2000, p. 38).

When it comes to coaching presence, we mostly work with what Wilber refers to as the subtle realm.

Some integral coaching researchers (Divine, 2009; Stoneham, 2009) have investigated their clients' level of attunement to how they interact with their complex world. They found that being in touch with their physical and emotional states has an impact on the environment in which clients work.

Reality check:

> How does my transpersonal system impact on how my client's transpersonal system can develop in the here and now of our coaching sessions?

Reality #4 – Presence as clean language and symbolic modelling

Developed by counselling psychologist David Grove[6] in the 1980s as a result of his work with trauma patients, clean language is a practice that focuses clients' awareness on their 'here and now' experience about themselves, instead of asking clients to describe their issues based on past experience. The idea is to use clients' own language that is clean of any interpretations, advice, criticism, leading or loaded questions, suggestions, metaphors, words or thoughts, symbols and meaning-making coming from the coach. Clients create their embodied metaphors and the coach guides them through the exploration of their metaphors by paying attention to patterns in the metaphor and how clients organize their ideas and how ideas interact in the metaphors they create.

It was found that without shifting the metaphors clients create, their embodied mind is likely to keep on working within the paradigm of the very metaphors created, clean language formed the basis for symbolic modelling in coaching (Lawley and Tompkins, 2000). The aim was to expand on clients' capacity to develop transformative coping strategies. It is a progressive questioning technique to design a metaphor landscape using clients' exact words. The coach works with the metaphors generated by clients to clarify their specific beliefs, goals, values, conflicts, skills, behaviour style and sense of self in the landscape of their metaphors to bring about meaningful change on cognitive, affective and behavioural levels. To date, this technique has been well researched in coaching (Doyle and McDowall, 2015), in social settings (Fetterman and Robinson, 2014) and psychotherapy (Rees and Manea, 2016) to provide solid evidence base.

---

6 Lawley, J. and Tompkins, P. (2000) *Metaphors in Mind: Transformation Through Symbolic Modelling.* London: Developing Company Press.

Reality check:

> How do I know that clean language and symbolic modelling as an isolated bubble of systematic questioning meet my client's need in the 'here and now' of their interaction with me?

Reality #5 – Presence is about rehearsing new behaviours

In the behavioural coaching literature, some scholars (Hawkins and Smith, 2013; Peterson, 2006; Strozzi-Heckler, 2014) argue that rehearsal in coaching can enable clients to take action. The idea is that if clients can physically act out possible behaviours associated with some insight they gain through somatic experiences in coaching, they can transfer this insight into their life space. Making new patterns habitual receives support in the following fields:

- Somatic leadership coaching (Hamill, 2013), which encourages practice of physical behaviours associated with a newly gained somatic experience.
- Integral coaching (Hunt, 2009), where the client's 'New Way of Being' (NWB) is enacted to replace the 'Current Way of Being' (CWB).
- Systemic coaching (Whittington, 2012), where representatives of the client's problem system enact a specific systemic scenario by feeling and saying whatever is pertinent to the client as the issue holder.
- Gestalt coaching (Cremona, 2010), which uses the 'empty chair' technique to have the empty chair represent clients and visualize clients' emotional responses.
- Multiple perspective taking (Harding, 2006) in the coaching room.

Reality check:

> While enacting new behaviours, how to ensure that my client's new lived experience is not just a new way of behaving but a valuable experience beyond being 'new' for my client?

Reality #6 – Presence as conversational intelligence: words create worlds?

As a neuroscientific approach to presence in coaching, conversational intelligence (Glaser, 2014) serves as a technique to connect, navigate and literally grow with clients through conversation. This means that through language we can trigger each other. Conversations in which clients feel good and introspective in positive ways help them connect to the coach.

Conversations of a connective quality trigger an entirely different part of clients' chemistry, the pre-frontal cortex where trust lives. Not only do our brains utilize areas of the neocortex for communication, they also synchronize with each other. A study (Stephens, Silbert and Hasson, 2010), using fMRI to record brain activity from both conversation partners during natural communication, shows how brain activities are coupled during successful communication. This coupling, or synchrony, disappears when we fail to communicate.

According to Judith Glaser, conversations have the ability to expand our brain and have three dimensions: biochemical (responsible for our bioreactions), relational (expressive of mutual needs such as trust, respect, candour in relationship with others) and co-creational (enabling the drive to create joint success rather than staying addicted to being right).

Used in leadership coaching, conversational intelligence is about enabling coaches to shape clients' mindsets and experiences by reducing fear and inner focus while creating connection and engagement in coaching.

Reality check:

> What might happen on a non-verbal/movement level in conversations when brains couple in synchrony and how might that affect play out in how clients grow and develop in this mutuality?

Reality #7 – Presence as a 'use-of-self' to experience the client

In presence-based coaching, Silsbee (2008) identifies five methods to practise presence as a 'use-of-self' to experience clients through 'three doorways to presence: mind, body, and heart' (p. 3):

- centring (bringing awareness to the body sensation
- building somatic awareness (moving to meaning-making of the body sensation)
- somatic self-observation (forming awareness of sensations in response to the client)
- working with urges (catching conditioned responses)
- taking up direct or indirect body practice (for example, yoga, pilates, mindfulness and meditation).

Influenced by psychotherapy, the concept of 'use-of-self' is sometimes referred to as counter-transference in coaching (de Haan, 2011; Lee, 2014; Orenstein, 2002; Sandler, 2011) as an agenda to work with unconscious dynamics in the coach-client relationship.

Various other notable influences on the 'self as tool' in coaching derive from work on focused awareness of the self in the 'cycle of experience' in Gestalt psychology (Bluckert, 2006, p. 139) or existential-experiential coaching (Madison, 2012). These approaches call for coaches to access the felt sense as a tool in the coaching process (see Reality #1). Integral coaching developer

Hunt (2009) argues that for coaches to manage the 'relational field', they need to 'hold the full complexity of another human being with somatic patience, presence and courage' (p. 19), while Kennedy (2013) finds that coaches using their immediate physical experience when being with clients will enhance presence and authenticity as well as the use of self as an instrument.

For some other scholars, coaches' access to their own felt response in coaching is applied to handle unconscious processes (Turner, 2010) or emotions (Cremona, 2010) by sharing their physical responses in the 'here and now' of coach-client relationships. While there are attempts to explain this phenomenon with mirror neuron theory, some researchers (Caramazza et al., 2014) warn that this development is still in its early stages.

Reality check:

> How will I know and manage that experiencing my client as a 'self-as-tool' will not become a manifestation of my counter-transference but material that reflects awareness of my client's material in the dynamics of our coaching relationship?

Landscape of eight myths of presence

Myth #1 – Presence is about 'I'm saying this from a place of presence.'

We often hear coaches say, 'I'm saying this from a place of presence' when they explain or disclose something about themselves. When I make this claim, did I really experience presence? If so, did I really understand my experience of that particular presence? Does my saying that I am speaking from a place of presence warrant being present, or is my claim some unheeded intention? Did the man who loved dragons ever experience or understand the experience of dragons? Did he really love dragons?

Practising habits is a behaviourist stance and implies that our actions express who we are: 'I do this, therefore I am.' Some critics (Searle, 2004) claim that acting in a certain way presupposes that we can understand our insights or internal experiences, which they argue is an illusion. Unless we have the experience of driving a car, we cannot understand driving the car even if we take a manual and training courses to make sense of how to drive a car. Even if we can use behaviourism to explain certain elements of what and who we perceive we are and what we do, it would be a huge mistake to reduce our insight to behaviour based on some way we found to perceive ourselves.

Reality check:

> How do I know that I am speaking from a place of presence? Where is my detachment from my lived experience?

Myth #2 – Presence is about 'being fully present'

This everyday coach-centred label goes back to the theoretical conceptualization of 'being-in-the-world' coined by Martin Heidegger (2010) and elaborated as 'being there' by Robert C. Solomon (1972). Being-in-the-world and being there occur by way of being as a body in a particular circumstance. The world is here and now, and everywhere around us. We are immersed in this world with others. So, how could we be anywhere else than here?

When speaking about 'being fully present', coaches refer to the idea that we as individuals are fully as we are without wearing any masks. Being present is about the coach and therefore implies a dualistic perspective. Coaches connect 'being fully present' with authenticity of their self although Heidegger argues that 'being' is inextricably 'being with' others and 'being-in-the-world' into which we were thrown. As such, we cannot be fully authentic as a self. According to Heidegger, there must be inauthenticity first, and human beings strive to continuously seek the authentic via inauthenticity. Hence, being-in-the-world is never being present-at-hand but in a mode of a state of mind.

Reality check:

> How can I be committed to being authentic as a separate self without being immersed with my body in a holistic environment (including my client)?

Myth #3 – Presence is about clients doing embodied exercises

Embodied exercises are quite popular with coaches to facilitate presence in coaching. In his embodied phenomenology, Maurice Merleau-Ponty (2002) describes how our embodied interaction with the world is the source from which we derive a sense of self and a sense of the world we are in. He argues that the body holds knowledge and that body practices can facilitate experiences and generate insight that language or external observation may fail to bring to light. In this light, the body is a perceiving instrument mutually engaged with consciousness and the world.

However, embodied exercises are not a dogma (Jackson, 2017), and scholars in established fields like psychotherapy (Soth, 2010) warn that after a decade of disembodied 'talking therapies' we cannot be serious about bringing back the use of the body just by introducing a few embodiment techniques or rehearsing physical behaviours. This seems to be even truer when it comes to coaching as a field of discipline that is yet to be fully established as a profession. After just a few years trying to get the body noticed in coaching, are we doing justice to the living body as the spontaneous, vibrant ground of a subjective sense of self when making it another coaching tool?

What do we mean by presence anyway? **23**

Reality check:

> Which principles do I need to further investigate in order to include embodied exercises when working towards also enhancing my client's presence?

Myth #4 – Presence as a neuro-linguistic programming (NLP) matching and mirroring technique

Using the neuro-linguistic programming (NLP) matching and mirroring technique as a form of verbal and non-verbal presence is widespread among coaches. In focusing and listening with the entire body rather than just with the ears, the goal is to build rapport with clients, prompt their sense of being connected with the coach and help them feel safe in coaching.

Assuming clients' behavioural style (breathing, body language, verbal language, para-language such as the tone of voice, pitch, volume and rate of speech) or kinaesthetic preferences (for example, eye movement as indicative of the client's preferred representational and cognitive system) is argued to be a mindful and purposeful way of establishing common ground (Bandler and Grinder, 1990).

The evidence base for NLP is widely discussed and contentious (Sturt et al., 2012; Tosey and Mathison, 2007). The biggest bone of contention might be that the matching and mirroring approach to presence in coaching appears as a directive, if not manipulative, style that is not attributed to skillful and ethical coaching.

Reality check:

> How can a conscious act on my part further my client's capacity to self-regulate, that is, notice and actively work with emotional, cognitive and behavioural material that emerges in the here and now of our coaching relationship?

Myth #5 – Presence as heart intelligence?

Heart intelligence is the flow of intuitive awareness, understanding and inner guidance we experience when the heart is coherently aligned with the mind and emotions (McCraty and Rees, 2009). The self-initiated freeze-frame practice, including the act of breathing, is argued to activate heart coherence to improve emotional well-being, as measured by the HeartMath software. The practice is claimed to change the heart rhythm pattern and create physiological coherence, characterized by increased order and harmony in mind, emotions and body. Coherence implies that we pay attention to the deeper intuitive inner guidance. In doing so, our ability to access heart intelligence increases.

During stress and negative emotions, erratic heart rhythm patterns travel from the heart to the brain rather than the other way around. The neural signal flow inhibits cognitive functions. This means that our ability to think clearly, learn, reason, and make effective decisions is limited, which might explain why we tend to act impulsively under stress.

Although HeartMath has been heavily criticized as a pseudoscience without published peer-reviewed studies being available, breathing fully and deeply as such is found to help control stress (McCraty and Rees, 2009). This indicates that it is more important than ever to stay in the moment and manage stress.

Reality check:

> How might the emerging trend in energy medicine support my coaching practice and my coaching effectiveness?

Myth #6 – Presence as cultivating the coach's self of mastery in coaching?

To some coach practitioners (Iliffe-Wood, 2014), coaching presence is about cultivating the coach's self as a well of inner wisdom. These practitioners claim that if we were to cultivate ourselves – and to some coach practitioners, coaching is a business that is all about changing, developing and growing the self – what is the essence of the coach's 'self' when it comes to being present with clients?

As a rather spiritual faculty to step out of the mind as an antidote to fear, worry and panic, coaches practise breathing and awareness of the inner space consciousness that goes beyond mere visual perceptions (Tolle, 1999) to be present. According to Eckhart Tolle, we lose the present moment when we lose ourselves in our thinking mind. Enforced stillness, which requires awareness of mental processes rather than some identification with those mental processes, is argued to help us recognize that what is going on in the mind is not helpful, as it is an illusory world that makes us suffer. Fighting our thoughts, we make them even stronger. Exercising our will power will break the cycle of racing fearful thoughts. Becoming aware of what is going on in the mind equips us with free will to see the futility and destructive nature of fearful thinking or heavy thought processes.

Another spiritual faculty of cultivating the coach's self is mindfulness meditation (Kabat-Zinn, 2005). Having its origins in Buddhist psychology, it involves breathing practice, mental imagery, a non-judgemental attentive awareness to experiences of body and mind, and body relaxation in the present moment. Although mindfulness meditation can reduce stress, promote concentration and self-awareness, it may engender negative effects, even in healthy individuals. Some cognitive psychologists (Farias et al., 2016) warn that meditation can cause dissociation, psychoses, trembling, sleeplessness, and the production of stress hormones during meditation.

Reality check:

> What happens if and where presence remains a self-reflective mastery and cultivation of my 'self'?

Myth #7 – Presence as presencing in coaching

'Presencing' in Theory U (Scharmer, 2008) blends the notions 'presence' and 'sensing' and works through 'seeing from our deepest source'. In Theory U, we work with spotting our blindness, in particular our lack of awareness of the inner place where our attention and intention originate. At its core, 'presencing' is a journey and goes beyond what most researchers and cultivators of cognition and mindfulness are occupied with primarily: the opening process of becoming present, paying little attention to the 'drama of collective creation that happens when we enter the right-hand side of the Theory U process' (p. 37). This side deals with intentionally bringing the 'new' into reality.

What emerges is a holding space that allows us and the system to sense and see itself in terms of both the current reality and the future that wants to emerge. Theory U is based on three instruments, as follows:

- *'Open mind'*: the mind works like a parachute: it only functions when it is open. It is the capacity that suspends judgement and seeks to enquire with curiosity.
- *'Open heart'*: this is our capacity to empathize with others rather than becoming cynical. It is about walking in someone else's moccasins for at least half a mile using our heart as an organ of perception.
- *'Open will'*: this encompasses our capacity to access our authentic purpose and is sometimes referred to as intention or SQ (spiritual intelligence or self-knowledge). It deals with the fundamental actions of letting go and relaxing into the unknown without being entrapped by our own anxieties over identities that we are not familiar with.

Reality check:

> What is the blind spot from which we as the field of coaching operate at present?

Myth #8 – Presence as deep listening and powerful questioning

The ICF describes coaches at MCC level as being almost telepathic, owing to their ability to listen to and understand clients, recognize their own mental, emotional and behavioural patterns in the moment, predict thoughts and behaviour and get close to their clients' model of the world, as coaches open up to the larger relational context. At this active yet calm and patient depth of listening, we get a sense of what clients are not saying, in addition to what they are saying and meaning. We get a sense of who the other person really is, as well as what they are saying, as we pay attention to the feelings associated with their words beyond empathy. Deep listening aims to understand, as one of our most basic needs is to be understood. Too often, we listen just enough to respond by spending energy on preparing an answer or response. Effectively, coaches practise deep listening with the expectation of hearing something new or surprising, which requires the temporary suspension of 'self-judgement and judgement of the 'other', and a willingness to receive new information – whether pleasant, unpleasant, or neutral. The space of deep listening is likely to give rise to powerful questioning, which is one of the core elements of effective coaching (Hauser, 2017).

Reality check:

> How does the drive to ask powerful questions bias my capacity to be truly present?

Conclusion

This chapter landscaped various concepts of presence that have emerged recently without claiming to be exhaustive or reductionist in nature. Nor does it intend to get us lost in concepts. It is designed to ignite reasoned discourse among scholars and practitioners on the essence of presence. However, I fully recognize that there is one dimension to presence that is devoid of any screen of concepts: the spiritual nature of presence which I will discuss later in the book (see Chapter 4, 'Integrative Presence', pp. 81–104).

Such a landscape can be of great benefit to all coaches, including novices in the field, as it can serve as a compass on the path of forming your presence through myths and realities. Losing sight of the path of your presence may put your coaching engagements to risk. Loving presence the way the man loved dragons does not guarantee your mastery in presence.

3 How movement synchrony embodies your presence – Forming through evidence base

Introduction

> What happens when we install two pendulum clocks on the wall? In 1665, Dutch scientist Lord Christiaan Huygens (as cited in Peña et al., 2016) found that two pendulums hanging from a common wooden beam started oscillating in line and in perfect synchrony – either in the same direction (in-phase) or in opposite directions (anti-phase). The same eerie phenomenon occurs with metronomes. It is as if the metronomes no longer existed individually and as if each metronome contained information on the other. Basically, the in-sync phenomenon can be applied to studies ranging from biology to engineering to sports. Fish shoals sync with each other as a survival mechanism. Human beings do it too. For instance, synchrony seems to be a useful indicator of how attuned a care-giver is to an infant: Not having synchrony with the mother presents a host of risks to babies and the adults they will become (Feldman, 2007). Recently, measurement scientists (Oliveira and Melo, 2015) have found that small vibrations travelling through the coupling device between two clocks are responsible for the 'odd sympathy' in the clocks. The vibrations are calculated to interfere with the swings of the clocks, eventually causing them to synchronize with the other.

What does this dynamic interaction mean for coaching conversations? How are emotional reactions amplified, attenuated or maintained through the 'unspoken', or what we refer to as movement synchrony? How can clients self-regulate (that is, notice, accept and actively work with emotions, thoughts, and behaviours in the moment) and attain goals through the unspoken? I will illustrate these relationships on the basis of:

- the hard facts of the coaching presence research project (quantitative data)
- the soft facts coming from participating coaches' lived experiences (qualitative data) in the research.

I will start by unrolling the questions and concepts that have helped formulate the research questions. As we move along, I will share three case studies as qualitative wisdom and finally divulge the quantitative research knowledge.

Formulating concepts and finding qualitative wisdom

What is movement synchrony and what is it not?

Movement synchrony is one form of interpersonal synchrony (IS) (Feldman, 2007). In principle, when we hear both 'what's said and what's not said' by someone – the verbal and non-verbal elements of communication – and show a response, that is when we are most likely to be in synchrony. Specifically, when responses show in the spontaneous and timed coordination of body movements in conversations, that is when people are reciprocally attuned with each other (Knoblich, Butterfill and Sebanz, 2011). The responses imply adaptation to each other's rhythms and cycles of activity.

Researchers in various areas of behavioural science have explored IS, either through word use (Ireland and Pennebaker, 2010) or by measuring eye movement (Brown-Schmidt et al., 2008), facial expression and gestures (Feldman, 2007; Ramseyer and Tschacher, 2011), vocal pitch (Reich et al., 2014), and breathing patterns (Yang, 2007). They found that when people sync with each other, they show increased liking, compassion and rapport (Hove and Risen, 2009), and are more socially conscious. Body movements transmit empathy and emotion (Hatfield et al., 1994).

In defining coaching presence, the International Coaching Federation (ICF) refers to this adaptive cycle of responsiveness as 'dancing in the moment'. Dancing does not necessarily mean that behaviours are similar (Chartrand and Lakin, 2013) or even the same in synchrony but that there is a non-verbal response to our conversation partner's experience in the moment. Conversation partners can also display different forms of response: one of the partners leans forward while the other one nods their head. This is defined as in-phase versus anti-phase coordination (Kelso, 1995). Both in-phase and anti-phase coordination are found to be stable modes of coordination with in-phase synchrony being the more stable mode. Attunement occurs without any conscious effort.

My two main tenets in movement synchrony for coaching

My first tenet is that our body does not lie. It responds spontaneously to 'what's said and what's not said' as it naturally embodies 'how we're doing' and 'what's going on for us' at any given moment. As such, responsiveness offers a gateway to instinctive, candid and honest expressions of ourselves. What if we masked 'how we're doing'? We can, certainly. And if so, is masking, as a conscious and deliberate effort to interact with someone not non-verbal material for exploration in itself? After all, 'one cannot not communicate' (Watzlawick et al., 1967, p. 51). Synchrony as an emergent interpersonal phenomenon involves spontaneous coordination of movements and people do not pursue the goal of performing these movements. As such, I argue that spontaneous responsiveness serves as a more trusted source of information than spoken words (see, Chapter 1, 'When the doorbell rings, it'd better ring a bell').

My second tenet is that synchrony involves reciprocity (Cacioppo et al., 2014), which occurs when all interaction partners synchronize their movements. The relevance of reciprocity can be traced back to attachment theory (Bowlby, 1969). Attachment theory posits that reciprocity is one important way to create a secure attachment between a care-giver and their baby. When a care-giver and a baby fail to respond to each other's verbal or non-verbal signals in a sensitive and timely manner, this is what will happen: not just the baby but also the care-giver will feel distressed. The mother may wonder, 'Why does my baby not respond to my billing and cooing?', while the baby might think, 'Why is this adult so insensitive to my needs?' This effect was also found in the 'still face experiment' conducted by Dr Ted Tronick[1] at Harvard Medical School, University of Massachusetts, Boston. The study shows that babies are extremely responsive to the emotions and reactivity of the social interaction that they get from the world around them. They can engage in social interaction. Both care-giver and infant work to coordinate their emotions and what they want to do in the world. Infants very quickly pick up when their mothers stop interacting with them. They then use all of their abilities to get the mother back. After only 2 minutes when they do not get the normal reaction from their mother, they respond with negative emotion: they turn away, feel stressed, and may even lose control over their posture because of the stress that they experience. This holds true for mothers too (Tronick, 1989).

Psychotherapy research (Ramseyer and Tschacher, 2016) found that non-verbal synchrony between therapist and patient strengthens the therapeutic relationship. Elsewhere, in the social and cognitive sciences (Dijksterhuis and Bargh, 2001), we learn that when conversation partners show coordinated body movements, they perceive:

- bonding (Vacharkulksemsuk and Fredrickson, 2013) as self-other boundaries disappear (Smith, 2008)
- successful cooperation (Valdesolo et al., 2010)
- perspective taking (Wheatley et al., 2012a)
- increased environmental receptivity (Valdesolo et al., 2010)

---

1 Dr Ted Tronick: Developmental psychologist in the USA. He carried out studies in 1970 which show that when the connection between an infant and care-giver is broken, the infant tries to engage the care-giver, and then, if there is no response, the infant pulls back – first physically and then emotionally.

- inclination to communicate (Anshel and Kipper, 1988) as perceptions lead conversation partners to become more involved in their interactions
- better joint performance (Cui et al., 2012)
- more effective communication (Jiang et al., 2014).

These findings imply that how we perceive others is linked with how we interact with others. Common to all theories including neurological research (Kokal et al., 2011; Wheatley et al., 2012a, 2012b) is that movement synchrony is a rewarding experience, as we feel understood, which is also essential to sustain our clients in coping with their issues and challenges in the coaching engagement.

How can these tenets relate to coaching presence?

The coaching presence research is the first attempt to investigate movement synchrony as expressive of presence in coaching. While some coaching researchers (Ianiro et al., 2013; Ianiro et al., 2015; Ianiro and Kauffeld, 2014) have already analysed verbal and non-verbal behavioural exchanges act by act in coach-client coaching engagements, their studies do not investigate presence in terms of spontaneous responsiveness between coach and client. Instead, these studies look at the level of dominance (that is, a characteristic ranging from high submissiveness to high dominance) and affiliation (that is, a characteristic ranging from hostility to friendliness) between coach and client and how these two key characteristics of social interactional behaviour (Kiesler, 1983) predict goal attainment in coaching (Biberacker et al., 2010). These studies are important as they show that dominance and affiliation through verbal and non-verbal behavioural exchanges determine the quality of the coach-client relationship. However, they do not look at how the coach-client relationship plays out in how presence leads to clients feeling psychologically safe, or what we refer to as clients' capacity to self-regulate. To what extent does presence through body movement foster trust?

As the first tenet is that the body does not lie, we can expect movement synchrony to produce authentic responses that both coach and client can trust. Presence as a way to tune in with each other through spontaneous body movements implies that the non-verbal interactions between coach and client are effortlessly dynamic and ongoing. The second tenet is that synchrony involves reciprocity, coaches' body movements potentially shape how clients respond spontaneously to coaches, and the other way around. Research in the social behavioural sciences shows that perception and motor movement are automatically linked (Dijksterhuis and Bargh, 2001; Wheatley et al., 2012b). This link provides a constant flow of behaviour that can be rapidly and effortlessly synchronized, even when people's attention is directed elsewhere (Oullier et al., 2008; Varlet et al., 2014). So, the effortless quality of synchrony guarantees an authentic exchange in conversations, which supports contemporary concepts of presence as an effortless and flexible attunement with clients, one that they can trust. Leadership theorists (Gardner et al., 2005) argue that authenticity is ultimately what employees will trust in leaders. Trust as expressive of bonding, goal and task agreement (Bordin, 1979) is important in coaching too. Trust and bonding are key contributors to the quality of the coach-client relationship (Boyce at al., 2010; Gyllenstein and Palmer, 2007) and have long been identified as a key to positive coaching results.

So, presence relates to the spontaneous and reciprocal coordination of body movements where coach and client can cultivate a relationship that is authentic and trusted.

Spontaneous responsiveness to what and to whom?

This question helps uncover two other questions: How well do we understand the dynamics between coach and client? If presence is about reciprocity and spontaneous responsiveness, why do we not look at the role that clients play in the dynamics of 'dancing in the moment'?

In the coaching presence research project, the idea is to look at the relational dynamics of presence. I argue that reciprocal and spontaneous responsiveness as expressive of presence is about both the coach and the client. Both have needs. Both are human beings. Since there is barely anything that we do in our life individually, why not explore presence as greasing the cogs of the coach-client world reciprocally? We understand coaching as a partnering process in which clients co-create the relationship, which implies that clients can influence the coach, and we are aware that clients do not want us to 'do coaching to them'. We view the coach-client relationship as the basis of the challenging coaching work to be done. So, reciprocity and spontaneous responsiveness in the moment may not be about the coach or the client alone. This perspective shapes how the research project explores presence as a function of the following three factors:

1 Clients have their needs met by how coaches sync with them through spontaneous non-verbal responses at the level of the whole body.
2 Coaches are aware of and can tease apart their needs and those of their clients to meet clients' needs spontaneously in coaching, which will show in their spontaneous movement.
3 Coaches' level of presence as expressive of their spontaneous non-verbal responsiveness to clients' needs is conditioned by how clients appear in coaching.

The coaching presence research project's perspective is unique as it recognizes that both coaches and clients partner in meeting each other's needs towards greater effectiveness. This phenomenon is referred to as 'emotional contagion' (Hatfield et al., 1994) in the social sciences. Emotional contagion happens when both conversation partners spontaneously coordinate movements (Hatfield et al., 2014) either on the micro level (mimicry, facial expressions) or the macro level (the entire body). Coaching theory supports the idea of emotional contagion, calling for coaches to practise empathetic connection while showing professional detachment (Diamond and Hicks, 2005) all the while acknowledging that it is the client who does the work in coaching. What is unclear is how emotional contagion is practised by coaches and how it plays out in clients' learning and development.

What happens when meeting clients' needs?

The coaching presence research attempts to deliver some deeper understanding of how coaches work with their needs and how coaches' needs influence clients' needs in the 'here and now' of the coaching relationship. What if clients needed to see coaches as human beings rather than as some detached functioning self? For instance, to feel safe in coaching. What if skilling coaches to work with their 'past, present and future needs' as an instrument in coaching is more valuable for clients' learning and development than exercising control to be 'fully detached' in the coach-client relationship? What do we know about the impact of our own needs on our level of responsiveness to clients' needs through spontaneous movement?

I argue that coaches' awareness of and skillfulness with mastering their needs is what clients require, if we are to claim that the coach-client relationship is a partnership with clients to support their development, growth and goal attainment (Theeboom et al., 2017).

When clients' needs are met spontaneously and when coaches' needs do not interfere as unconscious material with meeting clients' needs, clients will develop some sense of safety, trust and connectedness. They can partner with coaches authentically as they manage to self-regulate, that is, open up, become curious, autonomous and accepting of challenging moments and tasks, which is important for them to work on their goals or issues effectively.

Let us take a look at a research case in the case study 1, which illustrates the dynamics of meeting needs in coaching:

Case Study 1

Maria is a well-established executive coach with over 15 years of coaching experience. She has a female client whom we shall call Julia. In the coaching presence research feedback session, Maria reports that Julia is an ideal client. She feels that she uses the coaching that she was taught in her coaching training. She feels that Julia is ready for coaching and reports feeling comfortable with her right from the start. Maria's individual results on synchrony, however, show that Julia is highly 'responsive non-verbally' to Maria without Maria responding back to Julia. There seems to be an unequal distribution of non-verbal responses between Julia and Maria, as if Julia were working hard to get Maria's attention.

In feedback, Maria acknowledges that as she 'felt comfortable with Julia' and as she interpreted Julia's 'eagerness to do things right' as readiness for coaching, she missed out on sensing her own 'feeling comfortable' and sharing this felt sense with Julia. She realizes that she failed to discover what her felt sense might be about in the 'here and now' of their relationship. Maria discovers that she showed up as static – non-responsive – without her body emitting any responses to those emitted by Julia.

Missing out on the opportunity to spontaneously respond to her own felt sense and to Julia's physical responses in the relationship, Maria fails to create a safe space for Julia to discover that she is bringing a well-known pattern of hers into the coaching relationship: her need to do things right. What would happen if Maria sensed her internal state of being comfortable with Julia and spontaneously shared her sense making? What if Maria noticed and shared with Julia that Julia was showing up as an 'ideal client' for her? What if she self-regulated and noticed her bias? What might shift for Julia? Whose needs is Maria responding to when she says, 'I felt great in the coaching. Julia was an ideal client and I have feedback from her that she was very happy with coaching'?

What happened in Maria's coaching in theoretical terms and according to our conceptualization of presence?

The issue in Maria's case

Maria did not pay attention to her felt experience of comfort with Julia. She did not wonder why she might feel at ease with Julia while she might feel different with some other clients. Maria met her own need of:

- feeling comfortable with Julia, and
- doing coaching right rather than sensing that Julia was working hard to be a good client.

As a result, Julia did not feel safe with Maria.

While Julia was reporting success at the workplace after coaching and also gave the coach positive feedback on completion of coaching, in the post-session questionnaires, which she completed after each coaching session, she reported feeling unsafe in her process with Maria. Even if Julia reached her goals, the question remains: What might have shifted in terms of effectiveness for Julia if her pattern of 'doing things right' had been interrupted by Maria's responsiveness to her need to get her attention?

Maria's lack of spontaneous responsiveness and the reciprocal quality of responsiveness were reflected in the motion energy analysis of non-verbal interactions recorded over time (see Figure 1). That is, Julia's need to do things right impacted on how Maria showed up in coaching; Maria's needs were met and Julia's needs were not met as Maria was meeting her own needs. The lack of growth of Julia's self-regulatory capacities is shown in Figure 2 in

34 Coaching Presence

comparison with how presence developed as expressed through movement synchrony over the course of the coaching engagement.

A solution in Maria's case

Our 'sensing and regulation of self', coined as 'interoception' by Sir Charles S. Sherrington[2] (1906) and later researched in cognitive sciences (Craig, 2004,

Figure 1 This chart depicts the overall quality of synchrony between coach and client across all sessions. The x-axis shows the time lags per second on either side of the process (client on the left-hand side and coach on the right-hand side). The y-axis shows the level of synchrony as a value. One line (which is labelled) represents real movement synchrony; the other (also labelled) represents random movement. Where the real line is above the random line, either the coach (right-hand side) or the client (left-hand side) work towards meeting the other person's needs. Overall quality of synchrony is 54% as expressive of the client's attempts to synchronize with the coach.

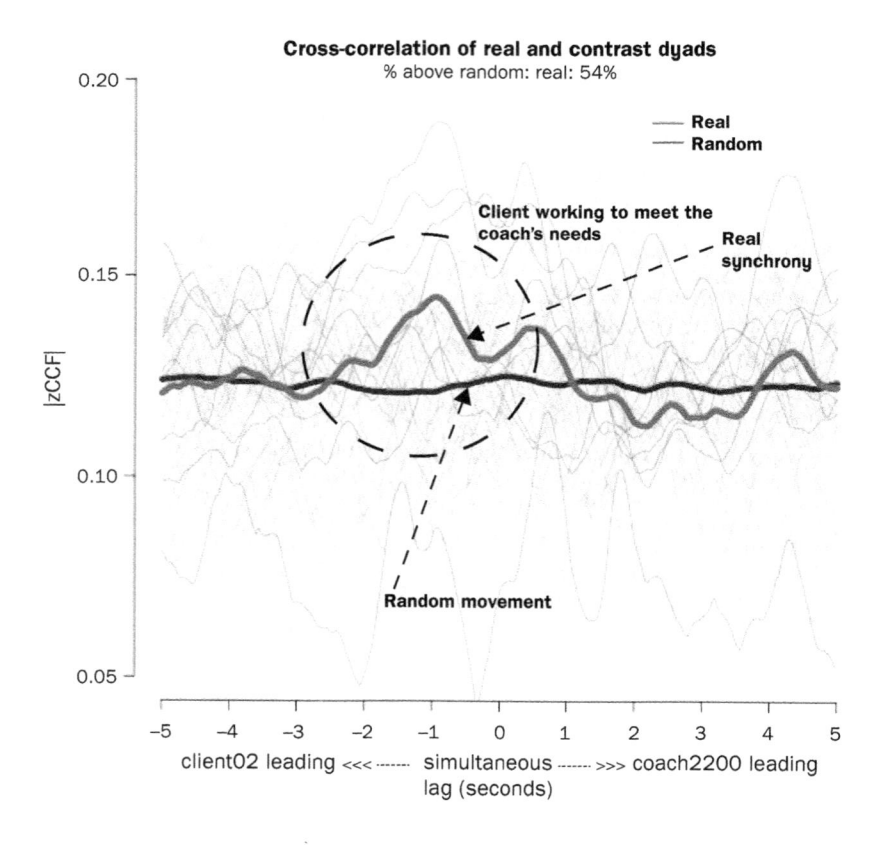

Cross-correlation of real and contrast dyads
% above random: real: 54%

[Chart: y-axis |zCCF| from 0.05 to 0.20; x-axis lag (seconds) from -5 to 5; client02 leading <<< ...... simultaneous ...... >>> coach2200 leading. Lines labelled "Real", "Random", "Client working to meet the coach's needs", "Real synchrony", "Random movement".]

---

2 Through his 1906 publication, *The Integrative Action of the Nervous System*, Sir Charles S. Sharrington disproved the theory that the nervous system, including the

Figure 2 The upper chart depicts the client's self-reports over eight sessions. The x-axis in the upper chart shows the number of coaching sessions. The y-axis shows the self-regulation values and the development the client reported for self-regulation over eight sessions. The lower chart depicts the development of synchrony across eight sessions. No synchrony development relates to no self-regulation development over time.

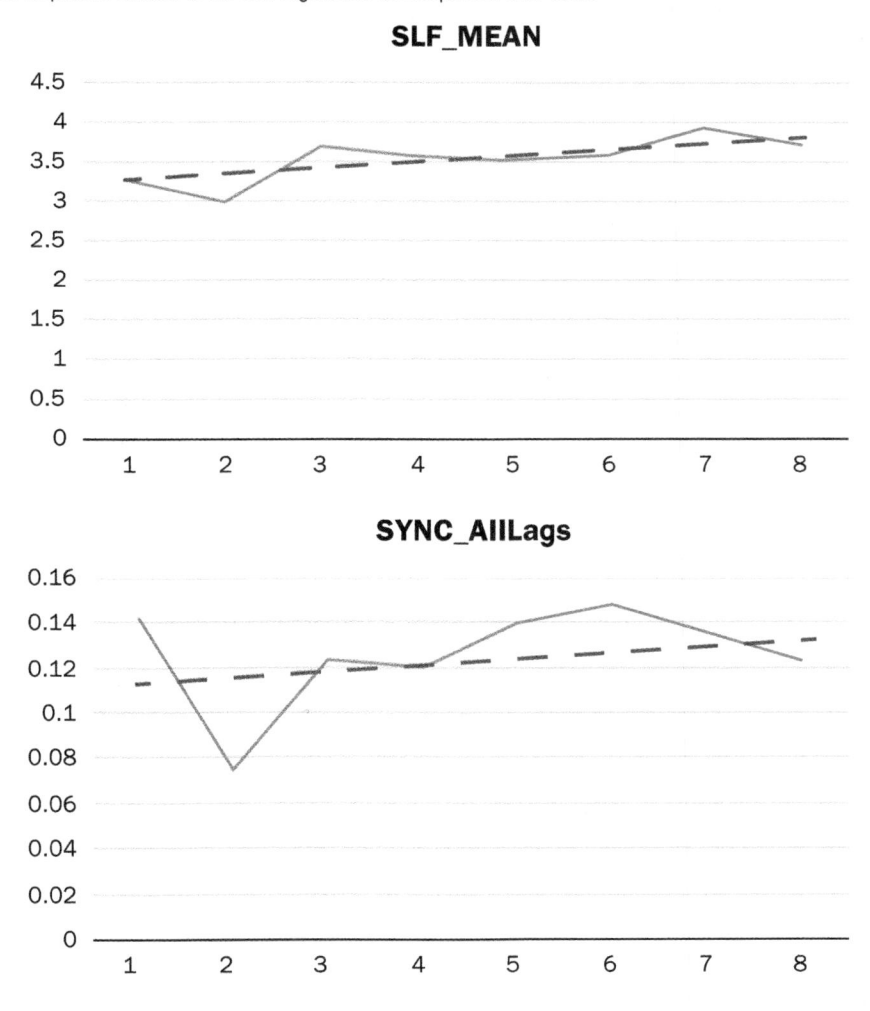

SLF_MEAN

SYNC_AllLags

2014), may be a gateway to non-verbal spontaneous responsiveness. If coaches can access their bodily sensations and are able to self-regulate, it may be easier for them to simulate clients' body states. This might result in relationally sensitive and receptive responses. If the goal of coaching is to facilitate growth or

---

brain, can be understood as a single interlinking network. His explanation of synaptic communication processes between neurons shaped our understanding of the central nervous system.

development, then coaches for whom it is easier to simulate clients' experiences may synchronize with them more easily, possibly sharing their felt sense with them. This is a relevant skill for both:

- for the coach to enable the client to feel attuned with them, and
- for the client to self-regulate, and thus attain self-directed goals effectively.

Although the concept of 'use of self' is an emerging concept in coaching, we will find it quite rarely present in coaching practice.

Fusing movement synchrony, self-regulation, and goal attainment in coaching presence

Defining and integrating self-regulation in coaching presence

What does it mean for clients to self-regulate as a gateway to self-directed changes and goal attainment?

As we essentially view coaching as a 'result-oriented, systematic process' (Grant, 2003, p. 254) and goal-focused activity (Gregory et al., 2011), the coach's role is twofold:

1 Facilitate clients' 'movement through a self-regulatory cycle' (Grant, 2012, p. 255).
2 Foster self-directed changes in clients (Theeboom et al., 2017).

The aim is to integrate clients' goal attainment without relapse (Prochaska and Norcross, 2018) and well-being or sustained thriving (Grant, 2014) in coaching as a transformative learning process (Mezirow, 1997). A competency that may be linked to this kind of integrative learning is self-regulation. There is only one study in coaching that indicates that if we work on the four factors that are required for mindfulness in coaching, clients will attain goals more effectively than through coaching alone (Spence et al., 2008). The four factors in psychological literature for mindfulness training are (Bishop et al., 2004):

1 Openness and curiosity towards present affective and cognitive material.
2 Monitoring what is going on emotionally moment by moment.
3 Accepting orientation towards emerging experiences as the two main forms of reflection (Schön, 1983): reflection-in-action and reflection-on-action (Dewey, 1933).
4 Refocusing our mental processes in the 'here and now'.

To account for both the emotional (i.e., affective) and cognitive aspects of how clients move through a self-regulatory cycle, we define self-regulation as the clients' capacity to do the following:

- regulate mood as expressive of positive and negative affect (Watson et al., 1988)
- self-reflect goals and problems in a result-oriented manner as guided by Greif and Berg (2011).

Measuring emotional self-regulation – Mood

In measuring mood, we adopt the perspective of the self-regulation resource model (SRRM) proposed by Sirois (2015), which reflects the balance of positive affect and negative affect as an indicator of successful emotional self-regulation. In principle, emotional self-regulation has been shown to reduce tendencies to avoid experiences (Barrett, 2017), which is important in coaching if clients are to be ready for coaching. According to Barrett, emotions are the result of meaning-making of our felt experiences In this meaning-making process, the brain prioritizes where to invest energy to generate the feeling of safety.

So, to what extent does movement synchrony support effective meaning-making of felt experiences, which is found to reduce the brain's processing load and save energy (Wheatley et al., 2012a, 2012b)? To what extent can movement synchrony help clients balance what is going on emotionally in moment-by-moment interactions in coaching? How are emotional reactions amplified, attenuated or maintained through movement synchrony?

Measuring cognitive self-regulation – Goal self-reflection

In measuring goal self-reflection, we refer to meta-cognitive monitoring abilities (Greif and Berg, 2011). The focus is on clients' result orientation rather than their aimless rumination (Greif, 2008). Cognitive processes amplify, attenuate, or maintain how strongly we respond emotionally to situations and people (Davidson, 2000). They have been shown to reduce tendencies to avoid experiences too (Hayes et al., 1996), suppress thoughts (Wegner et al., 1993) or over-engage in worry (Borkovec, 1994), employ rumination (Nolen-Hoeksema and Morrow, 1991), and over-generalization (Carver, 1998). As a result, these processes facilitate emotional self-regulation (Kumar, 2002), which indicates that cognitive and emotional self-regulation are interrelated.

So, to what extent does movement synchrony support clients in how they can monitor their thoughts in challenging moments in coaching? Some studies in clinical psychology show that synchrony is linked with individuals' capacity to express their thoughts freely in the face of experiencing worry (Borkovec, 1994): people ruminate less (Nolen-Hoeksema and Morrow, 1991) and over-generalize less (Carver, 1998).

Fusing movement synchrony and self-regulation in the coaching relationship

The question is: how will clients' internal regulation capacity impact on how they can regulate behavioural exchanges in their interactions with coaches?

This is a phenomenon that is referred to as co-regulation in relationship science (Butler and Randall, 2013). It is both an intrapersonal and interpersonal phenomenon. Interpersonal synchrony comprises both aspects of co-regulation (Koole and Tschacher, 2016).

Links between the intrapersonal and interpersonal aspects of synchrony were initially found between care-giver and infant in developmental research (Feldman, 2015). Where care-giver and infant were interacting synchronously, infants developed self-regulation skills as adolescents. Where toddlers felt emotionally safe, they showed affect balance later in life. Affect balance fostered their self-control abilities, irrespective of factors such as temperament, IQ, and maternal cycles (Feldman et al., 1999). Similar links have been found in close relationships (Butler and Randall, 2013; Ferrer and Helm, 2013; Timmons et al., 2015), where synchrony was shown to result in co-regulation as some healthy exchange of emotional responses rather than a mere matching of the same or similar emotional responses (Kleinbub, 2017). A mere matching of emotional responses implies only excessive arousal referred to as co-dysregulation (Reed et al., 2015) rather than a healthy equilibrium of emotions. Yet, the particular link between synchrony through body movements and emotion in relationships is not well established in the adult literature even if there are indications that the whole body can be viewed as an important 'signalling device' in emotional processing (de Gelder, 2006). One study examined the movement synchrony-emotion link during conversations of students (Tschacher et al., 2014). The findings of the study are consistent with the idea that synchrony is instrumental in fostering the capacity for self-regulation as a process of self (Koole and Coenen, 2007; Kuhl, 2001), which reflects clients' volitional and lasting adaptation (Nordham et al., 2018).

In coaching, we understand that self-regulation as expressive of feeling safe is a prerequisite for goal attainment (Spence and Oades, 2011; Grant, 2012). When clients and coaches exchange simultaneous affective or behavioural reactions to the same stimulus (Pinel et al., 2015), clients are more likely to adapt their emotional responses to challenging moments in coaching. So, the question is how do clients utilize self-regulatory resources in the sessions and across sessions to engage in successfully attaining their goals?

It is not surprising why it is difficult to study this phenomenon because self-regulation is not a 'switch-on' or 'switch-off' phenomenon but a process of self. It reflects the quality of long-lasting adaptation. It is this long-lasting adaptation, this 'ripple effect' that coaching may need in order to count as effective. Therefore, looking into self-regulation appears to be important when it comes to reaching goals in coaching effectively and in a self-directed manner.

Let us look at a second research case in case study 2, which illustrates the intrapersonal and interpersonal dynamics of self-regulation through body movement synchrony in coaching:

Case Study 2

Peter has 10 years of coaching experience and invites Lora to participate in the coaching presence research project with him. In the feedback session, Peter relates that at one point in the course of the research project, Lora felt that she had gained some key insight. The question for Lora at that point was what to do next. Peter explains that he invited Lora to reflect on what she might find most powerful to do next, and to act on that key insight, which was that Lora found herself to be over-controlling. Peter relates one incident, 'Lora is taking her time thinking. We are sitting there in pure silence surrounded by a calm environment where I have my office. Dead silence. While Lora takes her time to reflect, which goes on for quite a while, I suddenly hear a rooster doing his "cickeerickeee" in the neighbour's garden several times. It takes me a second to realize that it is too late in the day for the rooster to do his "cickeerickee" and sensing that, my face lightens up and I say, "I think the rooster is really crazy" and then I lean forward and burst into hearty laughter. Lora looks at me for what seems to be a few seconds and then bursts into laughter too. There we are, laughing together when she finally says, "Peter, you know, maybe I should be doing something crazy too."' Later, Lora told Peter that she was sensing the same urge to laugh but was not sure if she could allow herself to do it. When she found Peter simply sharing his sense of experience, she felt encouraged to let go of her sense of control, which actually helped her find her action-taking point.

In the feedback session, we then take a look at the individual research results of Peter's and Lora's coaching process. I shared Peter's and Lora's levels of presence as expressed through their movement synchrony and Lora's self-reports about her self-regulatory capacities over the sessions. We find that the levels of spontaneous responsiveness to each other's needs show robust values. There is strong synchrony and an equally strong growth in Lora's self-regulatory capacities. We are not surprised by this result as Peter's story confirms that he is able to use his self as an emerging instrument to work with Lora.

What happened in Peter's coaching in theoretical terms of the intrapersonal and interpersonal aspects of presence?

The coach's capacity to introcept using the felt sense of his 'in the moment' experience meets his client's need. Releasing the felt sense spontaneously by leaning forward and laughing invites the client to be confident to share her own 'in the moment' felt experience. Meeting the client's need in synchrony influences how the client learns to emotionally self-regulate and feel safe with her felt experiences, not just in the relationship with her coach but also in relationship with herself. This felt and shared experience prompts the client to refocus her attention, which leads her to be curious about how to discover what to do next. Figure 3 depicts the synchrony of Peter and Lora and Figure 4 shows

40 Coaching Presence

Figure 3 This chart depicts the overall quality of synchrony between coach and client across all sessions. The x-axis shows the time lags per second on either side of the process (client on the left-hand side and coach on the right-hand side). The y-axis shows the level of synchrony as a value. The blue line represents real movement synchrony; the black line represents random movement. Where the blue line is above the black line, either the coach (right-hand side) or the client (left-hand side) is working towards meeting the other person's needs. Overall quality of synchrony is 95% as expressive of coach's and client's attempts to respond to each other's needs equally and reciprocally.

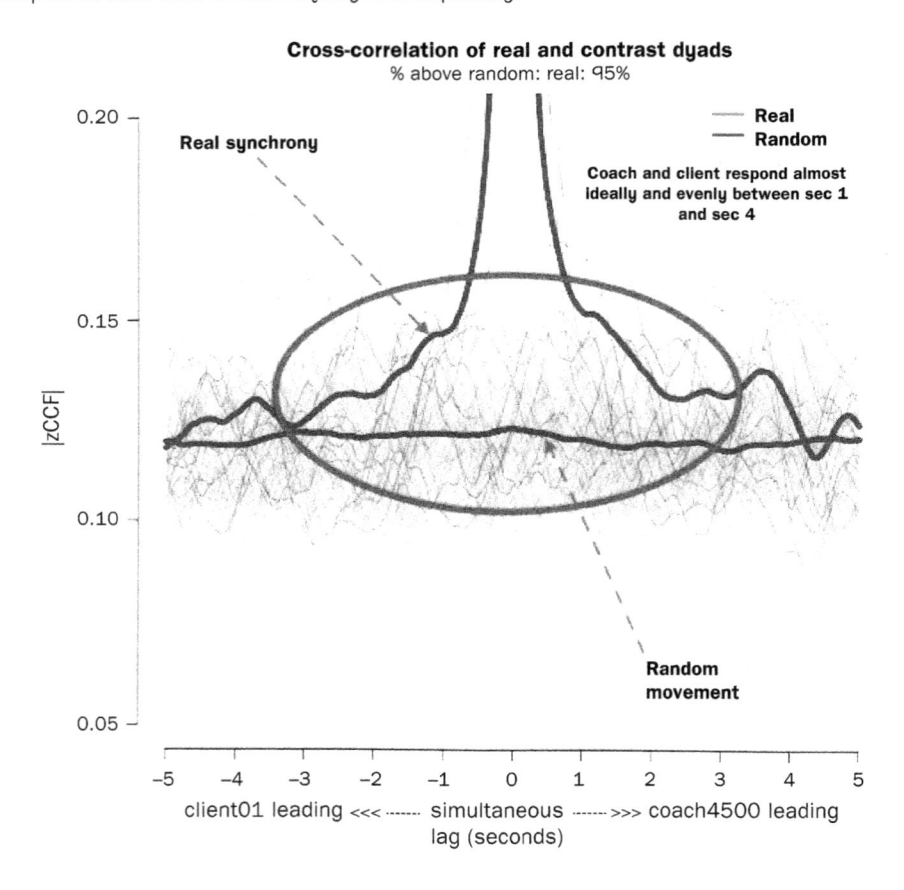

Cross-correlation of real and contrast dyads
% above random: real: 95%

Real synchrony — Coach and client respond almost ideally and evenly between sec 1 and sec 4

Random movement

client01 leading <<< ······ simultaneous ······ >>> coach4500 leading
lag (seconds)

Lora's self-reports in the upper chart while the lower chart shows the development of presence over time.

The qualitative wisdom on this case indicates how important it is to ensure that coaches are trained to feel safe to work with somatic awareness, somatosensory perceptiveness as well as flexible and courageous sharing of their felt experiences from within and outside the coaching relationship, if and where it relates to the material presented by clients. Movement synchrony as expressive of presence requires high levels of interoception, or the capacity to have a felt sense of the signals of our interior states rather than the brain's interpretation and

Figure 4 The upper chart depicts the client's self-reports over 10 sessions. The x-axis in the upper chart shows the number of coaching sessions. The y-axis shows the self-regulation values and the development the client reported for self-regulation over eight sessions. The lower chart depicts the development of synchrony across 10 sessions. Synchrony development relates to self-regulation development over time.

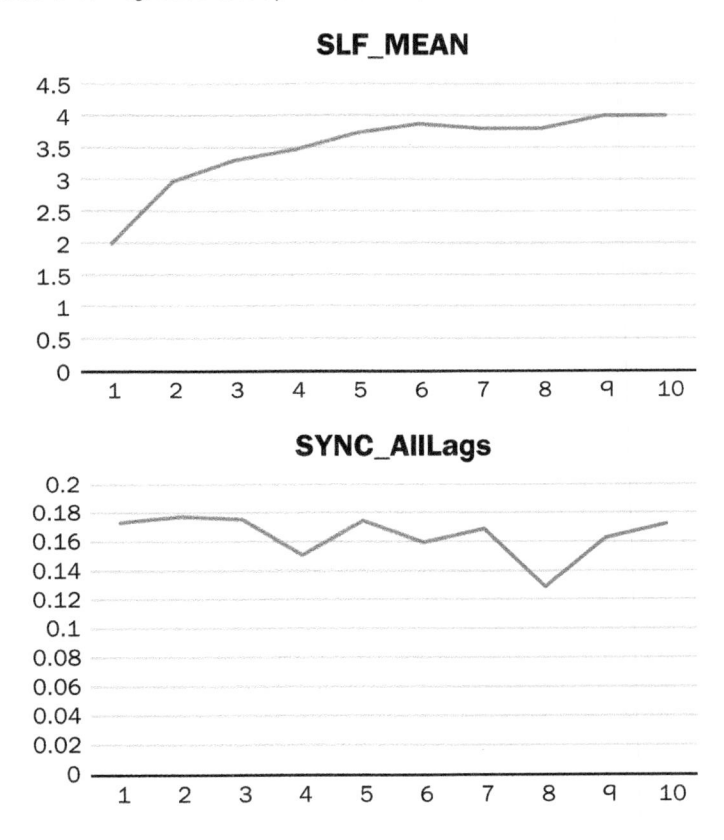

SLF_MEAN

SYNC_AllLags

prediction of those signals. What might have happened if the coach had felt inhibited by the rooster's behaviour, or if he had not noticed the rooster at all?

Strengthening self-regulation through the coaching relationship

So far, we have found that the quality of the coaching relationship is a key success factor when it comes to achieving overall coaching outcomes (Athanasopoulou and Dopson, 2018; de Haan et al., 2019; Gessnitzer and Kauffeld, 2015; Grassman et al., 2019; Grover and Furnham, 2016; Jones et al., 2016; Molyn et al., 2019). This does not seem to be true when it comes to how the effectiveness of coaching changes over the course of coaching (Molyn et al., 2019). The relevance of the quality of the coach-client relationship in coaching as a change process is not clear. Is it a factor that predicts outcomes in coaching or rather a phenomenon that strengthens or weakens how coaching leads to outcomes? Or something different? Additionally, the link between the strength of the coach-client relationship, self-regulation, and movement synchrony has remained unexplored. How do some more well-established related fields like psychotherapy address the link between the quality of the collaborative therapeutic relationship (that is, the working alliance characterized by goal orientation, joint task setting and bonding (Bordin, 1979)) and self-regulation in relation to movement synchrony?

While coaching is distinct from psychotherapy (and other related fields such as counselling or mentoring) in relation to how therapists work at emotional depth with patients and how coaches work with emotionally stable clients (Peltier, 2010), the recent qualitative meta-synthesis (Erdös et al., 2020) demonstrates that emotions play a key role in clients' learning and growth processes too. Therefore, we can expect that body movement impacts on clients' capacity to regulate the self to attain goals. This proposition is supported by coaching scholars (de Haan and Duckworth, 2013; McKenna and Davis, 2009), who argue that there are sufficient similarities (i.e., understanding cognitive and emotional responses, client-centred collaborative partnership) between these two fields of discipline for the relevance of psychotherapy literature to be considered in coaching process research to contribute to enhance coaching practice.

Psychotherapy research has explored the working alliance in relationship with interpersonal synchrony using video-based Motion Energy Analysis (MEA) (Ramseyer, 2020a) to automatically assess body movement in therapeutic sessions. Findings suggest that movement synchrony is an indicator of beneficial processes within sessions. In one study, patients were asked to assess their working alliance at the end of each session (Ramseyer and Tschacher, 2011). In other studies, patients and therapists self-rated the overall therapy levels (Altmann et al., 2020; Paulick et al., 2018; Ramseyer and Tschacher, 2016). Both approaches revealed similar results.

The In-Sync Model (Koole and Tschacher, 2016), which suggests that the alliance is grounded in the neural coupling of, for example, patient and therapist's brains, is one possible theoretical framework for these findings (see Figure 5). Inter-brain coupling facilitates complex social-cognitive processes which help form goals and intentions that patients can maintain over time. Yet, inter-brain coupling is achieved only indirectly. It takes the mutual coordination of the patient's and the therapist's behaviour and experiences to achieve this coupling. Furthermore, this coordination is developed through synchronous activities. So, movement synchrony helps establish a strong patient-therapist relationship, which in turn promotes emotion regulation in the patient and thereby good therapeutic outcomes.

However, recent studies indicate that the purported positive association between movement synchrony and alliance appears to be restricted to certain preconditions. A study (Ramseyer, 2020b) suggests that the association between synchrony and alliance may not be the same if assessed in a group that shares similar characteristics (for example, all participants are students). In other

How movement synchrony embodies your presence **43**

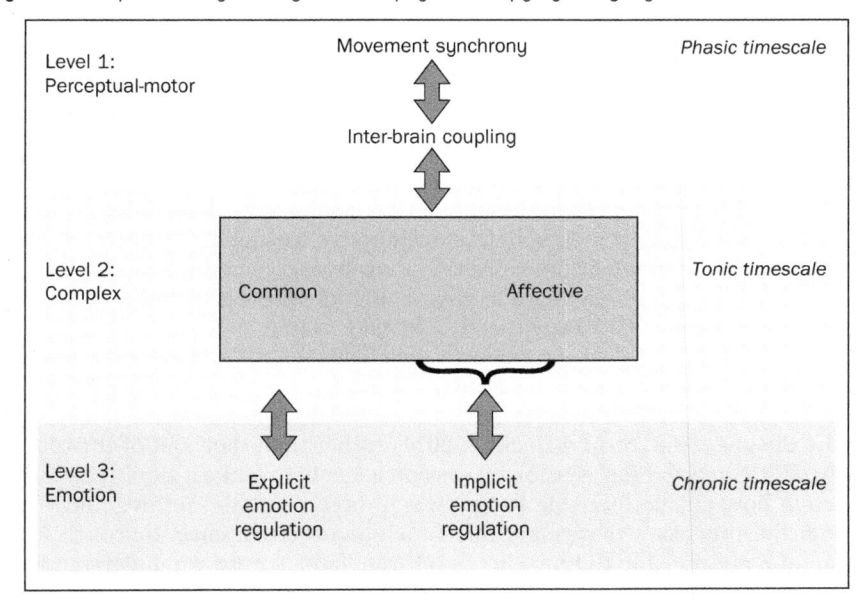

Figure 5 Interpersonal synchrony model in psychotherapy by Wolfgang Tschacher

```
Level 1:              Movement synchrony              Phasic timescale
Perceptual-motor
                      Inter-brain coupling

Level 2:                                              Tonic timescale
Complex          Common              Affective


Level 3:         Explicit            Implicit        Chronic timescale
Emotion          emotion             emotion
                 regulation          regulation
```

words, results depend on the specific properties of each population we investigate. These properties set groups apart from each other and greatly influence the level of associations that can be found between synchrony and the working alliance.

Psychotherapy research also indicates that emotion regulation has an adaptive property too. It arises to responses, exchanges and mutual sharing but does not have to do so unless the interactions meet the patients' needs in the moment. As a result, psychotherapy research claims that the strength of the patient-therapist relationship is tied to emotional processes (Greenberg and Safran, 1989). Overall, theory so far suggests that a strong patient-therapist relationship will improve clients' self-regulatory capacities and enable clients to deal with their emotions.

To date, we do not understand the extent to which clients' self-regulatory capacities will grow as a beneficial effect of the working alliance in coaching. First, based on what we know from coaching research on the working alliance, I believe that the working alliance embodies an interpersonal phenomenon that influences rather than being a factor that ultimately predicts coaching success. This means that it will change as clients and coaches change through their work over time. As an interpersonal factor, it will strengthen or weaken how movement synchrony and self-regulation relate to each other over time. Second, I believe that because the working alliance is an interpersonal factor, it will shape how clients self-regulate and will be shaped by how both coach and client dance in the moment to the beats of movement synchrony over time.

Fusing movement synchrony in goal attainment

In principle, the link between goal-directed behaviour and movement synchrony is established in psychology (Marsh et al., 2009; Valdesolo et al., 2010). This principle is rooted in the theory of the dynamics of self-organization of coordinated action (Fowler et al., 2008) and sustains the principle of 'behaviour before brain' (van Dijk et al., 2008). In other words, thinking emerges because we move rather than the other way around.

For coaching, this principle suggests that clients who are attuned with their coach in the way that they spontaneously move to socially interact are more likely to engage in mindfully reflecting their goal-directed behaviour. In turn, this will increase their capacity to engage in higher levels of self-directed goal attainment (Grant, 2003; Prywes, 2012; Spence, 2007).

What is the role the coach plays in the clients' process of self-directed goal attainment? Coaching scholars argue that coaches' way of 'being with clients' (Divine, 2009; Gendlin, 1969; Linder-Pelz and Hall, 2007; Madison, 2012; Sieler, 2010; Silsbee, 2008; Strozzi-Heckler, 2014) rather than their out-of-the-toolbox way of 'doing coaching' session by session is likely to make a significant difference in how clients feel able to attain self-directed goals. Yet, we know little about the processes that relate this coach-focused presence approach in the coaching relationship to how clients self-regulate. Nor do we understand how this coach-focused presence approach affects clients' capacity to self-regulate to achieve their goals effectively.

We will now take a look at a third research case in case study 3, which illustrates how movement synchrony relates to self-directed goal attainment in the coaching relationship as a process.

> **Case Study 3**
>
> Sue is a seasoned coach with over five years of coaching experience. She is very interested in learning and growing as a coach. Therefore, she invites John to participate in the coaching presence research project with her.
>
> In the feedback session, Sue describes her relational process with John as difficult. She says that John is rather rigid and has agreed to take coaching to see how coaching works rather than allow himself to learn and self-discover. She also says that John tried to 'lead and put himself above her' at the outset of the coaching assignment but that later he took steps to accomplish goals and self-reflect with her as a partner. Sue also acknowledges that she may put too much on John to struggle with and that John is the type of person who has high moral standards and a strong religious background. Finally, she says that she does not believe that John has reached his goals. She surmises that John may have well reached some goals after all but that it would have taken longer for John to experience coaching as an intervention that would make a difference for him.
>
> Looking at the individual research results, we find that it is only a few times when Sue and John move in synchrony and are present with each other. Data

> shows that most of the time Sue and John are uncoordinated and the motion energy analysis software cannot produce any clear results for true synchrony levels. The calculation shows that their movements are random movements rather than any spontaneous responses to each other's needs in the relationship.
>
> Reflecting on her results, Sue finds that she felt inhibited by the 'powerful' religious and spiritual background that John brought with him to the coaching room and that she just went with John's pace, very well aware that he was having a hard time taking action steps.

How does movement synchrony relate to self-directed goal attainment based on Sue and John's example?

The issue in Sue's case

Both Sue and John were reserved, as there is very little and low movement synchrony between them in the data analysis. From Sue's reflections, it seems that she adopted John's rigid stance of, 'I take coaching only to see how coaching works' by being equally rigid in how she 'put too much on John to struggle with'. Low movement synchrony levels reflect this 'rigid' stance and show equally low development of John's capacity to self-regulate. Sue was unable to respond spontaneously to John's needs of spirituality. Instead, she kept back as she 'felt inhibited by his powerful religious and spiritual background' and met her need to keep things smooth, despite knowing that her coaching was ineffective. John was unable to reach any self-directed goals as Sue and John got stuck with John's agenda of wanting to 'see only how coaching works'. Both Sue's self-report in the feedback session and John's sessional self-report over time show a very weak working alliance. Figure 6 depicts the synchrony of Sue and John and Figure 7 shows John's self-reports in the upper chart while the lower chart shows the development of presence over time.

A solution to Sue's case

What if Sue challenged John by telling him that she felt inhibited by the powerful religious and spiritual background that he was manifesting in the coaching relationship? What if Sue shared with John that she felt that the lack of goal-intention and the mere drive to find out how coaching worked were not what Sue felt coaching was about? What if Sue shared with John that she might show him how coaching worked but suggested that he find a true goal for himself first? What if Sue had the courage to face John's powerful background and was an equally powerful partner as a coach by challenging him about the way he was acting? What if she paid attention to how she felt inhibited by John's hidden agenda of 'just wanting to see how coaching works'?

46 Coaching Presence

Figure 6 This chart depicts the overall quality of synchrony between coach and client across all sessions. The x-axis shows the time lags per second on either side of the process (client on the left-hand side and coach on the right-hand side). The y-axis shows the level of synchrony as a value. One line represents real movement synchrony; the other represents random movement. Where the real line is above the random line, either the coach (right-hand side) or the client (left-hand side) is working towards meeting the other person's needs. Overall quality of synchrony is 48% as expressive of coach's and client's simultaneous responses: where there are responses, they occur in the same second. Overall, coach and client show no significant responsiveness to each other.

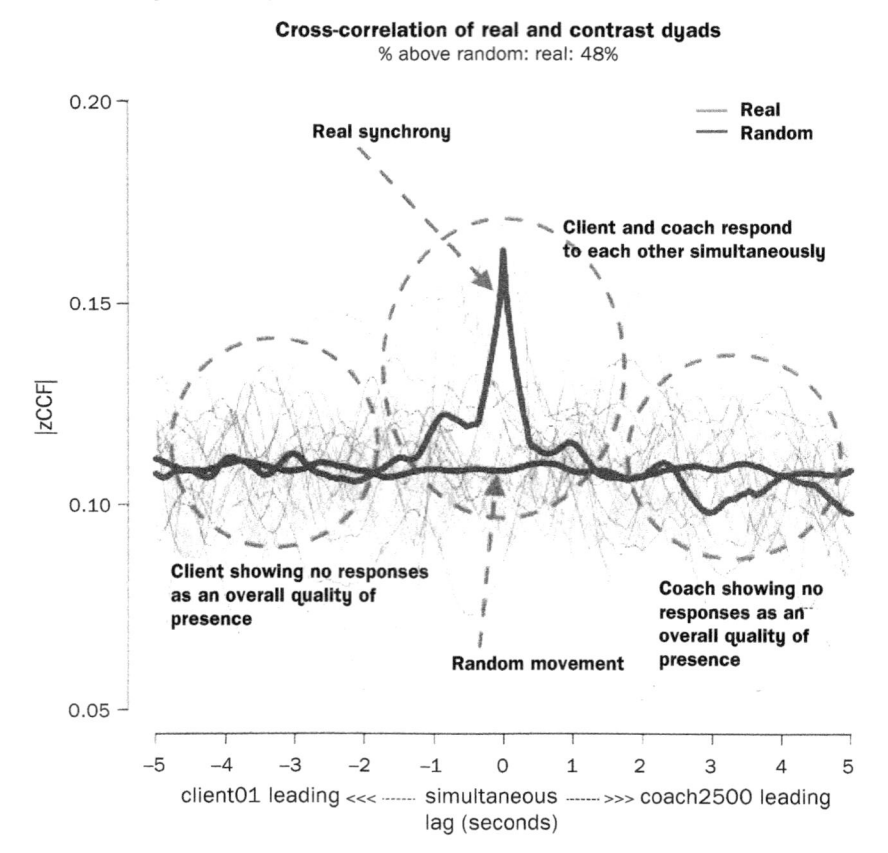

Cross-correlation of real and contrast dyads
% above random: real: 48%

[Chart showing cross-correlation with x-axis "lag (seconds)" from -5 to 5, labeled "client01 leading <<< ······ simultaneous ······ >>> coach2500 leading", y-axis |zCCF| from 0.05 to 0.20. Annotations: "Real synchrony", "Client and coach respond to each other simultaneously", "Client showing no responses as an overall quality of presence", "Random movement", "Coach showing no responses as an overall quality of presence". Legend: Real, Random.]

These questions alert us to the importance of interoception and the understanding of who we are in coaching globally: our explicit role in coaching for clients' self-directed goal attainment. We 'are not just there' to ask powerful questions or roll out tools we acquire in our coaching education and further development training but we are the powerful tool: how self-directed we are in why we do coaching may determine how well we can support our clients in reaching their self-directed goals.

Figure 7 The upper chart depicts the client's self-reports over 10 sessions. The x-axis in the upper chart shows the number of coaching sessions. The y-axis shows the self-regulation values and the development the client reported for self-regulation over eight sessions. The lower chart depicts the development of synchrony across 10 sessions. No synchrony development relates to no self-regulation development over time.

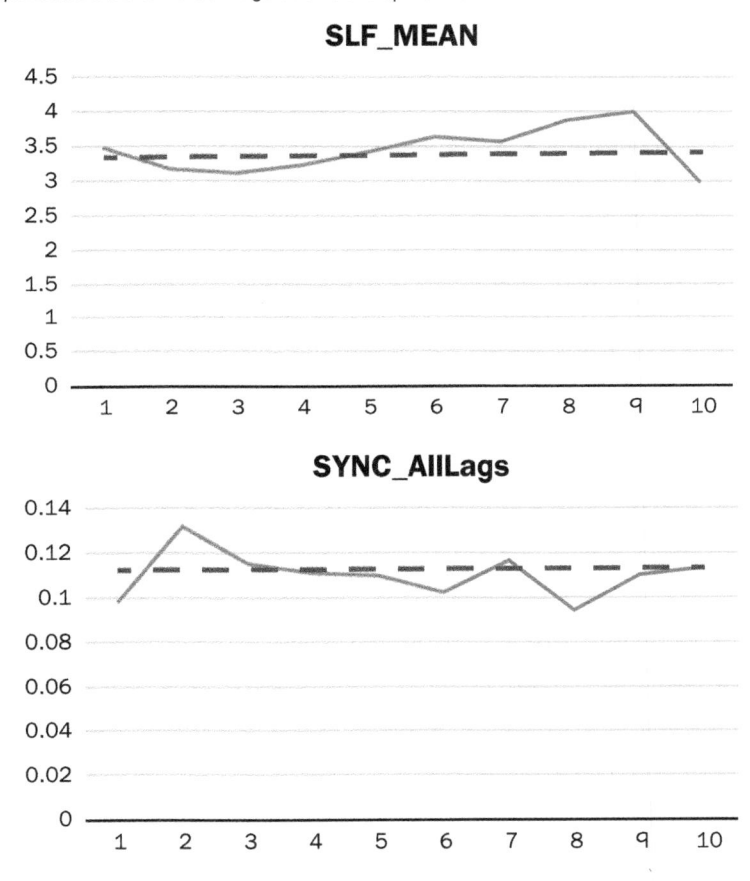

SLF_MEAN

SYNC_AllLags

Framing the quantitative results

> The seeds of great discovery are constantly floating around us, but they only take root in minds well prepared to receive them. – Joseph Henry

The coaching presence research project – exploring a comprehensive, multi-cultural sample of naturalistic coaching processes – provided a number of findings[3] related to both the process and outcome aspects of coaching.

---

3 You can obtain research data from the double-blind reviewed journal article cited as: Erdös, T. and Ramseyer, F.T. (2020) Change process in coaching: Interplay of

Overview of quantitative results

First, coaching has been successful for the majority of clients participating in this study. Second, it takes exploring coaching as a process to reveal that a solid working alliance, with high cognitive and emotional self-regulation predict successful goal attainment three months after completion of coaching. Third, only a complex network analysis uncovers the power of synchronous body movement in coaching as a process, as framed in the five points below.

Movement synchrony – A correctional mechanism?

Movement synchrony, the working alliance and goal attainment in coaching are associated in a peculiar temporal manner: The temporal network models show that lower synchrony in a previous session predicts higher goal orientation and higher goal setting as two out of three components of the working alliance (the third one being bonding, as discussed below), as well as higher goal of self-reflection as a key component of cognitive self-regulation in the next session. Does this association suggest that higher movement synchrony indicates some 'correctional mechanism' that emerges at a point where the coaching process is perceived to be deteriorating? It seems that it all depends on levels of goal attainment.

Movement synchrony and working alliance in goal attainment

In the group with an average coaching success (mid-33 per cent), movement synchrony in a previous session predicts a lower level of bonding in the next session (as evident in the temporal process network). Similarly, movement synchrony is also negatively associated with the level of bonding of the same session (as evident in the contemporaneous network: session-level analysis) in this group. These associations between movement synchrony and bonding are not found in the least successful group (low 33 per cent) or in the very small group that did not complete the post-coaching questionnaire on goal attainment. In contrast, in the most highly successful group (top 33 per cent), movement synchrony is positively associated with bonding of the same session (contemporaneous network). The negative relationship between movement synchrony and bonding in the group with average coaching success comes as a surprise. It contrasts findings by Ramseyer and Tschacher (2011) and Altmann et al. (2020). However, such an effect is not new in research on non-verbal synchrony. A recent study interpreted a similar negative association as an indicator that there is a difference between idiographic and nomothetic samples (Ramseyer, 2020b), that is in groups that have specific characteristics versus groups where we can draw more generalizable conclusions. Findings in psychotherapy settings point towards an optimal (middle) level of synchrony as desirable for a strong working alliance. Low movement synchrony is shown to be an indicator of drop-out (premature ending) and high movement synchrony

---

movement synchrony, working alliance, self-regulation and goal-attainment. *Frontiers in Psychology* (in publication).

is found to be a predictor of early termination (Paulick et al., 2018), which indicates effective learning and growth. This also falls into line with more recent work in psychotherapy settings, where movement synchrony in the third session of therapy predicted lower success later in therapy (Lutz et al., 2020).

Therefore, high initial movement synchrony may not necessarily imply good contact between coach and client. A similar interpretation can be found in past research conducted on marital conflict, where physiological synchrony (a different manifestation of non-verbal synchrony) during a couple's conflict discussion predicted later divorce (Levenson and Gottman, 1983). More recently, it has been found that students showed higher levels of non-verbal synchrony in discussions of a conflictual type than in discussions characterized by collaboration (Tschacher et al., 2014). In that particular study, the highest levels of synchrony were evident while students were engaged in a very specific 'fun task' (building a menu of disliked foods). This may mean that the level at which people synchronize depends on the situation or the task at hand. Similarly, people are most successful in collaborative tasks in weak coupling, that is, not in totally synchronous behaviour (Abney et al., 2015; Wiltshire et al., 2018; Wiltshire et al., 2020).

The particular associations between movement synchrony and the working alliance suggest a strengthening/weakening influence of bonding on how movement synchrony relates to clients' self-regulatory capacities. In other words, coaching is a dynamic learning process with each coaching session forming more than the sum of its individual parts. This implies that bonding as an aspect of the quality of the coaching relationship may be determined by 'how well' rather than by 'how much' coach and client are present emotionally, cognitively and behaviourally in each session. 'More presence' does not necessarily lead to 'more bonding' or 'more working alliance' generally, and subsequently to higher goal attainment. High goal attainment is warranted by how uniquely coach and client are present with each other in the same session without a particular session-level synchrony predicting a stronger coach-client relationship in future sessions. It is the quality of the moment-by-moment experience that may build coaching results beyond a linear input-output mechanism of 'more synchrony' engendering 'more working alliance' resulting in 'higher goal attainment'.

Movement synchrony as a process in coaching

In the sessions analyzed, dyads show higher levels of movement synchrony at the outset of the coaching process, and synchrony shows a linear trend for a temporal decrease. As mentioned above, these associations may imply some 'correctional mechanism'. At the beginning of the coaching process, greater effort is required in terms of 'getting onto the same page' or 'attaining the same wavelength with each other', which later becomes less important as coaching sessions progress. In dyads where progress starts to go off track, higher levels of movement synchrony indicate emerging efforts to correct the deteriorating relationship or the yet unproductive process.

Additionally, the temporal models show that six sessions suffice for clients to establish self-regulatory capacities where movement synchrony and working alliance are strong in each session, which implies that clients become autonomous after six sessions to attain goals in a self-directed manner.

Movement synchrony and self-regulation at session level and as a process

The influence of movement synchrony on self-regulation and the working alliance was most evident in the temporal network of the group with average coaching success, where low movement synchrony predicts higher positive affect (emotional aspect of self-regulation), higher goal self-reflection (cognitive aspect of self-regulation), and a more solid overall working alliance over time. In the session-level network analysis, clients report lower bonding in sessions with high movement synchrony, that is, in sessions where coaches may attempt to correct for the relationship or the coaching process being off track. So, the optimal level of movement synchrony may not only lie somewhere in-between too little ('bored-teenager-effect') and too much synchrony ('mime effect') as described by Boker (2004) and Ramseyer (2010), but it may depend highly on the contextual situation of coaching and the characteristics of the verbal exchange, the coach and client respectively. As mentioned above, the so-called weak coupling may indeed be an important condition for successful social or collaborative interaction (Wiltshire et al., 2018). Given the non-experimental character of the research project, this question remains unanswered. Future studies may try to control for and specifically focus on contextual factors of coaching interactions (Erdös et al., 2020). Such an approach is likely to complement our understanding of coaching as a dynamic learning process.

Movement synchrony, working alliance and self-regulation in interaction

Generally, the working alliance is found to strengthen/weaken how movement synchrony relates to both cognitive and emotional self-regulation. Specifically, in dyads reporting high levels of working alliance, movement synchrony is negatively related to cognitive self-regulation, while the reverse is true for dyads reporting low levels of working alliance (Figure 8B). In contrast, in dyads reporting high levels of cognitive self-regulation and high levels of working alliance, movement synchrony is positively associated with emotional self-regulation, while in dyads reporting low levels of cognitive self-regulation and low working alliance, movement synchrony is negatively associated with emotional self-regulation (Figure 8A). This is a highly differentiated matrix of findings.

These differentiated interactions indicate that movement synchrony predicts high cognitive self-regulation when paired with low task setting as one of the three components of the working alliance (the other two being goal orientation and bonding). This association does not exist in dyads with high task setting. This hints at coaching engagements in which coach and client

Figure 8 Panel A: Interaction between synchrony (SYNC, X-axis), affect regulation (PAN-AB; colour of slopes) and cognitive self-reflection (RoPS-tot, Y-Axis). Panel B: Interaction between synchrony (SYNC, X-axis), alliance (WAI-tot; colour of slopes) and cognitive self-reflection (RoPS-tot, Y-Axis).

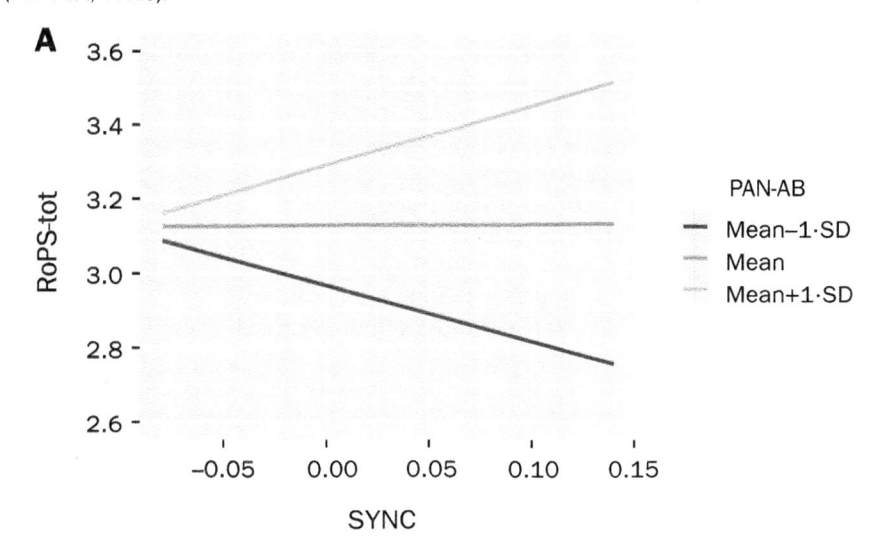

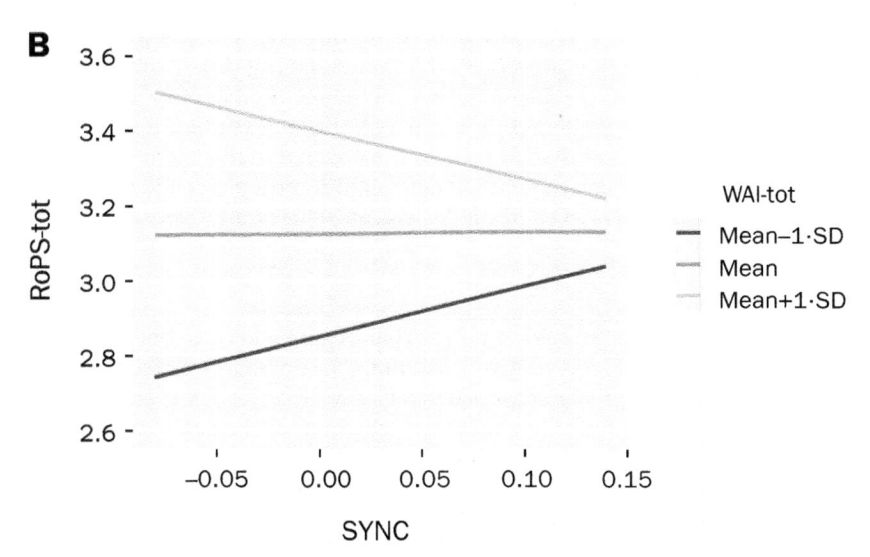

focus predominantly on goal attainment and where the working alliance is determined by the level of task setting. In other words, where task setting characterizes the coaching process, the extent to which coach and client synchronize becomes obsolete. This indication accords with Greif and Berg's

(2011) theory that a task-specific result-orientated reflection style renders coaching efficient with regard to clients' successful goal attainment and that this association may contribute to how we can develop self-regulatory theory beyond coaching.

The level of complexity we arrived at in exploring the working alliance as a strengthening/weakening agent through network analysis and differentiated interactions does not come as a surprise. Grassmann et al. (2019) report in their most recent meta-analysis that the strengths of the coach-client relationship is linked to but does not cause coaching outcomes. The debate around goal/task focus, trust and rapport between coach and client is attributable to how coaching as a context and as a process produces change in and for clients (Molyn and Gray, 2019). This raises two questions:

- What is the role of coaching as a change intervention?
- What is the role of the coach and the client in the coach-client relationship?

A recent qualitative meta-synthesis of client factors and contextual in coaching as a change process (Erdös et al., 2020) suggests that coach/client characteristics rather than specific techniques associated with a coaching intervention comprehensively affect the coaching process.

Findings suggest that a working alliance can most appropriately contribute to the evidence base in coaching if and where we view it as a process measure. The working alliance does not lead to goal attainment. This study shows that a working alliance works as an interpersonal factor rather than a factor that predicts outcomes. As such, it strengthens or weakens the direct relationship of movement synchrony and self-regulation. Findings in this study also indicate that because a working alliance is an interpersonal variable, it shapes how clients self-regulate and is shaped by how the coach and the client dance in the moment to the beats of movement synchrony in interdependence with clients' self-regulatory capacities in each single session rather than over time.

Conclusion

Synchrony through spontaneous non-verbal responsiveness between coach and client has so far received scant attention in coaching psychology. This approach to coaching presence represents a new direction for research, which has long been preoccupied with coaching techniques and what coaches need to do to support our clients' goal attainment. Both the quantitative and qualitative avenues I applied to explore presence through spontaneous movement synchrony show valuable, albeit unexpected outcomes. The qualitative explorations indicate that coaches need to do the following:

- *allow* themselves to be seen as vulnerable, emotional, feeling and sensing
- *acknowledge* that they may and can be affected by clients' vulnerability, emotionality, feelings and sense sharing

- *use* their awareness of self and interoception to attain professional proximity and work effectively, if we are to understand coaching as a 'way of being' in the world.

The quantitative explorations indicate the following:

- Working alliance does not strengthen spontaneous non-verbal interactional processes (for example, simultaneous behavioural reactions to the same stimulus).
- Only task setting as one element of the quality of the coaching relationship strengthens the spontaneous non-verbal interactional processes. This is contrary to what has been shown in psychotherapy and the behavioural sciences and implies that the In-Sync Model is too simple to provide us with reliable outcomes.
- We need to investigate the relationship between movement synchrony and the working alliance at a more detailed level, as the coaching presence research project has done.
- Clients adapt their emotional responses to challenging moments, using their emotional self-regulatory and cognitive resources beyond sessions to engage in attaining self-directed goals.
- Self-regulation has a ripple effect on clients' long-term goal attainment.

This is important for all coaches as we all need to learn and practise coaching presence as a spontaneous capacity to respond to clients' needs, as the key to clients' capacity to work on their issues with coaches. What is surprising is that the working alliance does not strengthen clients' capacity to self-regulate through movement synchrony. Only if coach and client keep agreeing on tasks will the working alliance strengthen that relationship. This means that we need to do more process research to better understand what is going on between the coach and the client and how the quality of their coaching relationship influences effective outcomes.

Findings at a glance:

- Clients effectively reach goals when the coach and the client are mutually present (as expressed in their movement synchrony, which is based on the premise that the body does not lie and will convey nuanced energies in the coaching room that clients will trust more than spoken language) and have a strong coach-client relationship (solid bonding, task setting and goal orientation) in each session. In other words, coaching is a session-to-session experience in which presence is not a 'quantifiable' phenomenon. This means that more presence does not lead to a better coach-client relationship over time. While coaching is a process, it is each session-level experience that eventually creates high levels of goal attainment.

- When coach and client move in synchrony and when the relationship is characterized by solid levels of bonding in each session, six sessions will suffice for clients to become autonomous.
- High initial presence in the early coaching phase (as expressive of movement synchrony) does not necessarily imply good contact (that is, bonding and more generally a strong working alliance) between the coach and the client. It indicates that the coach and the client do not have a well-functioning collaborative relationship and that coaches appear more present through movement synchrony to correct for the absence of a solid goal-orientated and task-setting partnership.
- High initial presence at the outset also indicates that presence (as expressive of movement synchrony) serves as some kind of 'correctional mechanism'. At the beginning of the coaching process, greater effort is required in terms of 'getting onto the same page' or 'being on the same wavelength as the other one', which later becomes less important as coaching sessions progress.
- Generally, analyzing presence as a process, it becomes apparent that where coach and client are not in sync they have a more collaborative partnership with high levels of goal orientation and task setting. This process also suggests that movement synchrony serves as some kind of 'correctional mechanism' that emerges at a point where the coaching process is perceived to be deteriorating.
- Establishing good contact or robust bonding depends on 'how well' rather than 'how much' the coach and the client are present and coordinating with each other emotionally, cognitively and behaviourally in each session.
- The optimal level of movement synchrony between coach and client depends on contextual factors, such as coaching as a task-setting and goal-orientated collaborative intervention (as evident through the quantitative findings) and the coach as forming the client's environment (as evident through the qualitative feedback sessions).
- Where task setting characterizes the coaching process, the extent to which coach and client synchronize and the extent to which coach and client are present with each other becomes obsolete.
- Emotions matter in coaching. Movement synchrony helps clients build emotional self-regulation, which supports task setting, goal orientation and bonding as well as goal self-reflection from session to session.

Part II

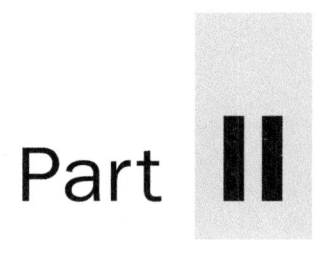

Framing the findings in practice

When making the matryoshka doll and after the mother doll is formed and set, the framing of the nested dolls begins. Just as our skeleton serves as the structure for our bodies, the frame of the matryoshka doll is the underlying as well as the encompassing structure of all the nested dolls.

In this part of the book, my aim is to integrate the research findings to frame the focus on what you can effectively do to enhance presence in your coaching practice. This implies that the style of writing will begin to change through to Part III as we turn our attention to applying evidence in practice.

There is also a switch in subject from 'I' to 'We', after introducing a model of presence that grew out of an emergent collaboration with Samer Hassan, one that can serve as a 'nested doll' to lead reasoned discourse about presence as a skill-based methodology. In doing so, we are aware of standing on giants' shoulders. We trust that by inviting coaches to think about reasoned discourse, we can frame how to account for our beliefs around where the 'I' stands when it comes to presence. Identifying where the 'I' stands and making meaning of why and how the 'I' stands 'there' appear as a professional stance in coaching practice.

So, by framing the findings in practice, we invite coaches to seek mastery by forming their beliefs through critical thinking beyond the 'echo chamber' of like-minded coaches. We invite you, dear reader, to reflect on how we know what we claim to and how our knowing differs from how things simply seem to us. Therefore, this Part is not about believing whatever we want but about forming judgement within a framework of foundations set in evidence and expressing our best current understanding in our quest to seek truths about presence.

4 Integrative Presence – Framing the findings with a methodology and philosophy

Introduction

In this chapter, which wants to emerge while I am away on a retreat in the north of Belgium, I first define Integrative Presence as informed by the findings of the coaching presence research project. In doing so, I deliberately draw on three theoretical frameworks as the giants on whose shoulders I want Integrative Presence to stand:

1 presence-based coaching
2 complex adaptive systems theory (CAS)
3 integral coaching theory.
4 I will reveal the reasons why.

Next, I will allow myself to be guided by a metaphor to inhale life into this concept. My aim is to illustrate its spirit as a fluid and emergent experience rather than a static postulation. The tender truth of the spirit invites the firm force of evidence. Don't you want to meet me there?

The three giants – Brief excursions into framing Integrative Presence

Presence-based coaching

Silsbee's (2008) presence-based coaching theory argues that coaches' 'presence evokes change in others' (p. 5) and that 'there are three doorways into presence: mind, body, and heart' (p. 3). Silsbee's theory addresses strategies coaches can use to show how to engage with becoming aware of, building, and developing awareness of our physical sensations in response to others without moving to meaning-making of these sensations either emotionally or relationally (see also, Chapter 2, 'What do we mean by presence anyway?'). However, as we are socially bounded in 'how we are' and how we behave with each other, the question how to 'build a body able to work in partnership' (p. 162) with clients' mind, heart and body interlocked in a system of dynamic interactions, as influenced by a larger social and global system remains unresolved. We face several questions:

- How does coaching presence impact clients from the coaches' perspectives?
- How do clients feel affected by coaches' presence?
- How do we know that it is through presence that clients truly grow and develop to reach goals?
- What if there is more to presence than the partnership with one's own mind, heart and body?
- Whose mind, whose body, and whose heart do we need to integrate to experience a fuller and more comprehensive sense of presence beyond individual physical sensations?
- What if presence is a more complex phenomenological experience?

Complex adaptive systems theory (CAS)

The assumption that there may be a fuller and more comprehensive sense of presence yet to be explored and framed was nurtured by the results of the coaching presence research project. Findings indicate that presence is neither about the coach nor about the client alone and that it can be explained only when we look at it both within each coaching session and as a process over time. As the findings reveal the interlocking system of how coach and client 'dance in the moment' in the coach-client relationship, and that presence can indeed harm rather than just help clients, it becomes apparent that we need to connect our view of coaching presence as an intrapersonal and interpersonal phenomenon with other scientific disciplines and theories.

This approach chimes in with calls in coaching psychology (Bachkirova et al., 2014; Cavanagh and Lane, 2012; Western, 2012) that developing the knowledge base of coaching per se requires us to apply complex adaptive systems theory (CAS; Stacey, 2011) for a deeper understanding of the process of coaching as an emerging phenomenon. Why do we not apply it to coaching presence?

As a set of complex responsive processes, CAS refers to how behaviour may emerge unpredictably and without any linear cause-effect explanation. For instance, ecosystems, the human brain or ant colonies are found to be the best examples of complex adaptive systems as each of these systems performs as a network of a chain of agents acting in parallel. The coaching presence research project shows that clients' responses to coaches will determine how coaches will behave right from the outset in coaching. As such, while coaches perceive themselves as offering the same 'way of being' with all their clients, just as parents firmly claim that they behave in the same way with all their children, motion energy analysis reveals that their presence differs not just from client to client but also from session to session.

Already well established in sports coaching (Bowes and Jones, 2006), CAS is becoming increasingly relevant for organizations as complex and dynamic learning entities (de Haan and Burger, 2005). Bowes and Jones (2006) postulate coaches as working in the paradoxical state of harmony and conflict, regularity and unpredictability, stability and instability (Stacey, 2011). Therefore, I believe that CAS is a viable avenue to understand the coach-client relationship as an unpredictable phenomenon that reflects more than the sum of the individual contributions (de Haan, 2008a) of coach and client. Formal research corroborates calls to understand coaching as a context-sensitive and socially constructed change process (Athanasopoulou and Dopson, 2018; Bachkirova et al., 2014; Cox, 2013). These scientists postulate coaching as subject to fluctuations of the properties of the coach, the client, the coach-client relationship and various contextual factors and claim that it is more than an input-output cause-effect activity (Cavanagh, 2013).

In studying coaching presence as a socially constructed change process applying CAS, we can offer an alternative perspective to the more widely held cause-effect explanations, not just on coaching but also on coaching presence. This complexity view puts the focus on coaches, clients and their immediate and wider contexts as integral to understanding how coaching presence might work and why it is effective. One major integral approach available in coaching to date is integral coaching theory (Hunt, 2009). It is this theory that we deliberately choose as a third cornerstone of Integrative Presence in this book.

Integral coaching theory

Integral coaching theory (Hunt, 2009) and integral coaching practice (Divine, 2009) are grounded in integral theory (Wilber, 2000). Among other components, the integral coaching model proposes six lines of development in coaching: cognitive, emotional, interpersonal, somatic, spiritual, and moral. For a brief description of presence in the integral coaching model, see Chapter 2, 'What do we mean by presence anyway?'.

Integral coaching practice looks at skillfully working with various realms of energy as a 'way of being', viewing presence as sitting at the heart of learning and change (Divine, 2009). It focuses on our sensitivity to the nature of our interactions with the world beyond the felt experiences of the coach and the client. According to integral coaching theory, the body is a key instrument in accessing integral sensitivity. This view mirrors Merleau-Ponty's noting in the mid-twentieth century that sensation, perception and cognition are inseparably connected to the physical body. 'It is through my body that I understand other people, just as it is through my body that I perceive "things" (Merleau-Ponty, 2002, p. 216). This observation also receives strong neuroscientific support, for example, in the domain of the perception of emotion (de Gelder and Partan, 2009; Zhan and de Gelder, 2019). Such an integral learning and development system is devoid of any links to specific methodical approaches (Bachkirova and Lawton Smith, 2015), which is why integral coaching theory was selected as the third cornerstone of Integrative Presence in this book.

How and to what extent do the body and, in particular, body movement as expressive of presence and as integrating cognitive, emotional, interpersonal, somatic, spiritual, and moral lines of development embody coaching effectiveness? This is the question that Integrative Presence as an evidence-informed methodology and philosophy seeks to answer.

Defining Integrative Presence

Against this background, I define Integrative Presence as a purposeful dynamic interplay that emerges as measurable non-verbal energy from the interpersonal interactions between coach and client through the doorways of the mind, body and heart, as each mind, body and heart influences and adapts to the other mind, body and heart as a relational phenomenon in clients' change process, implying that the coach changes in the dynamic interplay too. Presence integrates:

- the self of either coach or client (the I-Sphere)
- the relationship between coach and client (the WE-Sphere)
- the social system that the coach and client form (the ALL-Sphere)
- the universe as a global legacy of how we are and behave with each other (the OMNI-Sphere).

We will now focus on outlining the essence of 'self' of the coach or the client in Integrative Presence, and the essence of the 'relationship' between coach and client as it was found to be relevant for presence in the research project. We will allow the essence of the 'universe' (OMNI-Sphere) as a global legacy to unfold in this chapter as it wants to emerge from the ideas flowing in a state of presence, in particular, the metaphor of 'the sea'. Furthermore, we will discuss the essence of 'social system' the (ALL-Sphere) more deeply in a case study (see Chapter 10, 'Faceting leadership'), as I have a compelling contemporary case to share to illustrate its essence for Integrative Presence.

Self of coach or client – the I-Sphere

In Integrative Presence, I define self as the non-dual energy of our 'self':

- shaped by the emergent reciprocal interaction of mind, body, and heart
- as embedded in the emergent reciprocal interaction of our closer and wider contexts
- as coloured by the non-dual energy of the OMNI-Sphere beyond our mental consciousness. It is transcendental bliss and presence as a purpose.

This definition is guided by Wilber's (2006) seven levels of energy and consciousness in our development and carves out the aspect of 'self' as non-dual energy. The non-dual self is the emergence of the echo of our non-dual energy over space and across time. Our self is present as such integrating energy from all spheres, beyond material qualities and properties. Wilber (2006) refers to it as the spirit beyond quantum reality which certainly always implies some sort of dimensions and properties and opposites (for example, non-quantum reality). Yet, the 'echo of self' expressing presence as such is not quantifiable, nor qualifiable. It is emergent in its wholeness integrating all: the I-Sphere, the WE-Sphere, the ALL-Sphere, and the OMNI-Sphere. It is like a submarine sonar instrument. The moment of presence is like a sonar pulse while Integrative Presence is like a pulse.

Relationship between coach and client – the WE-Sphere

In complementing Silsbee's (2008) presence-based coaching approach, in extending Hunt's (2009) and Divine's (2009) integral coaching theory as well as engaging with CAS (Stacey, 2011), Integrative Presence relates to how spontaneous non-verbal responsiveness in the coach-client relationship has a ripple effect in coaching: the effect of 'coach one, coach all' as clients become agents of their own responsiveness. Clients can become agents of their responsiveness if and where we manage to acknowledge that our needs are just as important as our clients' needs in coaching. How come? If we are unaware of our own needs (for example, the need to have powerful questions ready, the need to be professional, preference for a costly coaching tool, sense of superiority over other coaches), this can thwart our effectiveness as we become attached to meeting our own needs rather than being responsive to what clients need at any given moment. Our attachment to our own needs leads to our lack of presence, which eventually limits our clients' capacity to experience relationally how to be present. Of course, meeting clients' needs is important too. If clients have their needs met, they become capable of meeting others' needs, including ours. The latter is important for clients as they can perceive us as human beings in a learning partnership with them. Unless we become aware of the dynamic depth of needs being mutually met and the role that our needs play in coaching, we cannot identify the potential patterns clients bring to the coaching room. For instance, a client's readiness to please me in coaching can easily go unheeded as a relational pattern and coaching material unless I am aware of how this readiness to please me affects my energy levels and is felt in my body as well as how I respond to that felt sense.

It appears that energy, as formed through spontaneous body interactions between coach and client, constitutes synchrony as an interpersonal interactive phenomenon well established in the social and relationship sciences (Feldman, 2007) but unexplored in coaching so far. However, movement synchrony is not a panacea: it can both help and harm clients. The research findings indicate that movement synchrony may lead to clients feeling safe or unsafe in coaching under certain conditions (see Chapter 3, 'How movement synchrony embodies your presence'). Therefore, becoming aware of our non-verbal energy as an antenna that receives and sends signals of how we are with each other at any given moment is fundamental to our coaching effectiveness.

What is energy in Integrative Presence?

Energy as measured in the research project is the fluid, reciprocal and spontaneous emergence of material from what we present and what we are presented with at any given moment and in any given situation. Energy as an emergent phenomenon of presence in coaching is contained in any word, emotion, space that contains us, in each individual, in society as a whole and in how ancestral influences shape how we behave in mutual interdependence. It is expressed through the body as the most reliable instrument to indicate how we are doing at any given moment: the body does not lie.

The long-lasting ripple effect of co-created energy manifests through the spontaneous emergence of how we are with each other. This is the very essence of quantum entanglement, which physicist Albert Einstein famously described as 'spooky action at a distance'.[1] Quantum entanglement as a fundamental property of nature (Moreau et al., 2019) occurs when two particles become intricately related, and whatever happens to one immediately affects the other, regardless of how far apart they are.

Coaching for Integrative Presence

Coaching for Integrative Presence allows sensations, mental, emotional or behavioural interactions, situations, moments, and human environments of cultural and ancestral background to shape effectiveness in coaching in total interdependence. Coaching for Integrative Presence is not about the coach's or the client's experiences alone. Sensitivity to practising coaching for Integrative Presence emerges from a somatic and embodied interaction with that sensitivity and interdependence.

The sea – The metaphor of Integrative Presence as a methodology

We often refer to coaching as a journey. A journey with a destination without knowing how we will reach the destination. We refer to it as clients' navigating their self-discovery and exploration of the self towards growth, development, and ultimately well-being.

As I am sitting at my desk in an apartment I rented in the north of Belgium to start writing about my own coaching presence research journey there, I find myself looking at the floor-to-ceiling windows spanning the entire width of the apartment facing the sea between Belgium and Britain. I am staring at the turquoise-blue-brown sea on what is a beautiful day in late autumn 2019. I sense the width, depth and immense vastness of the water and reflect back on how my client's awareness of her lack of safety with me in our coaching engagement inspired me to investigate movement synchrony in coaching. I am reminded of how she was working with the ripple effects of the water in one of the centring exercises we did on exploring presence in coaching.

Observing the turquoise-blue-brown sea unfolding in its breathtaking vastness in front of me, I see a ship on the horizon and notice how my body responds: just as this ship on the horizon moves in a steady dance of winds and waves rocking the ship's body, I sense that presence is about 'moving' in a dance navigating the stimuli of the sea of thoughts, emotions and behaviours in and around us.

---

1 Weidemuller, M. (2013) Quantum physics: Spooky action gets collective. *Nature*, 498 (7455): 438.

Of course, just like navigating a ship, coaching is a highly responsible act. Just as a captain is responsive to the movement of the winds and waves as they rock the body of the vessel on the sea, in coaching, both coach and client respond to their internal stimuli and the stimuli coming from others as these rock our body in coaching. As they move with each other through the waves and winds of their journey, both coach and client are in the process of navigating the accelerating uncertainties of their universe.

Sitting there observing the sea, I ask myself: 'What if the sea represented how we navigate ourselves? Let us call it the I-Sphere. What if the ship stood for how we navigate our relationships, with its vessel embodying our attention to Integrative Presence? Let us call it the WE-Sphere. What if all that surrounds the sea reaching from the wind to the waves to the skies to all the other ships that might cross our ship's path were our environment? Let us call it the ALL-Sphere. And what if we framed the sea of Integrative Presence as a picture? What if the wall we put the picture on were all aspects of the room the wall forms part of, the building the room is in, the city the building stands in, and so on? Let us call it the OMNI-Sphere.'

Every captain needs to be responsive to the movements on the sea. It fascinates me when I realize that responsiveness on the sea is exactly what makes up the quality of presence in coaching. In particular, spontaneous responsiveness emerges through physical sensation and movement as the sea interacts with the ship. It is the capacity that guides the ship through the accelerating uncertainties of how the waves, winds and skies as well as other passing ships interact with the ship. This very interaction is framed in the picture that hangs on the wall of a room in a building, in a city, in a country, on a continent of the globe that we are part of. Furthermore, I believe that spontaneous responsiveness, where it emerges, accelerates, establishing safety on the ship, which will manifest in how the ship:

- copes with extremes on the sea (in coaching: bouncing between 'chaos and order')
- resources itself in the ALL-Sphere (in coaching: gaining self-worth and trust)
- decelerates 'accelerating change' on the sea (in coaching: bringing balance as a state that we flexibly access rather than as an escapism).

The ship responds interconnectedly in the moment, seeing first how the wind, waves and skies behave – and that is what the ship notices while it is not aware of what is 'underneath' more deeply. Nor can the ship see beyond the horizon. The ship sees the space and distance it needs to navigate through the behaviours of the ALL-Sphere. Synching with the sea, the ship can move with the needs of the ALL-Sphere as it accelerates or decelerates and turns direction, if only it is ready to spontaneously respond to the sea and the ALL-Sphere. Movement by movement, moment by moment, the ship and sea regulate in how they dance with each other encompassed in the ALL-Sphere.

As the dance unfolds in the ALL-Sphere, I am left wondering: Can we see how this dance is integrated in the OMNI-Sphere of 'the framed picture on the wall of a room in a building, in a city, in a country, on a continent of the globe we are part of', or not? Why do we care? And if we were aware of the OMNI-Sphere, what would it consist of? How do we deal with our responsibility to become aware of the dynamics of the OMNI-Sphere in Integrative Presence?

The philosophical edge of Integrative Presence

These questions arouse my curiosity and I feel drawn to reflect on the truth of what strikes me as the spirit of the OMNI-Sphere in presence. As I watch the sea framed by the panes of the floor-to-ceiling windows in front of me, my eyes suddenly turn to my arms. My eyes scan my skin and my mind considers how our skin is multi-layered, containing our body, and I hear my thoughts trickling about how the OMNI-Sphere can be multi-layered, including an ethical, social human, biological, psychological and spiritual nature. While I am aware that there might be more layers to the nature of the OMNI-Sphere, I content myself with opening up a reasoned discourse around this sphere as our global legacy. I believe that exploring the OMNI-Sphere in coaching presence creates a platform for the truth of this sphere's spirit to invite the firm force of evidence around the other three spheres. Don't you want to meet me there?

Ethical nature of the OMNI-Sphere

Ethically, the global legacy that we can access through the OMNI-Sphere in Integrative Presence includes issues of ethics and value-based standards that can inform our understanding of how to act professionally in practising presence and practising coaching, more generally.

My parents taught me that a promise is a promise. They said, 'You don't back away from promises.' They learned this from their ancestors who used to work hard to make both ends meet. Those were the times when equal and mutual support among neighbours ensured a bare livelihood. While times have certainly changed, the legacy has not. So I might have a tendency to hang on to promises that will shape how I keep promises towards clients, thereby potentially appearing to be inflexible in situations where they have not acted on a task from a previous coaching session. Am I aware of my responsibility to become aware of how the OMNI-Sphere shapes my practice? Becoming aware of the role of global legacy in my coaching practice will give me the autonomy to choose. While I might take a promise seriously in principle, I might just as well back away from it if other responsibilities kicked in. For instance, I promise to help you move house, but my child needs medical care the very day you relocate. I might need to break my promise to attend to my child's needs. Or my own. This is nothing to do with whether I am egocentric but with how times have changed to allow me to make choices in life – unless, of course, breaking promises is something that I practise regularly. We have a choice, which has certainly got its own implications for later generations in how we pass our flexibility on to them.

In brief, the philosophical nature of the OMNI-Sphere appears to invite us to reflect on the extent to which ethics and value-based standards may affect our presence in coaching. I propose two perspectives that can complement each other in how we may choose to work with ethics and value-based standards in being present with our clients:

1 *Ethics as a pool of values and standards we have received from our ancestors.* This refers to the cultural embeddedness, the universal truth of how people choose to be with each other, what has been passed down to us and which we pass on to others following in our path. These values and standards shape how we are now. We co-create and replicate these values and standards in how we behave as coaches and how those following us can behave in their world. Therefore, becoming aware of the spirit of how we approach our cultural embeddedness when responding to our clients is important because we may meet clients in their own particular cultural embeddedness, which may challenge how we can be present with them, so that our presence meets their needs rather than ours.
2 *Aristotelian ethics as a disposition to behave in the right manner and as a means between extremes of deficiency (for example, no awareness of the 'use-of-self') and excess (for example, no control over the 'use of self').* Aristotelian ethics refers to moral virtue that we learn primarily through habit and practice rather than through reasoning and instruction. We acquire this habit from others, and others learn from others, and they learn from others. That is why the OMNI-Sphere is important because it is this sphere which equips us with this disposition. Awareness of how our deficiencies and excesses shape how we behave and how we cope with these extremes relationally and openly in coaching implies that we are aware that we make choices, and clients can learn how to make their choices and cope with the extremes of their deficiencies and excesses.

Social human nature of the OMNI-Sphere

As Integrative Presence is about developing our awareness of the dynamic depth of how our presence affects others beyond our I-Sphere, the WE-Sphere, and the ALL-Sphere, our awareness of our responsibility to society and humanity strikes me as greatly influencing how we behave as coaches. This particular nature of the OMNI-Sphere may be strange, as it goes beyond the obvious in the seemingly cocooned cosmos of coaching sessions, but it is a perspective that can have the highest impact.

Let me propose a point of view. What if the way that prisoners were dealt with in your society potentially had an impact on how your presence plays out in the coaching room? A far-fetched thought, you might say? Suppose, your society treats prisoners in such a way that they sense shame for their wrong doings or what we determine to be laws, which can vary greatly depending on the legislator's perspective in your society. Suppose, in your society, people apply punishment and behaviour correction as the means by which they educate, develop and grow as a society. How do you behave as a coach in that society? The way that a society instrumentalizes shame and the way any member of that society copes with issues of self-respect and shame may require us as coaches to explore at least a few questions around how we can be present to our clients in that society, such as:

- Who am I as an integral part of that society, when it comes to how I think of what is lawful and when it comes to making sense of my clients' behaviour?
- What is the spirit with which I decide what needs 'punishing' or 'correction', as I am called to adhere by my codes of ethics of reporting unlawful behaviour in coaching?
- How am I as a coach in the face of societal pressures: do I exclude or isolate clients in how I deal with my societal pressures?
- How does my way of coping with societal pressures play out in my coaching presence?
- What is my level of presence as a coach around how to navigate the uncertainties of my social and human responsibilities?
- Which societal and human values do I consciously apply in my coaching practice, as they will have an inevitable footprint on my clients' learning and how their learning will shape the next generation's learning?

Yes, quite a cartload of questions. There are certainly more questions that will escape my level of awareness in the here and now of my reflections. What cannot escape my awareness is that we are social creatures: we need each other to define each other. To define myself, I need to feel the lineage, the meanings that travelled through generations and time as they impress on me without my realizing it.

Let me propose an additional point of view: the impact of politics on your coaching presence. Let us suppose that your society has failed to undergo some essential innovation cycle (for example, the principle of due diligence in the government) to meet the needs of your people (for example, integrity), and your society is now about to collapse (for example, through riots): how would that development shape your way of being present with your clients' needs? How might the political circumstances that permeate your society influence how you are with your clients? How might these circumstances impact your capacity to show due diligence and integrity in how you create learning for your clients? How might your clients' sense of accountability in coaching be impacted by the ongoing political circumstances in your society? Furthermore, what is your level of awareness of how your mental programming through your coaching training (for example, the doctrine of asking powerful questions) plays out in your flexibility and innovative capacity to be present with your clients?

These questions appear appropriate to me as we have accumulated wisdom and scientific evidence for similar dynamics around how both coaches and clients are affected by the social, human and political agendas in the organizations they work with – the ALL-Sphere. We call these agendas parallel processes, and we are sensitized to consciously pay attention to how these processes inform our flexibility in how we work with clients. In this vein, social, human and political doctrines can have an important effect on how we feel enabled to innovate in our coaching practice, which is essential to stay present to our clients' needs in a rapidly changing world of needs. After all, the extent to which we feel permitted to innovate is the imprint we inherit in our learning of how 'we must be' in our society to be seen and accepted.

Biological nature of the OMNI-Sphere

The relevance of human biology for coaching presence might apparently appear not to be obvious, and even challenging to accept at first glance. Some might view it as outmoded. The point of including the seemingly non-obvious is that Integrative Presence calls for being inclusive rather than exclusive with our awareness of how we view presence in coaching. To quote integral theorist Ken Wilber, 'Integrative simply means that this approach attempts to include as many important truths from as many disciplines as possible, from East as well as the West, from premodern and modern and postmodern, from the hard sciences to physics to the tender sciences of spirituality' (Wilber, 2007, p. 19).

There is an obvious connection between human biology and coaching presence. Imagine that you have a zit. Biologically, while a zit represents some material that is pushed out from the body, it manages to seek a path for inclusion as the body is called to send more blood to the zit to nurture and integrate it. In this sense, biology appears to epitomize the integrative practice of presence: the body meets the need of the zit spontaneously and flexibly. This example is common knowledge and is meant to illustrate the agency of the body to naturally and spontaneously transform or recover over time. Of course, we know of other types of physical and biological transformation that will be engendered by some chronic illness or caused by an external event (for example, an accident). It is also common knowledge that our genetic pool is transmitted from generation to generation and that our body cells regenerate every 7 years or so, which means that biologically we become a different person in cycles of roughly 7 years, to name but just two additional examples. The biological nature of the OMNI-Sphere is understood to integrate any transformation that has an effect on our physical and biological state.

What happens on a physical level naturally and spontaneously in coaching is indicated through the coaching presence research project to be of essence in how we can be present with clients. The non-verbal responsiveness in the coach-client relationship as expressed through body movement is shown to be a key indicator of how we can help or harm clients in their growth and development. Therefore, the body has a key role to play as the container of our biological material and physical transformation.

What is our current level of awareness of the impact that any type of physical and biological transformation or genetic predisposition (for example, a female with a menstrual cycle that can create tension in the body) has on how we feel able to be present non-verbally to spontaneously meet clients' needs in coaching?

How do you pay attention to the slightest relevance that your physical or biological state might have on how you behave in coaching? How do you consciously integrate your knowledge about your biological and physical transformation in practising presence in coaching? If you had a pool of intertwined genetic material (for example, being half-British, half-Dutch), how would you pay attention to including awareness of the impact that such intertwined genetic material might have on how you behave with your clients? How do you include or exclude any knowledge of your physical or biological transformation (for example, age and developmental cycle in life) in how you are present with clients?

These questions are intended to sensitize you to a specific dynamic pattern in being present, that of how a potential biological condition or genetic predisposition potentially impacts on how you can be spontaneously responsive through your body movement in coaching, as this was found to be important to meet clients' needs in the coaching presence research project.

Psychological nature of the OMNI-Sphere

Psychologically, there are two key aspects that I find worthwhile mentioning here without claiming to be exhaustive in dealing with the psychological nature of the OMNI-Sphere.

The first aspect relates to our sense of belonging as a key basic client need to meet in coaching. For instance, in certain cultures, carrying one's father's name expresses lineage and it forms an integral part of one's identity through a clear sense of belonging. It is important for the psyche to carry that name as it will be in the person's passport, creating visibility not just for the person carrying the name but for all the ancestors: you see me, you see 'us all'. Developing a sense of belonging will be different for orphans who will experience the psychological pressures of having only one name, the other being assigned to them by the orphanage. As coaching is understood to be a partnering relationship between coach and client, the extent to which clients feel that they can develop a sense of belonging and disclose their identity freely in coaching will determine how they can feel psychologically safe to do the challenging work they seek in coaching.

The second aspect relates to the well-established relational dynamics of 'I am OK – You are OK', 'I am not OK – You are OK', 'I am OK – You are not OK', and 'I am not OK – You are not OK' in transactional analysis (Berne, 1964). The relevance of relational dynamics for our psychological safety is also addressed in Chapter 5, 'Somatic Thinking', where the WHO model describes how Somatic Thinking understands human beings to make meaning of their identity psychologically. Where do I source my self-worth – from 'how others see me' or 'how I see others' or both? If I source my self-worth from 'how others see me', my self-worth will be dependent on that external source and I will be trapped. If I can access my self-worth through 'how I see myself', I can gain an additional source of psychological safety that is independent of how others value me. Ideally, as is common knowledge, if we arrive at an understanding that 'I am OK – You are OK' and 'Everything is OK', we can have our need of being seen totally met.

How do we pay attention to what clients need to feel psychologically safe? How good are we at identifying when we are trapped by our own need to feel psychologically safe in coaching? While these relational elements seem obvious and well established in coaching, the coaching presence research project reveals through the feedback sessions with coaches that more often than not coaches are not successful in identifying to what extent their own need to feel psychologically safe (for example, I need to complete another accreditation before I can do coaching; I know that my clients will never want to participate in research) limits their capacity to be spontaneously responsive to their clients' needs in coaching. As motion energy can be measured with precision to indicate the levels of non-verbal spontaneous responsiveness between coach and client, learning about your presence may feel like revealing the matryoshka doll by doll and nest by nest to seek the truth about the impact that your presence or lack thereof has on your clients.

Spiritual nature of the OMNI-Sphere

What do we know about the spirit and the spiritual nature of the OMNI-Sphere? We understand it as some divine knowledge that we do not really understand through mental labels. The spirit is the secret of secrets we can believe or not. It is the X-factor quality of the spiritual nature of the OMNI-Sphere that can truly challenge our presence in coaching as it is beyond any screen of concepts we can hold on to.

Eckhart Tolle (1999) refers to the spirit of presence as the sacred inner essence of what we pay attention to. Deepening the access between our self and what we pay complete attention to is the sign of presence as we recognize our oneness with what we pay attention to. Eckhart Tolle encourages us to relate to nature as the primary source of our inner stillness before we attempt to access the spirit of presence in a potentially challenging relationship.

A lot earlier, Antoine de Saint-Exupéry[2] (1943) says to the Little Prince: 'And now here is my secret, a very simple secret; it is only with the heart that one can see rightly; what is essential is invisible to the eye.' Later, when the Little Prince complains about the rose being capricious, he adds, 'It is the time you have wasted for your rose that makes your rose so important.' The dimension of time appears all the more important to me in the context of the spiritual nature of the OMNI-Sphere in presence, as we were able to measure it in the coaching presence research project. Time spent on and attention paid to what we surround ourselves with manifest some sort of energy exchange and energetic exchange as if the pulses of our existence are measured through this exchange across time. For instance, this energy exchange means that the Little Prince can establish ties with the rose over time to recognize himself in it and the rose will recognize itself in the Little Prince too, and as he recognizes himself in the

---

2 De Saint-Exupéry, A. (1943) *The Little Prince* Translated by Woods, K. (1st edn). New York: Reynal & Hitchcock.

rose, he allows the rose to teach him stillness, to see the spirit of the rose through relating and forming an exchange of energy with the rose. We find this exchange of energy unfolding in how both coach and client are present with each other in the coaching relationship across sessions and over time.

So, can time condition the spirit? Supposedly, energy travels through time as we relate to our environment. Imagine that you wake up one night and sense that something bad has happened to your spouse who went out with friends that night. In other words, you get a feeling that your spouse has had some sort of accident. When your spouse comes home later that night, you learn that indeed there was an accident and you become aware that you could sense it without knowing it for a fact. The ties you have established with your spouse over time are abundant with energy that can travel into the future as the sacred inner essence of your connectedness. This spirit opens up a deep access to what you love and recognize yourself in.

For coaching presence, finding stillness in the moment as we connect to our clients will allow us to recognize ourselves in our clients' needs, which is when we 'know' which powerful questions to ask. It is not the other way around. We will not find stillness in rushing to ask questions to be powerful. It takes connectedness with the essence of our clients' experience to gain access to the question that meets the need of their experience. It is in the stillness of this connectedness that we can 'hear' which question the spirit of the 'unfolding future' is calling us to ask at any given moment in any given session.

What is your relationship to the unfolding future – the unknown - and what kind of ideology do you have to relate to the unknown? How will this ideology around 'not knowing' influence your decisions about how you behave and relate with clients? And ultimately, what is your relationship to dying? Usually, we choose to interpret this unknown phenomenon in different ways: as the ultimate divine, or the body dying and 'that's all', or reincarnation, or something different. Each approach means to pacify the need behind knowing what will happen after we are gone. How does your meaning-making of the unknown quality of endings in life or in coaching engagements influence how you can meet your clients' needs?

Through the depth of our connectedness, the unity of our consciousness with nature and the stillness that we attain by recognizing ourselves in nature, the physical separateness dissipates and we bring ourselves back to the experience of what we pay attention to.

Conclusion

In providing a conceptualization of Integrative Presence as an evidence-informed methodology and philosophy, this chapter sought to be both concise and comprehensive. In depicting the metaphor of 'the sea' and in deep diving into the dynamics of the OMNI-Sphere to mark the philosophical edge of Integrative Presence, the aim was to create a solid anchor for anyone interested in building awareness of how to bounce between chaos and order in applying presence in coaching. On the journey of building awareness of 'the sea', movement synchrony as energy exchange between coach and client became the incubator magnetizing Integrative Presence.

5 Somatic Thinking – Framing the findings with deliberate practice

Samer Hassan

Introduction

This book and this chapter on Somatic Thinking form and frame Integrative Presence as an evidence-informed methodology and practice. Both share the primary focus of demystifying 'presence', and this is where I would like to start. Coaching through presence is the art of being an authentic human in support of humanity, not objectives.

As framed in Chapter 4, 'Integrative Presence', presence is the innate ability any creature possesses; it forms the basis of each skill humans have ever developed. For us to learn, we need to be able to observe ourselves and our surroundings in interaction beyond what we can observe in our immediate environment. Our ability to observe is conditioned by how well we can stay present to the energy exchange manifesting in the space and at the time things happen and as we are embedded in a larger global legacy.

If Sir Isaac Newton[1] had not been in a state of presence when the apple was falling from the tree as embedded in his own global legacy, he would not have observed the apple that stimulated the idea of gravity, the foundation of his universal laws of gravity and all the scientific advances spawned as a result. What if he had stayed preoccupied about something earlier in his life, or something his wife Hannah had told him just before, or anything else for that matter?

As discussed in Chapter 3, 'How movement synchrony embodies your presence', presence plays a critical role in our effectiveness. It is the root competence that feeds all the other coaching competences. Presence in coaching is the ability to focalize what our clients are communicating – verbally, non-verbally, and universally. We cannot listen profoundly, or partner with our clients, or ask powerful questions, or be effective as coaches unless we are in a state of presence, without which a conversation transforms into anything but

---

1 Sir Isaac Newton (1643–1727).

coaching, potentially limiting both our clients' growth and our own impact through coaching.

Presence as a purpose in itself

Chapter 2, 'What do we mean by presence anyway?' details some realities and myths that have fuelled our wisdom and knowledge around presence to date. What we become aware of is that few coaching theories and practices (Divine, 2009; Hunt, 2009; Silsbee, 2008) focus on presence as a purpose in itself. The research project on coaching presence presented in this book is the first attempt to start measuring and making sense of the impact of our presence in coaching, as it explores how the energy exchange between the coach and the client feeds the dynamics of 'being there' profoundly for clients.

As this book pursues the aim of carving out presence as a purpose in itself, what can Somatic Thinking contribute to this end? How can it foster the book's purpose? How can we access presence by design through Somatic Thinking?

In a world that is fused by the need to survive, multitask, play many roles, put our head down and keep going and never having enough time, I wonder, how can we attain presence in a world of accelerating speed, chaos, uncertainty and unpredictability? What if you wished you could thrive but felt that you did not have the time nor the space needed in your life for a demanding discipline like presence? Presence demands that you are 'there' in the same way that Isaac Newton was 'there' when he became aware of the essence of gravity, and that is a lot to ask.

Who am I in this purpose?

I have been practising and teaching martial and healing arts for over 30 years. In addition, I have been working as a professional transformational coach for 15 years. A long time ago, after completing my master's studies in China, I returned to my home country of Egypt and opened the 'Dragon Academy' as a centre for martial arts, which was one of a kind at the time. Because of all the holistic disciplines we offered (meditation, Qi gong, Yoga, etc.), I started witnessing how people were attaining better relationships, greater emotional balance, deeper clarity, a sense of purpose, and more. Seeing all of this warmed my heart and fulfilled me until the moment when I decided to close the academy and move to Canada. I kept in touch with my former students but after a while I noticed that most of them started regressing, losing life-balance, discipline and motivation. They gradually stopped practising. Witnessing this was painful. I asked myself, 'What did I do wrong?' I surveyed my students to make sense of what had gone wrong. After a demanding but stimulating process of reflection and introspection, I realized the lesson of my life that later became my purpose.

I realized that I was teaching my students with passion to the best of intentions, the way my masters taught me – the traditional Far Eastern way – focusing on perfecting techniques with quality, not quantity. We held that if you practised diligently for years without interruption, you would reap your benefits of acquiring skill and cultivating balance in your life.

Indeed, my masters and I managed to reap valuable benefits for ourselves as our practice was our vital vocation. Yet, my students had vocations in life that were different to the practice they were perfecting with me. Of course, they would not commit the same level of time and effort that I would to sustain stable results. I realized that what had kept them going for so long were two external motivations: the allure of a safe community and the teacher who always motivates them. In the absence of these motivators, the business of life started taking over. Understanding what had gone wrong moved me to the core. I realized that I did not want to be the source of others' motivation. Nor did I feel like giving people short-term benefits that they could not maintain or foster. These realizations opened my eyes to my true vocation and who I wanted to become: a partner and companion, a peer inspiring people to dedicate themselves to growth and source their motivation from within. It took less than a minute to decide that coaching would be my stepping board for this newly discovered vocation. I joined my first coaching training programme.

After years of working as a professional coach, blending both Eastern and Western wisdom in my practice, I was finally able to pinpoint the one ability that, if activated, I found could open the door to limitless, unconditional growth: presence. We can find this ability integrated in Silsbee's (2008) coaching for presence approach and it is taught in coaching programmes offered by Hunt (2009) and Divine (2009), to name but just two. Indeed, this ability is innate in our human nature, albeit forgotten in a dark corner inside the self. Yet, it is there waiting to emerge into the light of our awareness. Once in our awareness, presence will turn every experience into an opportunity to learn, adapt and grow.

Somatic Thinking

Somatic Thinking was born from the question, 'How can I create space for people to experience presence by design?' Leveraging over 30 years of experience as a martial and healing artist as well as over 15 years of coaching individuals and groups on four continents in three languages, I felt empowered to build a shortcut to presence. I designed Somatic Thinking as a philosophy and coaching methodology with the sole purpose of creating space for people to experience presence and to encourage them to adopt presence as their predominant state of being in the world.

The word 'somatic' originates from the Greek 'soma', meaning the body. A human being is a meaning-making creature that interacts with life, through a physical form that is called the body. Life is a physical experience, a world that is rich with sensory information (Gendlin, 2003b). It offers us energies that stimulate the senses of our body, which is capable of sending and receiving sensory information. Once our mind perceives the stimuli, we interpret the sensory information, giving it some meaning, forming ideas, making decisions and then acting. In brief, the body shapes the mind (Pfeifer and Bongard, 2007).

'Thinking' is the ability to use the mind to consider something. 'Somatic Thinking' as a concept helped me describe the partnership between the body and the mind when experiencing life, which is widely known as embodied cognition (Mahon and Caramazza, 2008) and recognized in coaching through the embodied perspectives of physicality in coaching (Jackson, 2017).

Somatic Thinking is defined as 'experiencing life in partnership with the body for holistic awareness and presence as the predominant state of being'. The concept of body and mind forming a holistic partnership is well established in psychotherapy (Reich, 1972; Röhricht et al., 2014) and has been taken up by phenomenologists (Merleau-Ponty, 2002), sociologists (Waskul and Vannini, 2006), bioenergetic scientists (Cotter, 1996; Lowen, 1994) as well as coaching scholars (Jackson, 2017; Silsbee, 2008; Whitworth et al., 2007).

The steps of receiving and sending sensory information in the body and making meaning of this information through thinking form what I refer to as the human interaction cycle (HIC) in Somatic Thinking. For instance, this cycle is acknowledged in psychotherapy (Reich, 1972) and health care sciences (Jarvis, 2012) as shaping our relationship to current experiences and all our future relationships to similar experiences. Gestalt psychology (Bluckert, 2006) posits that it also helps us craft our values, beliefs, identity and behaviour.

The butterfly experience

Let us see how we might interact with life when life offers us a butterfly in flight (see Figure 9).

1 Sense (for example, seeing).
2 Perceive (for example, a shape, visual variations, motion).
3 Give meaning (for example,, butterfly, colourful, flying, gentle, spring, beauty).
4 Form ideas and emotions (for example, I love butterflies, I wish to see it closely).
5 Make decisions (for example, I will have a closer look).
6 Act (for example, moving closer to the butterfly).

Observing these steps, you will notice that the first step – sensing – and the last step – acting – happen through our physical interaction with the outside world. The steps in between form in our inner world – the mind – in interaction with our body.

The logic of this observation dictates that our body is the bridge between our inner and outer world (Jarvis, 2012; Silsbee, 2008). It exchanges sensory information between the flying butterfly and our experience in the moment. If we were visually impaired or suffered from colour blindness, our sensing would be different, resulting in us experiencing the butterfly differently.

Somatic Thinking – Framing the findings with deliberate practice **75**

Figure 9 Butterfly experience

A few inspirational questions for you to consider:

- What if your sight was sound, and yet you did not notice the butterfly?
- What if you perceived the butterfly and thought that it was a scary bat?
- What if you perceived a bat and thought it was a butterfly?
- What could distort our butterfly experience?

When sensory information, perception and meaning-making align with our presumed physical reality (butterfly) in the moment, we are in sync with that experience, which is what we refer to as 'being in the state of presence'. When sensory information, perception or meaning-making are misaligned with our presumed physical reality (bat), we are out of sync with our present experience fabricating a modified copy of reality. That is a state that lacks presence. This process implies that we have an inherent need to have our meaning-making met, which is evidenced in the coaching presence research project. For instance, if coaches think that they can be great coaches where they perceive clients as being ideal (see Case Study 1 in Chapter 3, p. 32), coaches and clients sync with each other: sensing, perceiving and meaning-making get disrupted on both sides. If coaches think that they cannot do great coaching work where they perceive clients as being unwilling to be coached, they compensate the perceived disruption by trying to sync more with clients. Clients start to feel distressed because they perceive their coach is missing their needs while coaches become frustrated and/or even deflect the situation by saying, 'All has been going very well with this client' because they think that they have been coaching 'from a place of presence'. Wishing to be present is not the same as being in a state of presence as we know from the story about the man who loved dragons (see Chapter 2, p. 13).

Somatic Thinking focuses on enhancing the communication process (see Figure 10) between your inner world and the outer world through building your ability to navigate perception and meaning-making 'from inside'. It also serves to heighten your capacity to sense 'from outside'. The result is a state of presence that you can intentionally access when interacting with yourself, others and all that surrounds you locally and globally.

Two minds and presence

I received an email that was recruiting professional coaches for a study on coaching presence. It said, 'Tünde Erdös is exploring non-verbal interactions in coaching. She will be doing this by utilizing the motion energy analysis (MEA) software to analyze coaching sessions.' Imagine what it feels like for someone that is called to work with presence to be invited to a research project on coaching presence. There is technology that has been validated to demonstrate how presence works between two people and it is used in this coaching research to discover the physical aspect of presence. I was ecstatic. It felt like finding the missing piece of the presence puzzle.

Although it took me a while to schedule an appointment for the initial interview, my interest did not fade. I felt determined to see this commitment through. When we finally met, I felt that Tünde was searching for her missing piece in the presence puzzle too. So, I decided to participate in the research but I also offered to bring in the 'how' element to complement the 'what' element of the research. I was not sure if my offer would resonate with Tünde, but I decided to act from a place of presence and shared my idea anyway. Tünde's excitement with and passion for the offer came as a pleasant surprise. We found that Somatic Thinking would add value to how to lay out the cognitive and somatic nature of presence in the framework of the research project and its potential findings.

Our collaboration has unfolded for us like the butterfly experience I describe above. It is an authentic example of how we can co-create effectiveness beyond goal attainment in whatever we do by paying complete attention to how we respond spontaneously to life emerging moment by moment. The way this collaboration unfolded naturally and spontaneously reflects our wish to lead by example in how being present to life can generate effectiveness beyond stated

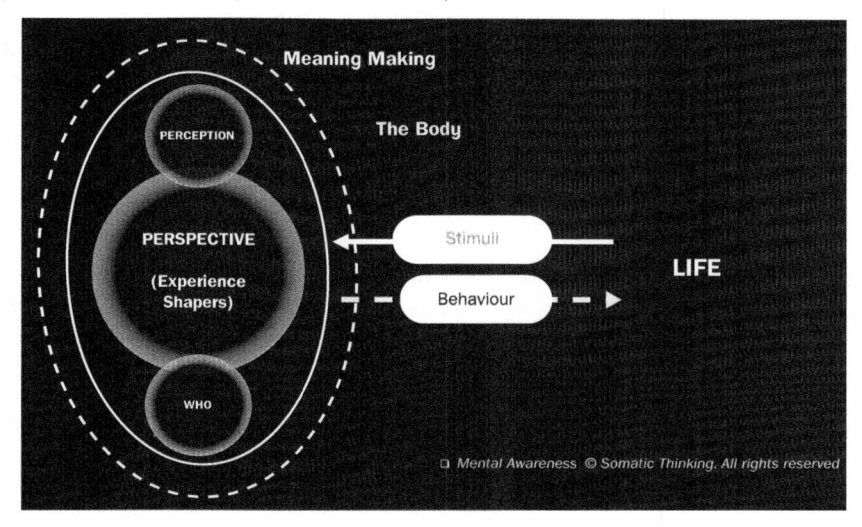

Figure 10 Somatic Thinking as a communication process

goals. The abundance of our current collaboration has culminated in the integration of Somatic Thinking into Integrative Presence.

Four steps to presence guided by Somatic Thinking

Leveraging Somatic Thinking in Integrative Presence, we follow a four-step process to guide coaches towards embodying presence as a naturally radiating competence in coaching:

1. Freeing the mind.
2. Clearing the intention.
3. Becoming aware of entanglement and synchrony.
4. Activating sensory and somatosensory perception.

Respecting the limited space that I have in this chapter in this book, I will detail only the first step, which comprises a pivotal module that we use to work with coaches (that is, the I-Sphere). The focus is on liberating the coach's mind from most of the distractions that clutter it in coaching: (that is, judgment, expectations, assumptions and the coach's story).

Freeing the mind

In a coaching conversation, the coach's mind can float between the past, future and present, wondering, 'Is the session going well? Am I helpful enough? How can I help my client? How much time is left? Why can't the client see the solution?' These are all thoughts that we struggle to keep in check. Staying present with our client in the moment without getting enmeshed in their story and/or our own story as coaches can be a challenge indeed.

To free our mind, it is important to ask, 'Who am I as a human being behind my role as the coach?' We can learn to see who we are as a human being behind our role as the coach by working with what we refer to as the 'Experience Shapers'. They equip us to effectively navigate our floating perspectives when interacting with an external event in real time.

Experience Shapers

The mind is our mental awareness, which is the container that holds who we think we are (thoughts, beliefs, views, identity and the mental image we have of ourselves, life and others around us). It also holds our perspectives and perceptions.

Thinking is our meaning-making process in our mind that shapes who we are and what we will do, while our perspectives are the lens that shape our perceptions and thinking.

Perspectives are key to shaping how we perceive a here and now event. In Somatic Thinking, we have three types of temporal perspectives that represent our unique ability to experience the same event in three different ways using either the Future Perspective, the Present Perspective, or the Past Perspective. Each perspective will shape our here and now experience differently.

The Experience Shapers represent three states that our three temporal perspectives can assume. They are based on my understanding of how our attention, temporal perspectives, perceptions, or mental awareness of who we think we are all interact in response to an external event in the moment. Two out of three Experience Shapers are influenced by our who.

1 *'Exploity' – future state perspective:* 'Exploity' is biased towards the future. It is most active when our mind is occupied with what we want to happen, paying little or no attention to physical sensations and what is happening in the here and now of a situation.
    - It needs: to move forward and become more 'non-stop'.
    - It likes: speed, stimuli, to expect, to possess, to explore, to exploit, unlimited experimentation, chaos, new experiences and curiosity.
    - It dislikes: waiting, boundaries, rationality, order and slowing down.
2 *'Mr Control' – past state perspective:* 'Mr Control' is biased towards the past. It is most active when our mind is occupied with what we know or what we want to know, exposing us to selective attention to our physical sensations.
    - It needs: to look back and know more.
    - It likes: to be right, to judge, to dictate, to hesitate, to rationalize, to slow down, to assume, boundaries and clarity, order, certainty, and to control the outcomes.
    - It dislikes: speed, uncertainty, the unknown, chaos, lack of clarity and experimentation without experience.

Figure 11 Exploity

3 *'Grandma Wise' – present state perspective:* 'Grandma Wise' is not influenced by our 'who'. It is bound by sensing the body. It is most active in moments in which we have an empty mind without expectations or the need to know, directing all our attention to our physical sensations and what is happening in the here and now of a situation.
   - It needs: to live in the present moment with all its offerings.
   - It likes: to accept, to be fulfilled, to sense sensations, to feel emotions, to communicate, to listen and to express, to be as curious as a baby, to be flexible, to experiment, participate and partner.
   - It dislikes: judgement, expectations, presumptions, assumptions, being right or wrong, possessiveness, hesitation, certainty and control.

None of the Experience Shapers is negative or positive. They are all important to help us navigate through life. Exploity is a force that moves us forward. Mr Control is a force that slows us down. Grandma Wise is the balance between both. The main difference is how these shapers interact and process information that we have through an experience.

1 *Grandma Wise:* receives physical stimuli => perceives sensations => feels emotions => thinks (consulting Mr. Control and Exploity) => reacts. This

80 Coaching Presence

Figure 12 Mr Control

sequence is ideal for real-time interactions with our outside world (that is, relating to a person, an animal or an object). Grandma Wise as a perspective state is the embodiment of presence.

2 *Mr Control and Exploity:* receive physical stimuli => think (past and/or future thoughts) => feel emotions related to the thinking => generate sensations => perceive sensations => feel emotions => think => react. This sequence is ideal for creating virtual realities that allow us to experiment with new ideas, imagine future results and test hypotheses in our mind (that is, goal setting, writing and art).

Do you remember the butterfly experience above?

The flying butterfly transmits all kinds of stimuli to our body, which transforms the stimuli into sensory information. On receiving the sensory information, our mind can perceive the butterfly experience in three different ways based on our three Experience Shapers (see Figures 11–13). Figure 14 depicts the three Experience Shapers which are described in detail below:

- If you are in a *Grandma Wise* state, it will absorb most of the sensory information without any alteration, allowing your perception to be in synchrony with the real butterfly. The result is that your 'who' will guide your thinking towards an action that is in sync with what is happening.

Figure 13 Grandma Wise

Figure 14 Human Experience Shapers

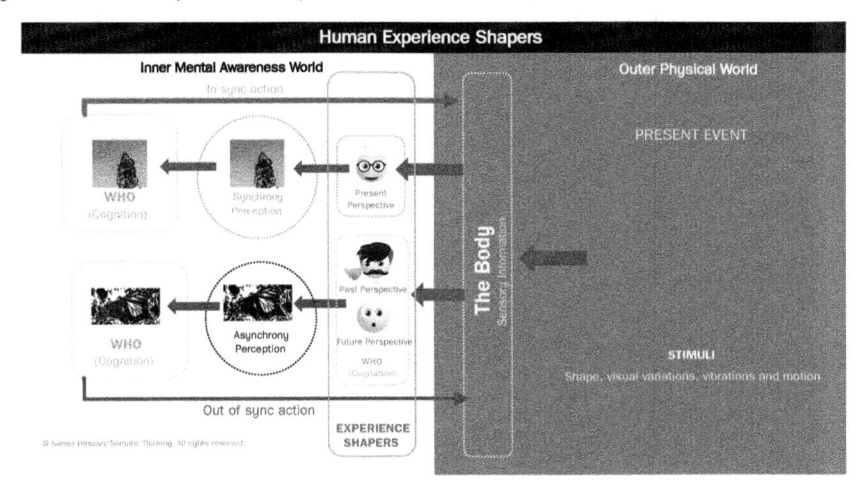

- If you are in a *Mr Control* state, it will be occupied with a memory that your who dictates, let us say your fear of bats. Mr Control will selectively absorb some of the sensory information and block the rest, rendering your perception out of sync with the real butterfly and perceive it as a bat instead. The result is that your who will guide your thinking towards an action that is out of sync with what is happening.
- If you are in an *Exploity* state, he will be occupied with the potential future that your who dictates, let us say going to meet your friends. Exploity will block most of the sensory information rendering your perception out of sync with the real butterfly and not perceive it at all. The result is that your who will guide your thinking towards an action that is out of sync with what is happening.

How to apply the Experience Shapers in coaching – Conclusion

We propose three steps that you can take when you start to apply the Experience Shapers in coaching:

1. You can start by expanding your awareness of the Experience Shapers and then training your awareness by paying attention to which shaper dominates your mind in conversations generally and in coaching conversations more specifically.
2. Start observing your thoughts and then sort your thoughts by assigning them to one of the three Experience Shapers.
3. Identify dedicated practices in your coaching sessions. You can start by identifying what you sense in your body in response to what is happening in the coaching room and continue receiving more and more sensory information, which will allow Grandma Wise to become the dominant shaper when interacting with your client and your outer world.

As a result, your ability to free your mind from the clutter of past and future thoughts starts expanding as you remove the main limiter to attaining Integrative Presence (see Chapter 4).

Part III

Feeding the findings with participants' voices

Throughout Part I and Part II of this book, we have concluded that in order to be a more effective coach, you need to cultivate mastery in coaching presence through deliberate practice that is formed by your openness to client feedback, your experiential wisdom as a coach, and empirical evidence collected through coaching research. We also offered a framework for how exactly you need to deliberately cultivate presence as a result of the coaching presence research to complement contemporary views on what coaching presence can embody. These were fairly fundamental questions that we needed to address, of course.

If presence were just about a screen of concepts and models, then all we would need to do is teach and learn more about models and theories and then we would be able to coach from a greater place of presence. Yet, we know, if we know anything at all, that theories and models do not automatically result in greater skills in coaching presence.

So, Part III is designed to integrate a third question. How about listening to those who will have a voice to share their first-person lived experiences of how their presence skills were forged and how they grew as a human being through their participation in the research project? Feeding in three coaches', three clients' and the researcher's voices, the aim is to round up the insights and the learning that we can offer through the research project within the limitations of a book as robustly as possible. These voices do not claim to be fully fledged case studies. Instead, they mean to inspire curiosity by feeding in participants' perspectives that cannot be reflected through quantitative results alone. In a logical next step, we invite you to do something that no book or training programme can ever do for you: experience the worth and gains of engaging in comprehensive coaching research yourself. We invite you to be a researcher or a research participant, be a reflective practitioner. After all, the proof of the pudding is in the eating.

6 Feeding in coaches' voices

From masquerades to just be whatever comes to the surface

Mireille Westerhuijs

I met the researcher when she was speaking about 'Dancing in the moment' at the symposium Coaching and Research of the Dutch Federation for Coaches (NOBCO) in 2018. She was investigating coaching presence and asked coach–client pairs to join her research. I was drawn to the subject and to the researcher's passionate way of talking about it.

At that time, I was at a crossroads of staying in human resources management or starting my own practice as a coach. For about 9 years, I worked as an HR specialist guiding re-organization processes in various health care organizations. Over time, I realized that it felt more rewarding to work with individuals than with and for 'the company' where I did not feel that I had found my place. I quit my job. I had been thinking of starting my own business before quitting my job though. I thought that I could do the work I loved with the people I liked and manage my agenda my own way. A dream come true. So, I signed up for a general coaching training programme and one on constellation work.

In my initial coaching work with clients, I found it sometimes quite difficult to oversee everything and act spontaneously in the moment. Habitually, I preferred to let information sink in and then respond. Therefore, participating in the coaching presence research project offered me the opportunity to learn from a coach who was more experienced in how to 'dance in the moment' with clients.

Unfortunately, my coaching practice did not want to come to life easily. I hesitated. It turned out that I needed to deal with some issues that were holding me back from being a coach. One issue was that I was asking myself, 'Would I be good enough to be a coach?' I did not allow myself to grow in my new role as a coach. I believed that to be a good coach, I would need to have the advanced-level competences attributed to a senior coach, such as many years of experience.

I scarcely got a good night's sleep and I started worrying a lot. I drifted into a depression where everything slipped through my hands. I did not bother about anything any more. I wanted to be released from the awful negative feelings I was experiencing. Of course, I knew that no one could do that for me except myself. Yet, I did not feel I had the power to do so. However, doing nothing was not an option either. So, I worked hard to exit my depression but I did not feel like doing this at all.

The progress I made turned out to feel rewarding and I felt encouraged to go on and make more progress. At some point, I stopped having negative feelings for a while. The time had come for me to slowly pick up some work. I became interested in coaching again and attended coaching webinars and workshops. That was when the offer to participate in the research project came in.

At that moment, I did not have any coaching clients. While I had no clients, I still intended to join the research with two clients instead of just one. I was looking for learning through comparison, 'Would my coaching presence depend on the client, or would I behave in the same way as is congruent in my style?'

I invited Frank Numan to be my client for the purposes of the research project. I invited him because we share similar interests in coaching. I experienced him as someone who was used to being in the lead. I felt that Frank would be a challenging client for me to guide. As I believed that I was supposed to be in the lead as a coach, my work was cut out for me.

My second research client responded to a post I shared on social media to participate in the research project. We knew each other professionally and my challenge with her was also to deal with the leading part. Apparently, 'leading' and 'guiding' were my main themes for my personal development. If I were to have a client with a different style of behaviour, I expected I would be preoccupied with my leadership skills. Those were my assumptions.

While on the research journey, I did not realize coaching presence was about the capacity to spontaneously respond to the client's needs at a non-verbal level. Responding in a flexible way without too much thinking, without any noise in the mind, and sharing what was going on for me physically – if that sensation had something to do with the coaching relationship – were aspects of coaching presence I had not been aware of.

When I received my feedback about my individual research results, I was both devastated and happy. I felt happy to benefit from receiving feedback about my coaching presence at an early stage of my coaching career. However, I felt devastated as it turned out that Frank and I were responding to each other's needs in a similar way but the responses were not much reflecting 'us being present'. We were both very reluctant to meet each other's needs. Our spontaneous responsiveness was found to be dampened by thinking; we both seemed to think first and then react.

Frank is someone who can use a lot of words to express ideas or even hide what he really wants to say. I often felt overwhelmed with that. I found myself losing the thread of his story. I coped by taking notes and preparing sessions thoroughly. You can say that I pre-cooked them to have a sense of control. Preparation and note-taking gave me a safety leash to hold on to with Frank. At the moment, I did not fully rely on my memory because of some health issues. It might well be that my health conditions at that point impacted on my presence too. It was not addressed.

After two sessions, Frank told me that if those were to be fully paid sessions, they should have more impact. We did not identify what he specifically meant by 'more impact' though. My response to his sharing was to introduce him to knowledge about constellation work, patterns and masks people use to hide feelings of unease. These were themes that really resonated with me. That did not happen to be true for him. His self-reports did not quite reflect what I had invested in the sessions. He did not practise the things we had been talking about either. The themes did not stick with him. It frustrated me. It looked like I was putting in more energy into making coaching work than he was.

Why did I not bring the unconscious material in the dynamics of our relationship to the surface? First, depression suppresses one's feelings and I was doing just that: suppressing my feelings, which led to lack of presence to interact spontaneously with Frank. Second, I value Frank and my idea was to allow him to be himself although his excessive talking annoyed me and I wanted him to shut up. In doing so, I did not allow myself from being me. I felt disempowered.

What would have happened if I had brought up these observations? Frank might have had a chance to recognize his pattern of talking too much. Our way of working with each other might have become collaborative rather than a battle between us over who was giving direction. Frank might have felt safer and we might really have been able to come to the surface. Frank might have improved on his ability to work with his issues.

As for Client 2, at one point I chose to share what was going on for me in the dynamics between us, which greatly shifted the process for me. We had a different process to the one I had with Frank, albeit with a similar feature. I was experiencing counter-transference of co-dependency between Client 2 and myself. There was a number of times when I wondered, 'Who is to lead and who is to follow? Who is there for who?' She was leading more, I was following more and sometimes I managed to reverse the situation. Feedback data showed that we were both meeting each other's needs, but that Client 2 was slightly faster in responding to my needs. In the second to last session, I felt brave enough to address the dynamics that I observed were developing between us. I told her that as she often took the lead, I was not experiencing the space to guide her at a deeper level. She recognized her pattern and challenge of needing to feel safe and in control in both her personal and professional life. Feedback data showed that this particular session reflected the lowest quality of coaching presence and the highest level of goal attainment. The quality of our coaching presence might be interpreted that we were reflecting a lot and responsiveness was minimal.

Let us now turn to comparing the two different coach-client outcomes in terms of coaching presence. According to research data, Client 2 and I were responding more spontaneously to each other's needs than Frank and I were. For example, the percentage of real versus random responses to each other were slightly higher with Client 2. The responses occurred faster too. A possible explanation could be that we did not share the pattern of overanalyzing like Frank and I did. Client 2 and I seemed to share the cooperative pattern of co-dependency.

Feedback data showed that Frank's goal attainment was steadily moving up. While Client 2's levels of goal attainment were increasing over time, the increase was rather inconsistent as the figure depicting our process showed ups and downs over time. While the levels of being in sync with Frank as expressive of our presence were increasing over time; they slightly decreased with Client 2 over time. I can only explain this development as being due to me inviting Client 2 to analyze our process in depth the way Frank and I did. This helped to shed light on our progress based on the research findings.

Participating in the research took some effort indeed, but I would not have missed it for the world! I am grateful for learning about the relevance of my awareness of whose needs are being met or not met during a coaching session. Am I serving the clients' needs or my own? Does my need to guide suit the clients' needs and goals? Can I just go with whatever comes to the surface during sessions and respond spontaneously to that emergence? Am I able to sense what is going on for me in relation to other people? Can I express my sensations to them if they serve their needs and purposes? How would I know that my sharing really served them? What if I just thought it served them in order to secretly serve myself in some way?

All of these questions helped me conclude that they were about getting to know myself better and become more authentic, letting go of control and seeing what wanted to show itself to me and figuring it out together with my clients. I concluded that I needed to be more in the moment.

I experienced the biggest shift in understanding coaching presence while writing down my story about my experiences for this book. Writing down my story prompted me to dive deep into my experiences and understand them in a way I had not understood before. The essence of coaching and all communication is about meeting my own and the other person's needs, seeing and being seen as well as understanding and being understood. For me, this insight brings clarity to why 'things work' between people and why they do not work. When 'things work', this working can reflect an equal give and take between people in a rewarding and inspiring way.

So, how did participating in research shape my practice? A coaching process is subjective. In the research, presence was measured at a non-verbal level using the MEA. The more objective data obtained through the data calculated via software served as a basis for reflecting on sessions in the light of presence more closely. In effect, I did some learning by doing, which I believe is the most effective and sustainable way of learning.

The entire process shaped what I thought about research. I assumed that research was time-consuming and costly, that it was theoretical, that people overvalued it and that the results of two research studies could even contradict each other. So, how much could research be worth?

What convinced me that it would be worthwhile participating in this research project was the researcher's own personal story about how she was prompted to be curious about doing research. I was convinced that her coaching experience, almost a moment of failure in her career, was a genuine place from where to start learning more about how to become a better coach for clients. This helped me trust her hypothesis about coaching presence. I could see her sincerity. I am glad the researcher took up this research project, as for me presence is the essence of coaching and life itself. This research showed me how meaningful and practically applicable research can be. I believe that those who feel attracted to such a legacy and the people around that legacy can benefit in a big way.

I am grateful to the researcher for inspiring me and encouraging me to embark on the journey. She lit my slumbering fire. I am also grateful to both my clients for trusting me, to go on this journey with me. Getting out of my comfort zone gave me the confidence to be a coach. You can do that too, whatever limiting beliefs you might have. We all have them.

Practitioner Take-aways

- Am I serving the clients' needs or my own?
- The essence of coaching and all communication is about meeting needs: seeing and being seen as well as understanding and being understood.
- I gained clarity around why 'things work' between people, in coaching relationships, and beyond.
- This research showed me how meaningful, practical and easily applicable research can be.

The journey of presence: From having to being

Katerina Bakunina

It is an undeniable truth that every person is different. This uniqueness also extends to what we dream of achieving in life. It appears that we are on a quest to answer some questions. Though most people know that there are various paths to achievement, very few fully comprehend that we already have most of the answers to whatever questions we might have or whatever obstacles seem to be in our way. Coaching is ultimately achievement-focused, orientated towards supporting people to take steps to move closer to answering their life questions. Each one of those steps carrying people forward is as diverse and distinctive as people's inner worlds. Where one person chooses to take a giant leap, another trots and wobbles, yet someone else just sways in place. The question that continues to intrigue me is how can the process of coaching invite clients to fully experience their own diverse and distinctive ways and not just plan the next step in coaching?

The first time in my professional coaching career when I got the chance to explore that question with coaching clients was when I made a commitment to participate in the presence research project. That was in February 2019. I committed to conducting 20 in-person one-hour sessions with two different clients, video recording each session and submitting my video files for analysis. For a coach with an already full client roster like myself, this was a significant investment of time and effort. Yet, my decision was a spontaneous one, fuelled by an inexplicable, powerful determination that seemed to radiate like a smouldering ember somewhere in my solar plexus. Later on, I would explain to my peers that the decision to embark on this six-month research journey stemmed from my curiosity and desire to grow my coaching competency. While also true, I wondered if the radiance I had viscerally experienced was the passion that I have for my profession, or something different. It is in this curious divergence of explanations that I am realizing the kernel of my insight: when we experience rather than explain, we can see possibilities beyond obstacles.

Let me share with you a memorable experience I had with one of the two clients on this coaching presence research journey, one that revealed the answer to my question of how the process of coaching can invite clients to fully experience their own diverse and distinctive ways and not just plan the next step in coaching.

It was a sweltering July afternoon in Manhattan, yet inside a small windowless conference room on the 4th floor of a large office building, it was chilly. I pointed the video camera straight at the two white armchairs positioned slightly at an angle to each other. Out of the camera's view, I pushed the heavy round conference table away and stacked extra chairs to clear the space for my stage. I was getting ready for my coaching session with Client 1 in the research project. The act of preparing for these coaching sessions became a ritual, a practice of drawing my attention to what was being studied – presence. And not just in a coaching session, but in my life more generally. For example, as I was waiting for my client to arrive, I started paying attention to what was surrounding us in the room. I noticed the muffled sounds of a vibrant office outside. The clacking of steps in the uncarpeted hallway. The unrelenting enthusiasm in a man's voice next door, the kind that one uses to deliver a well-rehearsed sales pitch. I noted the soothing comfort of knowing that I was prepared followed by an anticipatory fluttering in my stomach.

A call from the front desk jarred me out of this experience to alert me that my client had arrived. I got up, pushed the heavy glass door open and headed to the lobby. 'Hi! There you are!' I exclaimed as I approached. We chatted excitedly about the weather as we walked back to the conference room, our heels clacking in the uncarpeted hallway. 'Here we are!' the client announced. 'Yip! The same room, same time, last time, this time – next time.' We laughed again. I offered my client a glass of water and put my own glass next to my chair. I set my timer for 60 minutes and checked the image in the camera again as we both settled into our chairs. My chest felt hollow and open. I took a deep breath into that openness and asked, 'Are you ready? Shall I press the record button?' My client exclaimed, 'Yes! Let's go!'

We checked the homework and reviewed the progress made towards my client's goal. Yet, something felt off to me in the way my client was speaking.

The enthusiastic, brisk pace was the hallmark of our work together so far. This time, however, we uncharacteristically stumbled around different topics and themes and none seemed to gather any steam. Then I detected a shift. A pause, a break in speaking that had a peculiar quality to it. Like the silence between the lightning and the thunder. I asked, 'Something shifted just now in you. What is that?' My client seemed to be caught off guard not so much by my noticing something, but by her own awareness of the shift. 'I don't know. I should though, right? I've been just really … lost,' she said quietly as her shoulders dropped helplessly and her whole body sank into the chair.

I noticed the shoulders, the voice, the silence that followed. I took all of this as a clue to stay here, to experience 'lost'. In the past, a situation like this one would send me into a coaching tailspin. I would frantically rummage in my coaching toolbox for an exercise or some solution to assure my clients they were not lost, to fix something for them, or to save them somehow to help them keep moving forward. This time I did none of this. The practice of setting up the stage before each session and setting my intention on the purpose of study seemed to start paying off. Instead of taking another step in how to coach, I chose to slow down and look at what was happening in the moment with my client. As I slowed down and remained quiet, I no longer wanted to fix or prise out a solution. I wanted to remain a companion to my client, not be her fixer. So, I just listened, but it felt like I was listening with my whole body rather than just with my ears.

We both stayed quiet for a bit longer. I asked softly, 'What's that like for you right now, this lost?' As my client started describing it, with gentle curiosity, we both began watching the unfolding of sensations. First, my client noted humming in the pit of the stomach, that turned into a vast, foggy swirling that then tightened and finally released until it somewhat dissolved. I asked, 'Do you have a sense of what this was?' After a considerable pause, the client nodded and said, 'It's fear.' After another pause, I asked, 'And what's here now?' 'Relief!' said my client, her body softening, this time in relaxation. We both exhaled audibly. As the client looked up at me, words started pouring out of her at the more familiar quick pace. No longer lost and wandering, no longer scared and confused by the hidden emotion of fear, my client was once again firmly on her path, briskly walking towards her goal.

When the session was over and my client had left, I carefully packed away the camera, wrapped up the wires, and re-set the conference room. I flashed back to artful coaching demonstrations delivered by some master coaches at my coach training seminars. I remember being in awe of the powerful insights that emerged for clients who were coached by these masters. During the debriefings, I was often puzzled by questions such as, 'What did you notice about how the coach was being?' It seemed important to remember the questions that the master coaches asked, to identify their tools and figure out the script as if coaching was a scene-by-scene theatrical play. What I was not looking for and seem to have failed to appreciate was how they were creating a relationship with their client.

Standing there in the small windowless conference room on the 4th floor of a large office building, I sensed a pang of regret reverberate in my stomach.

How many times did I focus on getting my lines right rather than being fully in the experience of my coaching relationships? I realized that presence cannot be scripted and performed. Moment by moment, our inner worlds unfold, demanding to be experienced, felt, and sensed. Practising presence ultimately means being alive, keenly attuned to and connected with our bodies. While our minds can dream up visions years ahead or keep a sweet cherished memory alive, our body is the vessel of our experience in the present moment. The work of coaching gets done in these rarefied moments of presence, not when following a script.

How can I best support my client's transformation? This is the question that all coaches ask. Beyond the obvious professional development opportunities available to coaches, such as in-person seminars, attending webinars on coaching techniques, reading books and articles, doing one-on-one coaching with clients, and engaging in regular coaching supervision, a new profound option has become available to me. This option is participating in coaching presence research. The growth that I experienced in my coaching competencies has been accompanied by a distinctive sense of professional pride and belonging to the outstanding profession of coaching. After participating in the presence research project, I am starting to comprehend the beautiful complexity of coaching as an art and science. Most importantly, I receive feedback on my relational presence as a source of further self-enquiry. Foremost, this experience has given me an opportunity to connect my actual impact of and contribution in a coaching relationship with the discipline of coaching in an experiential, rather than theoretical, way.

Practitioner Take-aways

- I received an answer to my question about how the process of coaching can invite clients to fully experience their own diverse and distinctive ways and not just plan the next step.
- The work of coaching is done in these rarefied moments of presence, not when following a script.
- I am starting to comprehend the beautiful complexity of coaching as an art and science.

The dance of caring and daring

Solange Boasman

I have been passionate about learning for more than 25 years. With an educational sciences background at Master's level, my curiosity about 'how people learn' and 'what helps them learn and develop in life' has been my steady companion. Learning gives me a special thrill. I sense that I can take a step forward in life and in my role as a coach. Moving forward helps me connect with and better understand others. I believe that connection is one of the basic human needs and one of the requirements for learning (Stevens, 2009). Eventually, learning helps me discover possible tunnel views and helps me find my way out of those tunnels. It is a flexing exercise that keeps my mindset receptive to signals of discovery, which encourages me to keep connecting with others.

Joining the coaching presence research project was just an act of following my heart's calling and my curiosity to learn more about presence in coaching. In my coaching training, I learned a lot about asking the right questions, goal determination, goal attainment and professional distance. I learned less about clients' emotions. Yet, I am learning that emotions are the key to our development. On finding out about the research project on coaching presence, I was touched by its focus on attachment theory (Bowlby, 1969), which is the dynamics of human relationships. Through attachment theory, I learned about the importance of relationships in life and body awareness in guiding relationships. As a result, I have been seeking to integrate the focus on feelings and emotions into my coaching practice.

What was my learning on this journey? In the very act of writing this chapter, I experienced deep learning. However, allowing this learning to emerge is not simple. Let me share. When I started my writing as an adventure in itself, there was a moment when I noticed a gap in the level of my insights. I wondered, 'Did I reflect and learn enough on the research journey?' This gap appeared between the period of the recordings and the period of writing. I felt restless, which I could sense in my abdomen. I realized that I was concerned about appearing vulnerable in sharing my learning process. I felt concerned about revealing my imperfections. The voice of fear said, 'What would other coaches think of you and your reflections?', and 'Will they blame and shame me for being a bad coach?' I noticed that I needed to listen to these emotions. They had a strong pull. Eventually, I decided to allow myself to truly learn and manifest my vulnerability in this moment because I think this is exactly what the research is about. I believe that understanding presence through the very experience of working with my fear is of much greater value than my fear of rejection.

Looking back, I realize that the insights I gained on the research journey through feedback on my results were precisely about how to become more confident about sharing my emotions: the daring part of disclosing while caring not to overwhelm others, in particular, my clients. It helped me start consciously directing my attention to emotions in the coaching room because the findings showed me that emotions influence the effectiveness of coaching. This is of great value to me as I am learning to be more focused on feelings that emerge in the moment of the coaching relationship. This development helped me become more open, gentler with myself and, at the same time, firmer and more direct, confronting, courageous and risk-taking in my coaching relationships. I can see that this development improves the quality of my connections. Specifically, I learned that I could have coped with my client's fragility and my own vulnerability in specific moments if only I had shared more about my moment-to-moment experiences with my client. If I had paid more attention to my own experiences, I would have been able to perceive when my client himself was reluctant about sharing his experiences with others. I could have responded to those experiences by being curious, 'I can see, it touches you. What do you feel in this moment?' We could have started an enquiry into his feelings and he would have felt safer about learning more about himself and I would have felt safer about learning more about myself.

The research took place at a tremendously stressful period in my life. There was a lot going on with a massive impact on my environment and myself. The changes and transitions that emerged resulted in great loss. I felt extremely tired and tense. I tried to cope with what was emerging in the best possible way because I felt I just had to 'hold on to it'. In the coaching room, my head went like, 'Just (try to) be present and just do not let your client know about your struggle in life.' I was afraid of projection in coaching. Later on I realized that by avoiding projection, I was actually manifesting it. Basically, I wanted to avoid a situation where my client would want to take care of me. I also stopped supervision sessions for a while because I had so many 'other things' to cope with. Afterwards, I realized that what I needed most were those supervision sessions to create a safe space for my client. Of course, I was aware that my mood and my ways of coping with life events affected my presence in coaching. Yet, I was very determined to complete the project successfully because it was very important for me to contribute to research in coaching.

When the project ended, I picked up my supervision and intervision sessions. My supervisor and I spoke about my level of functioning in my practice during that stressful period and I (re)learned among other things that:

- I need to take my own feelings seriously to be able to connect with my clients on a deep(er) level and recognize my clients and myself in a loving way as caring helps people feel safe.
- I relearned why I found it difficult to share my own feelings in that stressful period and how it was impacting my practice. I learned again that sharing helps us discharge and connect. Asking 'what's happening in the moment' is being present and it is also an important condition for synchronicity, as a spontaneous responsiveness to others' needs.

On completion of the project, I received feedback from the researcher and we reflected on my research results of the recordings and my client's self-reports. I could see how my coping mechanisms reflected my lack of presence. It was painful to see the results because, in essence, I had a deep desire to be present. I had accumulated knowledge and focus on attachment, safety and emotions, and yet I had to acknowledge that I was not there. It was a fair confirmation of what I felt was going on in the process of participating in the research project.

In effect, my great shift in learning occurred through my reflections and through feedback from my supervisor and the researcher. The critical incident that we reflected on was when I felt resistance in coaching and I did not say anything. It was one moment when my client started a long monologue telling me about 'this and that'. I think he started his monologue because I was mentally absent when I should have been present as a coach. In that moment, I felt like a schoolgirl. I felt small, unfree and disconnected, and I longed for a dialogue and connection. As I was distressed in my mind and body, I did not address my issue with him.

Through reflection, I realized that I let stress overpower me. I rediscovered that I have the choice to accept everything that is happening in the moment. I can trust the process by creating an intimate space for my client and for myself. I also relearned that my role in coaching is to make body signals negotiable because these signals are about connection. I could have told my client about the stress I was dealing with. He could have seen that I was also dealing with issues. I believe it would have strengthened him in a profound way. It could have normalized his fear, and also mine. Perhaps it would have given him a deeper recognition of his life and the fact that moments of uncertainty and stress are normal. It could have helped him see that all of us have to go through such moments and that those periods pass. Perhaps it would have given us both the opportunity to synchronize on that issue.

A paradigm shift took place, allowing me to move from professional distance (as I learned it in my coaching training) to professional proximity. Today, I allow myself to be gentle with myself while being caring and daring. I am more open about my feelings and initiative-taking to see and connect with others in my private relationships. For example, I invite my whole family to have weekly video calls during the "corona quarantine'. It enables us to keep in touch, encourage each other and share our mixed feelings about the crisis.

If I had not embarked on this research project, I would have missed out on being confronted with how my own stress levels impact on my clients' change process. I believe in process research. Studying processes helps us coaches reflect in a focused way, for instance, on our capacity to self-regulate. It helps us make sense of what is really going on in the coaching room. As I learned through my research results, the value of paying attention to emotional self-regulation has a universal purpose. Process research has universal value. If we had a better understanding of the value of emotion regulation, then there could be greater happiness in the world, deeper understanding and forgiveness in families, relationships, organizations and nations.

My participation in this project brought me back to my level of understanding of emotions. It has been an interesting theme ever since I experienced it in my role as a teacher. The strongest bonds I had were those with the students who came to me after class to share their vulnerabilities and the students with whom I had to compete. I realized that I had to bond first before bouncing forward with them. So, the research project deepened my insights about coaching being about finding the 'balance of daring and caring' in the moment.

Practitioner Take-aways

- I need to take my own feelings seriously to be able to connect with my clients on a deep(er) level.
- I learned again that sharing helps discharge and connect.
- I learned to allow myself to move from professional distance (as I learned it in my coaching training) to professional proximity.
- Participating in this project brought me back to my level of understanding of emotions. The strongest bonds occur when we share vulnerabilities.

7 Feeding in clients' voices

What is life about, so to speak?

Frank Numan

In recent years, I have become very interested in personal development asking myself, 'What is life all about?'

I guess this question kicked in during my forties when I realized that half of my lifetime had gone. It also grew out of several stressful events affecting my physical well-being, career, private life and housing situation.

Maybe, just like you, as a young man I had a good education, started a proper career, worked hard and long hours, started having a family, raised three beautiful kids, purchased a house, paid it off to keep the family safe and secure, worked extra hours thinking that saving some money was a good way to go in life, and on Friday afternoons I would say, 'Have a good weekend, guys. I'll see you tomorrow.'

Does it sound perfect? Well, it was not. I lived my life as if material possessions, my health and our monetary convenience were a given. I even took it for granted that my parents would always be there.

Looking back, my life was not in balance with my personal needs. It seems that something essential was missing. I might have perceived the signs of that missing 'link' earlier when feeling somehow jealous of other people who opted for a 'simpler' life. But then, what did I know about life in my mid-twenties and thirties? By the way, why is 'life lessons' not a mandatory subject at high school?

Luckily, growing older has brought more peace to my life. I know now that there is always a choice to value and do things differently and that creating a world full of possessions around myself results in a false sense of security. I concluded that, 'There must be more to life than this,' and that I wanted to explore my options wondering, 'Am I happy? What is happiness anyway? What is my role in life for the future?' I started enquiring into personal development themes such as NLP,[1] meditation, non-dualism, human-affective relations and ego, to name just a few. I figured that time was the most valuable possession I had in life. In effect, every day is a brand new 24 hours I can spend. The question is, how to spend this time? Nobody knows how many of the 24-hour cycles

---

1 NLP: Neuro-linguistic Programming (Bandler and Grinder, 1990).

we can enjoy in decent health. So, we had better spend it wisely. But making the real choices is sometimes hard, out of comfort, out of reference to what we learned when we were young. This is exactly why I was looking for coaching. I was seeking answers for myself, maybe acknowledgment, and yes, maybe also the guts to make different choices.

I did not hesitate to say yes to this research project. My coach spoke enthusiastically about the researcher and I trusted my coach's sense of judgement as she has a solid background in human resources management. I had a good feeling upfront because I knew that we shared a common interest: the coaching profession and the human factor in it. I know that I could trust my coach fully. I thought that being video-recorded would not make much difference for me as my coaching journey would be about genuinely interacting with my coach and this turned out to be true. Additionally, I wanted to help my coach start up her coaching business. If participating in coaching research could help drive her purpose, well, we would both benefit. The icing on the cake was that I found the research theme very interesting. It was designed to investigate the non-verbal interaction between coach and client without looking at the conversations. I value the concept highly as I think that if a coach is sensitive and responsive to what is beyond the conversations (that is, body language, non-verbal interaction and responsiveness), she can guide the coaching process in a powerful way. The individual feedback we received on our coaching process and level of presence confirmed this. Last but not least, the research theme matched my personal enquiry about coaching, 'How can I be more in the present rather than in my mind?' So, I figured that this research project would contribute to understanding how coaches and clients can be more present.

What was the feedback we received? The objective way of measuring our non-verbal interactions with a dedicated software were matched with many questions I had to answer within 24 hours after each session about how I was feeling right after coaching conversations. On receiving the individual feedback on our coaching presence, I recognized a specific moment when I experienced a dip in feeling safe after session three. I remember indicating that lack of safety in the questionnaire after the session. Specifically, in that session, I felt that my coaching question was not going to be answered if we continued the way we did. And there we were; the research results showed clearly that I was non-verbally manifesting lack of presence on feeling unsafe in session three.

Through feedback it was also confirmed that I act more as a thinker than a feeler and that I interact with others as a thinker more or less consistently. In other words, our level of presence in sessions was shown to be low. This result brought me back to my coaching question about my role in life again. What drives me to be a thinker? Being a thinker, I tend to drive conversations taking the lead when I should have sat back, relaxed and enjoyed the journey from the backseat. The feedback results confirmed this tendency on an energy level. As we are energy, how am I shaping my conversations as a thinker?

Another unhealthy pattern that became apparent through the research results was note-taking. My coach's note-taking of our conversations was not very helpful for me. I noticed that her taking notes was distracting us from having a real conversation and, of course, I realized that this is a pattern I have too. I like to write everything down. I like keeping notes and making summaries. Notes are my anchor. Then my coach changed her approach, and that worked much better for me. This pattern of note-taking might be yet another reason why the results indicated that we did not always have a high level of presence in sessions. Generally, we might need to pay attention to whose needs are driving the sessions. Is the coach meeting her own needs when taking notes or meeting the clients' needs? If a coach is eager to test some new coaching tool after paying for some expensive training, whose needs will the use of the expensive tool ultimately serve? Or when I am talking too much, what do I try to avoid saying? What is the true thing I want or need to say? In what way would that meet my conversation partner's needs? Sometimes, my coach reminded me to get back to the point and find answers to what I really wanted to enquire into. I noticed that when talking too much I might simply be talking to myself as a way to provide insight into my own way of thinking – literally talking through my thinking as a way to control my ideas. We hear it so often; you learn more when you listen than when you talk, and yet, I talk more than I listen. Would that meet others' need in a conversation?

All these insights help me work on shifting my focus from being less in my head to acting more from the place of my heart without the head driving my conversations too much. Feedback showed that many times our non-verbal responses were not matching one another. This time lag effect might be due to my tendency to reflect before I say something. As my coach has a high intellect too, we might have been a perfect match in terms of how our heads were driving our interactions rather than our sensing and feeling being the engine for our sharing in sessions. This was clearly showed in the research results.

What are my hopes for coaching? I trust that with our contribution and that of other coach-client contributions, the insights will lead to the development of valuable tools for training presence in coaching. At least, the insights might teach us how presence works in real coaching sessions and what the effects of presence are on clients' outcomes. These insights might be beneficial beyond coaching. I can imagine that with the insights I have gained through this research project, I will be able to communicate more effectively both with my own clients and with anyone in life.

What else happened for me? My coach helped me be less in my head. I learned that happiness is not a state of being but more an attitude to life and that my happiness does not depend on others but on myself, on acceptance, on wanting what I have rather than on wanting what I do not have or cannot have. I came to understand that eventually the most important thing is to enjoy what is there rather than focus on what is not there, see life, see people, and see the beauty of creation, realize how sophisticated nature is, and see how everything is interconnected as we can witness it with the COVID-19 pandemic. The world does not revolve by our design; we only think it does by the false sense of security we create.

However, despite all the conversations we had, the biggest realization came a few weeks after our coaching sessions were completed when I met my coach again. She gave me a photo she had taken of me at a coaching session. On that day, I was early and I sat outdoors in the sun relaxed, waiting for the session to start. She thought it was a good picture and she wanted to give it to me. I did not even realize that she had taken that photo of me. Looking at it I noticed that with the coaching engagement now over, I was starting to lose my purpose again. The photo reminded me that I had to make some new choices in life to avoid having to learn from life's teachings again. Now, I am having the photo framed and it will take a prominent place in my home so I cannot miss it. This is also the power of coaching, I guess. Sometimes the unexpected generates the biggest impact.

To sum it up, the coaching conversations within the coaching presence research journey helped me rethink who I really am and want to be as well as what the key values are that I want to live by. But here I go again. You see how I am using the word 'thinking' here? Thinking is my very comfortable way of making sense of the world. I seem to be very good at it. So, let me rephrase my learning. The sessions helped me develop my capacity to feel more and realize who I really am and want to be as well as what the key values are that I want to live by. How does rephrasing my learning feel? I feel free. I have choices in life. From this 'presence' exercise here, I conclude that learning is not a static thing; you do not learn and then pass on to the next goal. It is more about starting to ask a question, finding your answers, and then moving on to the next question as a form of development. It is a progression of many steps without any specific ending.

How did the learning moments shift my way of being? I might have become more aware that learning is a process rather than a particular outcome. I realize that I am still not fully following my true dreams in life, and I find myself still partially limited by my thoughts and perceptions of impossibilities. And that is fine.

What is really important to me? This question is not answered, and I am more at peace with not having an answer to it than prior to coaching. At the beginning of the research project and the coaching conversations, I was not satisfied with the session outcomes. As we moved on with our process, coaching started having greater value for me as I was leaning more into the learning process rather than meaning to control a particular session outcome. The feedback results reflect this insight pretty accurately as they indicated a development in how I became more present in coaching too. I seem to have become more responsive to my coach. That created a shift for me. Through feedback, I learned that both coaches and clients have needs and that these needs will inevitably play out in coaching conversations no matter how much coaches try to hold back or how much they get paid for coaching. Why would that be an issue? Why should we act as if coaches did not have any needs? Would that serve clients' needs?

So, what is the real value of research for coaching practice and for clients?

I wish everyone might have a competent coach. Some might disagree, but I believe that coaching is a profession and it has standards. Professional coaches will have standards and will know how to keep their knowledge and skill levels up to date by exploring new insights, partly through engaging in research. Taking coaching training is not enough to keep abreast of latest developments as coaching is still very young as a profession.

Professional coaching is anchored in a good mixture of skills training, life experience, self-reflection, awareness of strengths and weaknesses, recognizing when these strengths and weaknesses operate, and participating in research to receive real feedback on coaching practice in action.

To build coaching as a profession we need in-depth coaching research that is designed in such a way that coaches can receive feedback on their current practice. The research project I participated in produced practical learning moments for me as the client. The value of this particular research on coaching presence is therefore high as results will not remain mere figures but will serve as a basis for learning for both coaches and clients.

> **Practitioner Take-aways**
>
> - As we are energy, how am I shaping my conversations as a thinker?
> - I work on shifting my focus from being less in my head to acting more from the place of my heart without the head driving my conversations too much.
> - I came to understand that eventually the most important thing is to enjoy what is there rather than focus on what is not there.
> - I learned to lean more into the learning process rather than meaning to control a particular session outcome.

Permission to dream

Wasfiyah Talib

Throughout most of my adult life, I have been searching for something – something I did not have, something I wished I could put a finger on and say, 'That's what I'm searching for, that's what makes me feel alive, complete, whole.' I felt I needed to accomplish something significant and say, 'That's what I leave behind – a mark of something that represents me.' I felt like finding the essence of who I was, giving purpose to my somewhat insignificant life, a life filled with many turns, noble dreams that were often dashed and then replaced with other dreams that were eventually realized but which did not always fit in with society's definition of 'success'. I finally decided that writing a memoir of my life's story as an immigrant, a single mother and a domestic violence survivor would manifest the essence of who I was.

The initial thrust for embarking on this particular journey was the person introducing it to me. I saw my coach as the younger version of the person I wanted to be – smart, creative, vibrant, compassionate, generous, intensely curious, and a go-getter. She also had maturity and good judgement – and a great sense of style to boot. I saw her as someone that was fun and always trying something new and innovative.

There were other equally appealing reasons for getting on board the research project. I was presented with a unique opportunity to see if I could make a breakthrough in the personally momentous task of writing my memoir. Writing my memoir would help validate my own life to some degree. It would help people understand domestic violence better, give purpose and meaning to my life and leave a legacy for my son, family and friends to understand exactly what I had gone through in my early years. It would also allow me to heal, after a 15-year-long self-imposed wall of silence on these events, by giving voice to my experiences. These were no small tasks that I had chosen to work on in coaching.

Finally, the nature of the project was a completely out-of-the-box experience for me. When my coach presented the project to me as the study of non-verbal communication between coach and client, the topic did not exactly excite me, to say the least. My main concern was being self-conscious and feeling uncomfortable with being observed and videotaped. I have always avoided being the centre of attention in relationships and social gatherings. I did not want the equipment to intrude as a silent technical third eye looking at our sessions, even with the microphone being disabled. Then, I thought about my own experiences on stage – as a teacher, actor, singer, student attorney, debater and orator – and remembered that I had learned to overcome those fears. So, I decided I was not going to worry and that being watched would be more like initial stage fright that would quickly go away after 5–10 minutes and would be easier to deal with after a few sessions. I had everything to gain and nothing to lose.

The learning that I take away from allowing myself to participate in this research project – a unique opportunity originating from a totally different part of the world from New York, in a field which was outside my usual range of interests – was that I am now able to give myself permission to step out of the box. Choosing to join the research project would have been unthinkable earlier in my life. I certainly used to take up new hobbies and start new side businesses like catering while running a real estate business and holding down a career job in public service communication, but I did not feel free to take on projects which challenged my way of thinking or my way of life. I would have opted out of the opportunity to join the research project back then as it would have challenged the status quo of a life where the needs of others took priority over my own needs and wants.

Saying 'yes' to the research project shows me how far I have come and the progress I have made since those days. Even today, some of my friends, who have known me for many years, will raise an eyebrow when the topic of the research project comes up in conversation, chalking up this latest project as yet another one of my now routine out-of-the-box undertakings.

This research project including video recording, my coaching sessions and the subsequent writing journey made it possible for several discoveries and important developments to happen.

First, videotaping did not pose any intrusion on or interference with the quality of our sessions. I did not feel self-conscious about my appearance or the content of our discussions as we focused on each other rather than the equipment. I also trusted my coach, knowing that she would maintain our privacy and disable the audio recording.

Second, my coach and I were able to develop a successful professional coach-client relationship that has become the best helping relationship I have ever experienced in my life. Our connection deepened as I shared easily and honestly not just my hopes, desires and intentions regarding my memoir writing project but also my life's routine activities and anything else that happened to affect me. Even as tissues became essentials in our sessions, I had little concern that the videotape would capture these teary moments or our laughing spells. Our sessions became a little show-and-tell for the research project, and it was fine with me.

The most striking shift for me over the course of the research project has been giving myself permission to dream and pursue the wildest dreams. I would not have experienced the exhilaration – and fear – of being exhorted to abandon all earthly limitations and thoughts to imagine the wildest dreams I could ever imagine for myself. Each time my coach would urge me to go higher, just one more degree of near fantasy to reach my dream of dreams. And I would push back and declare, 'But I have to put one foot on the ground!' and we would laugh. I learned to ask myself the questions she would ask me, exploring and challenging possible limits. But why? Why not? What if? So, what? Eventually those limiting beliefs would be dispelled and I would arrive at a vision that felt attainable and not too overwhelming for me. I am still unaccustomed to giving myself total freedom but the coaching sessions helped me feel okay and lessened my guilt about giving myself permission to follow my heart's calling.

I have already begun to act on pursuing my wildest dreams. Having remarried in Turkey, gaining a college-age step-daughter, and returning with my new family to my home in New York, I was challenged to revisit my initial plans of travelling the world one country, one year at a time as a single woman working as an English teacher. It was at that time that I undertook this research coaching project. When I was invited to write this chapter contribution, I was about to return from 3 months of solo travel to Singapore and Indonesia. So, I am living my dream of travelling and discovering the world on my own. The difference is that it would be 3 months each year instead of being a working resident abroad, which had been the original plan. What happened as a result of giving myself permission to continue travelling despite my new family situation? Notwithstanding the fact that I had been a Singapore native, I rediscovered Singapore with new eyes. I joined a procession of Thaipusam devotees in Singapore, video recording their self-mutilating acts of religious piety. I met my Indonesian relatives for the first time in my life and discovered my cultural roots. I swam with dolphins in North Bali and I stumbled upon an opportunity to work with Afghani refugees living in Bogor, West Java, Indonesia (a project that was shelved due to the COVID-19 outbreak). These are all experiences I would probably not have considered having if it had not been for the permission I learned to give myself at my coach's urging – to push a little harder, dream a little higher, and truly step out of the box and see the world with a child's eyes.

So, I learned to give myself permission to challenge any and every preconceived notion of how we do things. Permission to question every barrier and limitation that came my way. Permission to be as creative as I could be to make that dream come true. Permission that nothing was too wild or crazy if that was what I really wanted to do. Permission to see that what other people think did not really matter. I understand now that it is what I think that is important.

Another striking shift for me over the course of the project was how easily and readily I could express my emotions and how emotionally open I could be in the coaching process. This capacity to express my emotions, I think, reflects the rapport I shared with my coach. She has been of one mind and heart with me all along the process. My ability to express my emotions has made it easier for us to identify and confront my misconceptions and find the cause of the conflict I was working on. One such example was the purpose of my memoir. Rather than validating my life or keeping my memoir to serve as a legacy for my son, I could choose to write it as an act of giving voice – my voice – to a serious and misunderstood social problem that I wanted to share with real people, girls whom I felt needed to hear my story from me.

If I had not joined the research project, I would not have been able to completely revise my memoir on my own. The coaching sessions pulled the plug on my emotions around the memoir. They removed the blocks to my writing, allowing me to re-approach it without angst, fear and anger. Instead, I felt a sense of calm and eagerness to tackle the job. I tossed out my old chapter list of interrelated short stories and wrote a new detailed outline from the beginning to the end of the memoir based on my new focus and scope. At the end of our 10 sessions over 5 months, I had written my first draft of the first four chapters following my specific outline, which removed a lot of the indecision that usually accompanies the start of each writing episode.

In effect, I am not sure how research can shape practice in coaching based on what I have experienced on this research journey. I prefer not to speculate on a subject I have little knowledge in. I trust that my contribution both in being video recorded and my chapter writing will help researchers understand the coaching practice better and how they can help improve clients' learning process.

What I can imagine is that the research project on coaching presence might have intimidated many clients, and people in general. The relationship between client and coach as well as the content shared in coaching sessions are confidential and sacred, especially to clients. The fact that these sessions would be recorded, albeit without the audio, might intuitively go against every sense of privacy expected in coaching. I personally had trust in and great regard for my coach and her ability to assess the research team's integrity and trustworthiness. This is the reason why I did not hesitate to participate in the project on coaching presence.

Practitioner Take-aways

- Through allowing myself to participate in the research project, I am now able to give myself permission to step out of the box.
- The most striking shift for me over the course of the research project has been giving myself permission to dream and pursue the wildest dreams.
- Another striking shift for me over the course of the project was how easily and readily I could express my emotions and how emotionally open I could be in the coaching process.

Reborn through being

Aloys Bos

Before anything else, I need to admit that when I said 'yes' to the coaching presence research journey, I was not aware of the scope and level of complexity of the project. I believe it is impossible to know. Thinking back, I believe that I was driven by the need to simply 'learn more' and maybe be provided with tools that would help me cope with the struggles and challenges I was facing at that time. I wanted to learn more because it is my calling to face life itself. Facing life itself is important for me. Basically, I want to understand life, grasp life's energies and make sense of life in a spiritual way. What is also important for me is to be able to pass on my learning to others. I feel the urge to help humanity. Another reason for embarking on the research project was to develop deeper insights into life. Insights give me the opportunity to move beyond the five senses. Learning to see through insights means moving towards gaining some overview of life. I think life is the journey itself. I see this project as a part of my life's journey.

Allowing myself to embark on this coaching presence research journey taught me that there is no bottom. Life is bottomless. Life is as open as you need or want it to be. There is no bottom to land on, no bottom to stand on. I just keep falling, dare! I learned that opening up means to me that I show vulnerability. My vulnerability will eventually show my human side to whoever is the other person beside me. My coach gave me the space to open up, even cry, and share whatever I felt like sharing. Opening up was a process though.

At the beginning, it was hard to let go of my ego. However, once I did, a whole new world opened up to me. A world devoid of ego, just being who I am. I encountered a world of harmony and equilibrium. I felt I was living in a world where there was harmony with all living creatures. When we create 'do's and don'ts', I have the sense that we create a life full of ego. I see ego as the distorted part of our human existence. I see our ego as a defence mechanism developed from fear. Before coming onboard the coaching presence research project with my coach, I developed lots of fear and lots of ego. The past had my throat. I was angry and I played victim to my ego. Coming onboard, I learned that I can let go of my fears.

Generally, the learning I took from the research journey and coaching was to be who I am. It taught me to be as human as possible. I learned to perceive before I react. I learned to experience my ego triggers and allow them to emerge without acting on them directly and impulsively. I learned to be without any boundaries and excuses. I learned to just be! Just be where I am from a place of acceptance. I learned to figure out my emotions, figure out my ego and use these internal responses as signposts that indicate some direction for me to take. My emotions will not disappear. I remember that I showed my emotions over and over again in the coaching process, expressed them in tears, in anger, and whatever needed expressing. Indeed, that is precisely what I learned; to express my emotions instead of becoming my emotions. I learned that becoming any emotion clouds my perceptions, which is not helpful. Learning this will help me more generally in life and through me it will help others in living their life.

If I had not embarked on the coaching presence research project, I would have missed out on a lot. For instance, I would not have experienced contact with my coach, by which I mean that it was my coach who created the space and time as an opportunity for just being me! I would have missed out on inspiration. I received inspiration from her working place, which was like home. I was inspired by my coach's capacity to adapt. I would have missed out on the opportunity that there is someone who truly listens to me! My coach is capable of sharing her full attention, most of the time. She gave me the lead and then followed me. She gave me tools to become aware of myself, which I can use to help others develop greater strength too, as there is always a way.

Specifically, in terms of learning, the more I reflect, the more I believe that I learned most from the session about negative beliefs. I learned to trust my own ways and that my way is not anyone else's way. Today, I understand that I have to stick with my way and not with anyone else's way. My way is my process, somebody else's way is their process. In a sort of way, I used to believe that everybody sees what I see. In other words, I used to believe that my way is everybody else's way. Today, I am aware that there are other ways to perceive the world. I learned that one of the most difficult aspects of us as human beings is our history. I learned that history is constantly repeating itself until you start to see your own history and negative beliefs in that history. One of my negative beliefs was 'knowing why other people do what they do'. This negative belief triggered me to clamp down without me even noticing it. Once again, I learned what opening up means. I learned to reflect my self, have the courage to face my self with an open mind again and again. Over the course of the research project, each time I entered the coaching room I saw myself talking and showing emotions, finding my drive and mission. Finding myself, and losing myself. Through this project, my mission has become to 'be the child' every day. In other words, I want to face the world with childlike enthusiasm every day.

Applying all this learning is difficult. The most difficult part is to remind myself again and again that negative beliefs are constantly developing. They never disappear. They are constantly developing because one part in us is ego. Simply becoming aware of this ego part can erase a negative belief. Basically, negative beliefs are not me but perceptions of my ego, perceptions of my emotions. So, applying my learning lies in watching them, facing them, and letting them go. Although it is difficult, the best way to apply my learning is to remind myself to press the 'reset button'. Ultimately, what I can do is to become a new version of myself over and over again. I can mould myself in each newly encountered situation and in each newly found contact with anyone, even while simply having a conversation.

My journey turned out to be an ongoing process, just like life itself. In a way, the entire journey felt special to me. I am not sure I can say that there was one particular moment that felt critical. One thing is for sure, opening up in front of a camera was a totally new experience. I found myself wondering whether or not I should have the courage to be who I am. Prior to the coaching research project, I was in a state where I had lost confidence in myself, and probably in the world. Reflecting here, I think that a potential critical moment might have been that I felt I had permission again to be who I am. That is the only thing that really matters to me. That is maybe an experience I can refer to as a critical shift in the process, which emerged in the course of the session about 'all my selves'. My coach shared a metaphor with me. It was about all the selves sitting in a bus. The bus was my life and I was the driver with all my selves in the bus – in my life. The sharing of the metaphor represented a turning point for me in that I felt I could allow myself to just be me fully capable of ignoring any nasty passengers in my bus. On working with the metaphor, I remember that even my voice changed and my energy was shifting. All my selves helped me get a grip on my emotions in a pure 'state of being'. In this state, my energy is clear, enthusiastic and humorous.

The value of these moments of 'shift' is enormous for me. The whole year of being on the project was, and still is, worth it. I am saying that fully aware that a year is a long time and that many things happen along the way that can potentially thwart any worthwhile experience. The way I see it is that everything we worked on in the coaching research project somehow worked its way through me over the course of the months. The entire year became one integral part of the journey which I was on. The immense value I feel I gained through the coaching presence research project is that I experienced my coach as just being herself. She was not a role or a coach or … She was just my coach. My coach dared to be herself, which I thought created the right level of energy. I believe that if my coach's level of energy had not been right, I would not have opened up. I probably would have remained stuck in my emotional state. For me, it is very important to know that when we are talking, we are talking as humans, not as egos. In what felt like a new way to me, my coach showed me possibilities how to cope with life. She did so simply by offering me different ways of looking at a problem. I think everybody can use these insights on their life's journey.

What I would like to pass on to you, dear reader, is that you cannot push the river! It flows and the river decides. In this metaphor, the river is life and we are swimming, floating, surfing, rafting, drowning, sailing and making the best of it. Before coming onboard the coaching presence research project, I was fighting the current more often than not. I learned that fighting the current exhausted me. I learned to stay on my path, in my current. Now, the difficult question is how the research conducted on this journey can shape coaching as a practice. How can it shape my experience as a coaching client? How can we measure something that is our inner self?

To my mind, coaching is about the moment. I mean to say that the only possibility to create a positive impact is in the act of coaching that takes place at any single moment. Coaching is the moment of connection and contact in the moment the person you are with at a specific place. This moment of connection is a kind of opening through which the 'self' dares to emerge. This moment is about perceiving and listening with all our senses, including our intuition. If I observe someone with my senses, the other person can notice whether or not I am listening. This happens independently from the emotional state the coach or coachee is in. This leads me to conclude that if anyone wants to research coaching, they need to measure the state of awareness in a person and between the interaction partners. It might be that this is exactly what happened. If I can notice whether or not someone is listening to me with all their senses, why should it not be possible to measure it?

My participation in this project was about making myself available to provide insights into the theme, which was presence as energy flow – the connection and contact in the moment. I am still to find out how the results can reveal the dynamics.

Even though I believe that research is something valuable, in my capacity as the coaching client, I see the value in the coaching as it was delivered to me rather than in research itself. This raises the next question, How can you research 'doing coaching'? Maybe coaching is not about 'doing coaching' but about 'being' with the client and 'using the self' as the instrument to create the connection and contact that I experienced as valuable in the process. And this is after all what I believe in: pure being.

Practitioner Take-aways

- I felt I had permission again to be who I am. That is the only thing that really matters to me.
- I learned that fighting the current exhausted me. I learned to stay on my path, in my current, and then ...
- Negative beliefs are not me but perceptions of my ego and perceptions of my emotions. So, applying my learning lies in watching them, facing them and letting them go.

8 Feeding in the researcher's voice

Answering the door: My journey of meeting with my mentor – serendipity

When I realized on hearing the doorbell ring that 'I want to investigate presence' to mature individually and professionally, I was ready to remove the 'No Soliciting' sign from the front door and open it to my visitor.

Meet my visitor 'serendipity'. More often than not, on meeting serendipity we mistake it for chance and good luck. We often hear people say, 'Ah, I just happened to be in the right place at the right time' as they discover something they did not mean to find. Actually, serendipity has a different identity. Serendipity is an active mentor in the process of any journey of discovery you embark on. As your mentor, serendipity requires you to be curious and open-minded to unexpected and unprecedented observations, and flexible in thinking to be free for discovering new directions. Serendipity also requires you to build on well-established knowledge and be constructive about how you explore whatever you may encounter on your journey of discovery.

In simple terms, serendipity requires you to be present to circumstances at any given moment, reminding you that, 'Chance favours the prepared mind' as Louis Pasteur,[1] renowned for his discoveries of the principles of vaccination, microbial fermentation and pasteurization, used to say.

Serendipity has been an invaluable mentor in pushing the boundaries of my professional coaching performance and coaching as a business in my quest to thrive at the peak of the industry. So, let me share my journey of discovery with my mentor below and let us see if you feel inspired to remove the 'No Soliciting' sign from your front door next time the doorbell rings.

The research project on presence as a journey of discovery was serendipity's supreme sandbox. It is difficult for me to say with certainty how I came to that sandbox. One thing is for sure, I was not planning to do any research at the time when I stumbled on the fateful feedback from my client that I was moving my body back while saying, 'I understand you' early on in our coaching engagement. While I found her feedback useful to investigate, I was looking for something else at that time: performing perfectly on behalf of a CEO who hired me to coach his newly appointed executive leader how to be more assertive.

---

1 Louis Pasteur (1822 –1895): https://www.quotes.net/quote/37635

On receiving my client's feedback, I felt various voices competing to get the micro on the stage of my inner theatre and win the discourse over the question, 'Am I OK?' I had the sense that my body was like a cauldron holding a hot poisonous potion of cynicism, judgement and fear. My heart was unable to empathize either with my client or with myself. My mind was not curious enough to take in the feedback, and I felt unwilling to accept the 'unknown' about my practice. I did not understand why but I knew that these voices typically kept me from gaining my balance in how I could meet needs in relationships: for others and mine.

I noticed that something 'unhealthy' was going on without being able to put my finger on it. What was my challenge? What sort of operating mode was I in? I noticed that I was driven to 'perform as a coach' to please my client's CEO who had literally given me a 'command' to 'better make the coaching be a success'. My need to be accepted by the CEO tensed up my body and the pressures of 'needing to please and needing to do it right' overwhelmed me. Eureka! What was this need to be accepted about?

Who was the person I could not accept? The question felt like a fresh breeze giving me a wake-up kiss. It took me some time to open my eyes to the discovery that I could not accept my own successes. Why was I looking for them in the first place? I started feeling the resourceful power of empathy slowly building up in me. Like a glass that you start slowly filling up with water.

How could I actually source myself to emerge as a new person? The desires to learn and grow have always been my greatest assets. The minute I started imagining the learning and growth that would come with staying with my client's experience, something shifted for me. I could see in my mind's eye where we would be: in a healthy mode of relating. That raised my spirit. But I could not feel it. What kept me from feeling this healthy mode of relating with my client? What was I still grappling with? I noticed that I was holding energy that was directed ineffectively towards 'grappling'. It was this energy which kept me from being in a state of self-acceptance.

So, what were my primary sources of energy in difficult moments? I remembered back to when I had to resit a huge exam in my Master's studies and how I dealt with the sense of shame and failure. Back then, I did some mourning, shed many tears, and analyzed the reasons that I thought had led up to the failure. Most importantly, I sought out a few people I trusted to share my story with them. Through the trusted exchange I felt that my batteries were recharged enough to get back onto my feet and dare a second attempt at my exam. But something still felt wrong about this coping mechanism.

Reflecting on my usual coping mechanism, I discovered that I used to treat myself as a machine, albeit a human one, that had buttons anyone could push to 'create change' or 'make things move forward'. I acknowledged that the CEO had no choice but to treat me like one too. He was meeting my need of being a high-performance apparatus. He just needed to push the button to get me going. This discovery felt like a breakthrough moment, one that helped me become curious about 'who I was as a human being rather than a human machine that could perform well'. At that point, I noticed that while the reflection process was challenging, I was enjoying the gift of serendipity – this freedom of my mind 'wandering' and 'wondering'. So, I continued wondering.

Who was I surrounding myself with? I acknowledged that these were people who generally had high expectations of me the same way I was having high expectations of myself, and they would leave me once I failed to meet their expectations. I noticed the sheer one-sidedness of my human relations. Actually, I was not attracting human relations but performance-driven tools into my life. Everyone seemed to have the same hopes and expectations of me, and I wondered what I would expect of myself if I were in their place. I could very well imagine that my client felt like 'exiting coaching': Could she make out the human being in her coach?

Wondering who could offer a different perspective on how I was showing up in life, I suddenly had flashbacks of my childhood. My younger self was smiling at me, encouraging me, 'Do you remember when I had fun and felt happy?' As I was wondering what else my younger self would say about me if I met her, I felt fear of allowing my younger self to see me. Would she judge me? Would she accept me? I felt thrown back into my cauldron of hot potion of poisonous cynicism, judgement and fear. And then I heard my younger self say, 'You have a purpose. You remember? You wanted to go out there and do magic in the world. You loved dressing up as a magician. Your auntie sewed the green tulle coat for you while you sewed what you called Aladdin's slippers. You would not allow your mom to help you with making the magic wand for you. You wanted to take the cardboard box and even cut your finger, excited as you were to go on stage at school and perform your magician's story. You remember?' What a liberating moment! I just needed to give myself permission to pursue my purpose in life: doing magic, having fun.

How could I turn my circumstances into a magic moment? Instantly, I knew: the magic lies in relating to my client to discover our relationship and in sharing my serendipitous experiences with others in the coaching community to create value, rather than in performing for anyone. Navigating the waters of coaching as a perfect machine producing perfect end results for others is not fun, but co-creating with others is. I felt ready to fulfill my purpose. I felt the bliss.

As I felt inspired to go beyond perfect performance co-creating value around that particular critical moment that I experienced, owing to my client's high level of perceptiveness and ability to articulate what was going on for her in our relationship, I felt grateful to her. I felt grateful for my client's contribution to my learning. I realized that without the gift of serendipity my research question would never have been born to investigate presence in alignment with 'how I want to thrive with my clients'.

I started out on my part-time PhD with no real idea of how I would investigate presence. In hindsight, I ended up in a full-time project that rocks my world even after completion: it is fun continuing to co-create value with others around the findings. Serendipitously, my younger self knew that I could be in this world that was about having fun. Sometimes I am asked, 'You are investing yourself so much in this project, what are you going to do with this once you're all done?'

and the only thing I can truly answer is, 'I don't know. I just feel that I want to do what I need to do, and I want to do it properly. I will know what to do with "it" when I am done.'

I am also grateful to my younger self for reminding me that I have a choice: I can simply perform as a perfect apparatus, or I can do magic and embody excellence without mistaking excellence for perfection, a potential illusion in the equation. It is OK to allow joy to kick in on expressing 'something of who I am' in the process of doing research. There is no need to wait until the end results of the research to experience joy. Giving myself the permission to do research with joy and curiosity feels virtuous beyond perfection. The Greeks called it eudaimonia: the dynamics of being happy by staying in action as the expression of being 'excellent'. How often do we allow ourselves to flourish as a human being by paying attention to the energies of the soul that is constantly in action seeking happiness in doing research? And how is that in our coaching? How often is the 'how of what we do' in full alignment with 'what we do': being more and doing less as expressive of how we need to be with our clients rather than what tools we want to use to facilitate coaching effectiveness?

Being the researcher for the researcher's sake: what sort of success is that? I don't know. What is success? George Leonard, the 6th Degree Black Belt Master and author, suggests that we ought not to be so serious about our success. Instead we may want to understand the joy and fun of our successes being willing to see just how far we can go (Leonard, 2005). The pure quality of success is about being real, being human. Being human and staying human in what I do formed the discovery I felt my mentor serendipity meant to reveal to me, and there was some more to come.

Deep purpose seems to have its good place in my coaching presence research project. I learned to appreciate it highly in one dark moment of the project, in which it came to my rescue. Darkness hit when I entered the recruitment phase to get 150 coach-client pairs into the boat. Given the project's complex design, longitudinal character, and technological twist, I was facing a major challenge to find coaches who would be ready to engage in the process with me – and not just with me but with two clients of theirs. In hindsight, if it had not been for the bliss of the discovery of serendipity, I would have thrown in the sponge. After the umpteenth selection interview, each lasting one hour, I felt like I had yet again turned into some sort of machine – a slot machine – that would stubbornly persist in yielding the gains: the number of participants that I knew we would need to establish statistical relevance. I was surprised by how easily my body was coping with being exposed to this performance pressure, the anxieties around failure and shame, and the isolation I was experiencing in the recruitment phase as a result of social deprivation. I discovered that deep purpose runs deeply – and works the body.

Another noteworthy event is that without being specifically intent on attracting funds for the research, I was able to source financial support for my project from no fewer than three different institutions. It did not even take much effort. I was stupefied. I reasoned that the funding success was owing to the research design, which was found to be 'excellent' and as such, it simply pulled in the funds. Yet, my mentor serendipity evoked the power of the muse's perspective in which all things happen effortlessly. Indeed, creating the research design was like carving the design out of a marble piece that was simply there rather than the design being carved out of a marble piece that had been made to order. Just as Michelangelo[2] would create his Pièta: I took the freedom to carve out the 'figure' the way it wanted to emerge without needing to make too many compromises. It accumulated an energy that bore the mark of excellence. In effect, as my mentor signalled to me, the passion and happiness of doing research seemed to hold the pressure moments in place and ooze some attraction that was difficult to withstand. I eventually understood why my body could cope that easily.

How did you enjoy serendipity's presence and the discoveries made in serendipity's supreme sandbox so far, dear reader? What are you inquisitive about in your practice? Serendipity as a mentor can guide us powerfully to grow beyond our limits as we stumble over discoveries we have not been looking for at all. We become profound observers as we are helped to sharpen our skill to see patterns, associations, or implications that have previously gone unnoticed. Paradoxically, serendipitous discovery wants us to have a good enough idea of what we are looking for to be surprised. It also wants us to have time for reflection. Lack of spontaneity and complacency of spirit can be a threat to serendipity in coaching research and practice.

Where am I looking to be surprised next? So far, I have discovered that I do things because I am happy when doing them. It is as if 'balance' came naturally through the willingness to make mistakes and tolerate ambiguity as well as a readiness to be creative and seize upon chance events.

Maybe the place to start is to ask myself, 'Who am I in this world now and what am I called to do? When I am done, who will I be as I look into how I will be?' That is where coaching is so meaningful and valuable to me. It provides an opportunity to explore self-awareness, without which the whole discussion here would be utterly futile.

Practitioner Take-aways

- Allow yourself to feel inspired to go beyond performance in creating value.
- Experiencing joy doing what I need to do is blissful.
- Experimenting with curiosity while doing what needs doing makes virtuous excellence.
- Perfection is nothing to do with excellence. Passion and virtue do.

---

2 The Pietà (1498–1499) is a work of Renaissance sculpture by Michelangelo Buonarroti. It is housed in St Peter's Basilica, the Vatican City in Rome. It is the first of a number of works on the same theme by the artist.

Part IV

Fusing Integrative Presence into wider fields of practice

In my view, integration also has a forward-looking quality, which calls us to explore the implications that Integrative Presence can have in the wider fields of our practice for the future.

So in Part IV of the book, I turn my attention to fusing Integrative Presence into two of the wider fields of our practice that we certainly need to take into consideration in the modern world of coaching. I could choose more fields to integrate the essence of Integrative Presence, but these are the two that I deem to be the important ones at this moment of coaching history:

1 *Coaching training programmes*: Trust in coaching training programmes has suffered a severe drop as I showcase in the Introduction. This trust crisis is driven by a recent surge of pseudo-credentialling mills that churn out diplomas and coaches with few prospects and low credibility scoring. Add to this the slow progress in establishing an independent regulatory body that sets and monitors globally applicable codes of ethics and standards of acting professionally in coaching, and you have a vacuum of respect for existing knowledge and wisdom in coaching. Integrative Presence invites us to assume social responsibility for how we fuse existing knowledge and wisdom in coaching training programmes as the flagships of credibility of coaching. So Integrative Presence needs to be the core of the development of any professional coach.
2 *Leadership development:* I argue that leadership is synonymous with coaching: leadership is coaching and coaching leadership. As presence plays a critical role in coaches' effectiveness, so will leaders need to have awareness of how they behave with peers and employees to be effective, if they are to guide people to excellence beyond task achievement and goal attainment. In this view, leading is not a picnic in the park in the twenty-first century. Neither is coaching. Leaders and coaches need to engage with the complex realities of those whom they lead and coach as sometimes leaders lead from a place of coaching. That is why I put Integrative Presence on the shoulders

of three giants, one of which is complex adaptive systems theory (Stacey, 2011). Presence is a complex skill with a multi-layered essence. If leaders are to engage with those whom they lead in a state of presence, they need a frame of reference that can meet the needs of the complexities of their organizational realities. Samer Hassan and I will argue that it is our responsibility to develop leaders such that they adopt an integrative sense of presence and leadership.

We apply an embodied style as we have done everywhere else in the book as our main focus of attention in coaching presence is what the body has got to say when it comes to cultivating presence, either in the confines of coaching training programmes or leadership development.

9 Future flowering of coaching training programmes

Introduction

More often than not, I hear coaches complain that coaching education and training are a costly enterprise. It is as if it were a luxury that coaches cannot afford. Is engaging in professional education and training not what we ought to view as a social responsibility that we owe to our clients and the coaching profession? Ironically, coaches feel very well entitled to make a lot of money. They tend to complain when clients or client organizations refer to coaching as a 'luxury' they can rarely afford. What is our level of awareness of how we assume responsibility for providing and receiving education and training in coaching that reaches beyond 'renewal of certification' or 'becoming the new' coach? How can we be a flagship of credibility in our profession?

Integrative Presence invites us to assume social responsibility for how we provide and receive learning in coaching training programmes as the flagship of credibility of coaching. It invites educators, training providers and coaches alike to get involved in learning in a 'state of being present' to what emerges in our modern world of coaching. It invites all to engage in transferring and integrating existing knowledge and experiential wisdom on the coaches' path of renewing certification or becoming a coach.

This chapter looks at how coaching students can adopt an attitude of Integrative Presence towards becoming credible coaches in the service of clients and our coaching community. This approach puts responsibility for growth in the clients' hands and sends them on the path to discovery and development. Integrative Presence evokes precisely that sense of responsibility in those who aspire to become and further develop as coaches. It advocates a socially responsible learning process for coaching to be a sustained profession in the future. It aims to reduce the domination of certainty in coaching education and training based on past knowledge and wisdom as it seeks to counter the avoidance of intellectual challenge.

I will address three out of four concepts of Integrative Presence (that is, I-Sphere, WE-Sphere, and ALL-Sphere. See Chapter 4, 'Integrative Presence', and Chapter 5, 'Somatic Thinking') as they reveal themselves to be relevant to how we can advocate a socially responsible learning process. These concepts are formulated as three questions and are followed by observations and findings in the coaching presence research project. The aim is to inspire specific positive action steps which coaches can take to become more effective in their practice and which coaching training providers can integrate into their programme to increase the programme's strength and efficacy when it comes to supporting the flowering of coaching training programmes in the future.

Questions to adopt an attitude of presence

I-Sphere – What will coaches overlook without spontaneous responsiveness?

The qualitative findings in the coaching presence research project indicate that coaches' capacity to spontaneously 'use the unspoken self' is a reliable instrument to observe and measure the implicit reality and explicit quality of the coach-client relationship at any given moment. The study is the first empirical attempt to explore the impact of coaches' non-verbal presence on clients' capacity to feel safe and self-regulate in coaching. This study reveals that coaches' 'use of unspoken self' impacts how clients can become spontaneously responsive in the coach-client relationship.

Lack of spontaneous responsiveness implies that:

- we cannot sense our clients and we are not truly aware of what our clients' needs are
- our state of being inflexible (for example, moods) is energy that our clients will respond to with their own energy (for example, moods)
- energy through our physicality is more dominant in the coaching conversation than language and clients will respond to our physicality rather than our language
- as our body does not lie and our energy shows in our physicality, we transmit a lack of flexibility through our physicality
- effort to 'do' coaching (for example, effortfully expressing our understanding and questions) leads to clients' lack of feeling safe
- we respond to our own impulses faster and more often than we might like to acknowledge
- we are barely aware of how our momentary feelings guide our responses
- we fail to create lightness and energy when we are 'serious or rigid about coaching'
- we lack the confidence to work with strong emotions
- there may be lack of purpose for coaching, which is energy that shows in how we behave with clients
- we cannot meet our clients' needs effortlessly which shows in our physicality

- the quality of our listening (for example, selective) is focused on the verbal aspects of communication, which does not allow for a holistic understanding of our clients' world
- we are rigid in our perspectives and fail to experiment with new possibilities for how to show up and act to meet our clients' needs
- the way we see the world is more present and we cannot respond to our clients through sensing, listening, feeling and speaking to, thinking of and behaving with the client
- we are not aware how our needs change with each client and in each relationship
- our drive to focus on the powerful questions that we 'must' ask in good coaching deprives us of being able to sense 'how we are' in the moment
- the urges we have are significant material that needs noticing and potentially responding to by sharing with our clients
- the pressure of being not just a good coach but a great coach creates cognitive noise that dampens our capacity to be present
- we are meeting our own needs while believing that we are meeting our clients' needs
- our own meaning-making of our processes blocks us from being spontaneously responsive to our clients' needs
- the 'we' are the source(s) of our own resistance patterns failing to self-regulate in coaching
- we are not open to not knowing and unable to notice how we rush to 'know' and 'explain' to our clients
- that we mistake our insecurities for intuition (for example, intuition is a creative force; 'I don't know why but I feel like doing it' while saying that 'It's a gut feeling, you should not take that decision' is fear driving logic)

What we observed in the research project is that if and where coaches are either too inexperienced or too much of an 'expert', they fail to respond to their clients' needs. In the qualitative feedback interviews which we conducted after we analyzed the motion energy data quantitatively, we observed either a lack of confidence or over-confidence to drive coaches' spontaneous responsiveness as expressive of coaching presence.

Specifically, coaches at the low end of expertise and years of experience appear too focused on rolling out coaching tools (for example, ones they have developed a certain liking for; have invested money in; have been trained in) while coaches lodged at the high end of expertise and years of experience seem to be guided by the impression that they have already got the highest certification to warrant their effectiveness. They are subject to what I refer to as the Snow-White Phenomenon© (Erdös and Iglesias, 2020). In the fairy tale, the queen refuses to listen to the mirror. She is not open to feedback. It is difficult for her to be objective about her beauty or, for that matter, her own weaknesses as she believes that she is the 'fairest of them all'.

I argue that coaching training programmes can provide a suitable platform for coaches' to either build up their low confidence or equalize their over-confidence to be able to be truly present as the purpose of effectiveness in coaching.

WE-Sphere – What happens when coaches fail to be aware of reciprocity in coaching?

The findings of the coaching presence research project show that presence is not about the coach's or client's separate embodied cognition or embodied experience alone. This is supported by some earlier coaching research, for instance, engagement with counter-transferential material (Orenstein, 2002; de Haan, 2008b; Sandler, 2011; Lee, 2014), that is relevant to how presence can emerge in coaching. It is not surprising that in one coaching survey (Turner, 2010) involving 235 practitioners, 90 per cent of the surveyed practitioners indicated that coaching training should include skills designed to handle unconscious processes. So, the need to integrate the development of solid coaching skills to work with reciprocity in coaching training programmes is essential.

In the qualitative feedback interviews, we observed that when coaches are unaware of the dynamics of reciprocity in coaching, they fail to notice:

- that clients are aware of how we are doing in coaching and when we are able/unable to spontaneously respond to their needs
- how clients respond non-verbally to our energy in the room
- how parts of our feminine and/or masculine energy influence how clients respond either with parts of their feminine and/or masculine energy
- when clients notice if we trust or do not trust our inner knowing and how not noticing clients' noticing drives clients' responses in the relationship
- the difference between empathy and being enmeshed with clients' emotions
- how our own counter-transference drives how clients can respond to us on a physical level
- when clients work hard to meet our needs (for example, idealization as a defence mechanism)
- how clients strive to get our attention in unhealthy ways when we choose to detach from them, believing that we ought not to allow our emotions to enter the coaching room
- how our emotional detachment in the pursuit of professionalism blocks our capacity to be spontaneously responsive to our clients' needs
- how our urge to see coaching as some calling to 'help' impacts clients' energy in the room
- that where we mistrust our own autonomy, clients will feel incapacitated to build up autonomy
- that lack of autonomy (that is, I am not enough as a tool) drives our coaching motivation and diminishes our effectiveness

- having one specific way to work with clients (that is, even where we believe that we must work with presence as the 'one' way to support our clients) affects how clients behave as rigid in working with their issues
- keeping it safe for clients (for example, I cannot possibly tell the client that I feel bored with him) is energy that blocks them from being risk-taking and becoming autonomous in their own social systems
- the needs that emerge in the coach-client relationship must be sensed, noticing and sharing as relational material as they potentially emerge in response to relevant client material
- the quality of our sensing of 'how we are' in the moment will determine how we are receptive to clients' needs in the moment and how our clients 'can be with us' in response
- our lack of flexibility in how we respond to clients impacts their lack of flexibility in how they can work in coaching and vice versa.

The findings of the coaching presence research project show that coach and client coordinate their responses dynamically and spontaneously at the non-verbal level to meet each other's needs. They engage in reciprocity, which creates emotional contagion (Hatfield et al., 1994). It seems that clients need to feel that they are in partnership with us to strengthen their sense of safety. It is as if they did not want to have coaching 'to be done' to them. Instead, it is as if they wanted to be on an eye-to-eye level with us on their learning journey.

I argue that our clients' need to partner with us calls for acknowledging that for clients to self-regulate and for coaching to create a ripple effect in how clients can be effective beyond coaching, coaches need to be trained to practise professional proximity rather than detachment.

ALL-Sphere – What happens when coaches fail to integrate the ALL-Sphere

In coaching, we have a theoretical framework known as the Multiple Perspective Model of Coaching Research (Grant, 2017). It is a network of six perspectives and underlying categories (client personal system, coach personal system, client organization, proximal and distal systemic impact and client-coach relationship) from which to classify different contextual factors as relevant to coaching. In essence, it maps how the ALL-Sphere relates to coaching outcomes. While it provides a direction for coaching research, this model also serves as a valuable structure from which to describe the ALL-Sphere in coaching practice. In Chapter 4, 'Integrative Presence', I refer to the ALL-Sphere as past or present context or milieu-related conditions specific to the coach or client with either proximal or distal impact that affect, and are affected by, the other three spheres: I-Sphere, WE-Sphere and OMNI-Sphere. The nature of the ALL-Sphere is inherent in the circumstances governing a situation (for example, workplace, location, nature of coaching setting, organizational or social support, client-coach relationship, coach system and client system).

The findings in the coaching presence research project indicate that coaches fail to notice:

- that cocooning the client through focus diminishes rather than increases our capacity to be present with them (that is, being in the 'bubble' reduces our ability to sense globally)
- that impulses from our immediate environment (for example, noise outdoors or silence) have an impact on how we can work with our clients
- our perception of what presence 'should be' is a cognitive bias and decreases our awareness of how we can be present to the ALL-Sphere as an integral part of presence
- our judgement about the essence of presence foreshadows how we will pay attention to the impact of the ALL-Sphere on the WE-Sphere
- that session settings (for example, face to face or online, on the phone or in nature) have a bearing on how we can work and that each has its own dimension, quality and impact
- that visual presence (that is, seeing or not seeing either online or phone settings) affects the quality of our presence and how we perceive, sense and make sense of the client
- that the location of the coaching sessions (for example, light conditions and window size, sound) has an impact on our physicality (in the I-Sphere, WE-Sphere and ALL-Sphere)
- the power of the ALL-Sphere as relevant to clients' progress
- not addressing the ALL-Sphere affects our coaching effectiveness
- how the distal environment (for example, CEO, peers and social support) influences our embodied self and our capacity to sense, perceive and make meaning of our self and the client.

The qualitative findings of the coaching presence research project show that paying attention to both the more immediate and wider context of the coaching engagement is a key function of presence. This is also true for how we make meaning of our embodied experiences in these contexts. What stands out is that attention to the ALL-Sphere in the coaching relationship allows a shift. The shift happens in the moment of leaving the 'comfort zone' as both coach and client share how they perceive the immediacy of these contexts on their physicality and how they might 'change' some aspects of their context to do effective work. For example, when a client is seated such that the sunlight is reflected in her glasses and if and when you notice and have the courage to address this issue with her, what will happen is that both you and your client create space:

- to shift your seating position to feel more comfortable meeting both coach's and client's need to relate fully
- to work on learning to leave the comfort zone by taking the risk of addressing a phenomenon that would otherwise go unheeded

- for clients to show up with confidence themselves, which helps them become more autonomous
- to authentically share needs as a precondition for being seen by the significant other in the relationship
- to learn to build up skills to cope successfully with impact that our more immediate and wider contexts inextricably have on how we can be effective beyond coaching.

Conversely, what might happen if you simply keep feeling disturbed by the reflection of the sunlight in the client's glasses?

Conclusion

In this chapter, I formulated questions to address three out of four concepts of Integrative Presence which I deem important to integrate into coaching training programmes to enhance coaches' effectiveness through presence in the future. I offered an approach that involves asking questions through the positive power of negative thinking (Watzlawick, 1983): What do coaches fail to notice on becoming and developing as coaches? The aim of this approach was to refine the meaning of the three core concepts of Integrative Presence to develop coaching training programmes in the future.

10 Faceting leadership – The focus of Integrative Presence

Introduction

> Two CEOs in a mid-sized enterprise have a habit of replacing their assistant each year. Serving both CEOs, the assistants habitually end up in a salad bowl of cruel conflict. At the end of each year, the assistants receive the attribution of being a 'failure' and a golden handshake to leave. According to the CEOs, the issue lies with the internal recruiting staff that keep selecting incompetent assistant candidates.
>
> What is the level of the CEOs' presence to what they co-create? What is the CEOs' level of awareness of how their organizational culture and wider context feed what they co-create? Is change really unpredictable?

As we witness in the anecdote above, the two CEOs deflect conflict and victimize others for their own failure to be successful co-leads. Instead of shining the spotlight on the change that needs to happen in each of them, between them, and the conflict going on between them, these leaders externalize uncomfortable change moments. In this chapter, I illustrate the extent to which Integrative Presence can be applied to faceting leadership to this end.

What needs faceting in leadership

We know from the coaching presence research project that coaches do not respond spontaneously to what emerges in the coaching room when there is some fear fuelling their heart (for example, 'Will I succeed in helping my client?') and when there is noise cluttering their mind as a consequence of that fear (for example, 'I do not have the right model to answer the client's question'). We can predict their behaviours and responses. Their disruption is predictable, perceptible and provable.

How many leaders say 'I'm grateful that I've failed', or 'Let's see how this crunch can help' or 'It's OK that we're falling behind' or 'We need this crisis'? And how many leaders say 'I'm afraid, we need to cut jobs as this crisis hits us' or 'We've no way to afford the luxury of coaching now. Our focus is on our daily job' or 'We'll invest to innovate when times get better'? How about coaches?

Leading effectively and sustainably in an ever faster spinning world of changes certainly creates complexity and challenges (for example, pressures to adapt to globally emerging demands while being bound by locally governing requirements; cutting budgets and workplaces while striving to reach higher peaks of performance). The bigger challenge I see is to become aware of how we have co-created the complexity of paradoxes and challenges which we need to cope with today. It is also about how we assume responsibility for how we guide people, teams and organizations through this co-created complexity to sustainable success, in which everyone has enough gains.

What needs faceting in leadership is the awareness that adaptability or agility to change, conflict and complexity is not a matter of catalyzing a new approach to leadership but a matter of principled profound responsiveness, ideally in good times to better manage bad times. It is a matter of fearless nimbleness to focus on unpacking the drama of co-created inefficiency and ineffectiveness, paying attention to how we behave as leaders – coaches – at any given moment: presence.

Leadership presence

Leadership or executive presence is an emerging concept (Dagley and Gaskin, 2014; Grant and Taylor, 2014) associated with leaders who make us notice them with 'what they care about', who win our trust and have charisma (Harding et al., 2011). They inspire us to follow their lead. It goes beyond the barriers of accomplishment. Leaders who have presence appear credible and comfortable in their own skin. It shows in how they move effortlessly. It is as if presence were a 'state of embodied mind' rather than a skill based on style, energy or mood, and character (Bollas, 1992). Although we find leadership presence taught as a skill, it manifests more as a 'way of being' in this world even beyond a 'state of embodied mind', similar to how coaching does (Kennedy, 2013). It is recognized (Hewlett, 2014) that presence is about being perceived as a leader rather than the position one holds as a leader. Yet, the interaction between those 'leading and those being led' and how spontaneous responsiveness plays out in leader-led interactions reciprocally is under-researched.

In coaching, one particular case study (Stoneham, 2009) that uses integral coaching theory (Hunt, 2009) looks at how to help leaders develop a leadership style that is more attuned to the complex environments that leaders work in. It seems that there is a need to address how coaching presence can benefit leadership presence as a way of staying responsive not just in uncertain times but more generally as a core element that can bridge the gap between leadership merit and leadership success (Hewlett, 2014).

Integrating spontaneous responsiveness in leadership presence

I argue that spontaneous responsiveness in leadership is not just about being 'fast or agile' as a full-on business buzz among the ranks of 'synergy', 'disruptive', and the all-time great buzz 'thinking outside the box'. It is a way of being with each other in good times to better cope with bad times. What is this 'way of being with each other'?

Contemporary wisdom holds that 'you can take a horse to water but you cannot make it drink', which implies that the way leaders respond to people's needs determines whether those they lead will embrace what needs embracing. It takes more than an avalanche of change processes, versatile skills to be a generalist, knife-edged instructions, heavy-set documentation methods and a fast move-forward inclination in leadership for 'people to drink the water'. Structures – in particular, informal structures such as psychological safety through leadership – influence action-taking in human interactions. If leaders fail to be present holistically by spontaneously responding to:

- their own visceral responses to change (I-Sphere)
- the needs of those they lead (WE-Sphere)
- the organizational structures they are embedded in (ALL-Sphere), and
- the cultural boundaries they need to manoeuver beyond organizational legacies (OMNI-Sphere)

then only limited adaptability will be possible in the 'here and now' of interactions.

Integrating leaders' level of spontaneous responsiveness in leadership through the I-Sphere, WE-Sphere, ALL-Sphere, and OMNI-Sphere is paramount for their effectiveness beyond what we perceive as an era of rapid change, heightened unpredictability and disruption. It renders change and disruption predictable.

Case study

Let us look at the following case study as an example of an organizational reality that reveals relatively many facets of dealing with complexity. As such, it serves as an excellent biotope for exploring agendas of leadership presence and how to address them in a state of Integrative Presence. In consideration of this example, let me invite you to pay attention to inconsistencies in the initial situation.

Once founded as a family-owned business and successfully established as a production site, BIG operates today as an international group of companies headquartered in Vienna. It has various locations worldwide, each responsible for a unique field of competency. As such, it undergoes continuous transformation both internally and externally.

After turning BIG into a plc, the location based in Lower Austria had to move employees to Vienna to establish the company's HQ there some 10 years ago. Employees who moved to the HQ are now perceived by those who stayed in Lower Austria as superior and there is a feeling of constant push and pull of subjection and repression by HQ. This situation goes hand in hand with a sense of loss of identity.

To give Lower Austria a new developmental drift and after a few failed attempts to put an externally recruited CEO in charge, group leaders reinstall a long-standing CEO who is regarded as a 'pater familiae' among staff in Lower Austria.

The group as such is exposed to politically charged structural changes with big investment and buy-out decisions also affecting Lower Austria. Long-standing employees find it difficult to accept decisions made at group level. Controlling is one of the divisions that is heavily affected by these investments and buy-out decisions. The group plans to establish Controlling as a 'competence centre' with global responsibilities. The goal is to advance this division to a global service provider, which is expected to consolidate resources worldwide. However, physically, the division would remain in Lower Austria.

Lower Austria is boiling with rumours; the location's estrangement from HQ progresses with fast steps. Despite 'prophylaxis initiatives' to prevent conflicts and serious social engagement to calm the waters, employees respond with dissatisfaction and burnout. Employees leave even though Lower Austria serves as the biggest workplace provider in what is known to be an isolated region with unfavourable geographic conditions.

Amidst these circumstances, a conflict kicks in between the newly hired HoD for accounts payable/accounts receivable and a long-standing staff member we call A in Global Controlling. It is noteworthy that there have been three attempts to install a suitable HoD in this division over 2 years. The conflict turns into an open dispute and lands on the desk of the location's CEO. After a few emotionally charged discussions with the HoD and several failed attempts by HR and works council to facilitate an amicable agreement between the conflict parties, A goes on sick leave.

The Head of Global Controlling's loyalty to her HoD is carved in stone. She considers dismissing A. She is based in Lower Austria but reports to the HQ in Vienna. Despite herself, she decides to hire an executive coach with a mediation record to get support on how to resolve the conflict. Her motivation is, 'I want to finally know what is going on here. We cannot just wait until A returns from her sick leave.'

Faceting leadership by Integrative Presence: An *amuse-gueule* of basic interventions

Faceting leadership by Integrative Presence implies building awareness for the following agendas:

- Presence requires more than adaptability to differences of perception: conflict is more than some incompatibility between people and situations.
- Conflicts can be rooted in inherent organizational mechanisms: lack of clarity around these mechanisms leads to staff responding negatively to the implementation of change initiatives.

- Information deficits are the mother of 'rumours: information is a difference that makes a difference' (Bateson, 1972, p. 459). Lack of information about differences and sameness in human interactions (for example, purpose of global HQ and local division) harbours risks and opportunities for experiencing relational and material success, which is an existential basic principle (Buber, 2008).
- Presence requires sensing and perceiving dangers emanating from unresolved organizational development programmes: open 'construction sites' and an obsession with habits hamper staff's capacity to accept change initiatives.
- Organizations undergo cyclical phase changes (Adizes, 2004): it is risky to miss that perceptions of 'where we are with our development' collide.
- System ruptures (that is, when established rules are broken) bind energy; ignoring system ruptures leads to staff finding faults with the system and change (for example, external CEOs were not accepted by the existing system).
- When a company's structure is hit, staff feel pain; lack of responsiveness to this pain reduces staff's energy to adopt changes and paralysis kicks in.
- Where qualifications, skills and tools needed for work are not pooled objectively, staff either fight, flee or freeze when facing that discrepancy.
- Presence requires creating space for all to address 'hot issues' that surface only in moments of change (Schein, 2006) without fear of punishment for addressing those issues.
- Leadership and works council need suitable platforms for close collaboration and mindful alignment in moments of change to avoid 'two-party realities' (Eckardstein et al., 1988).
- Presence requires perceiving one's own responsiveness to change as a character; personal traits and states impact on how leaders respond to moments of change (Riemann, 1961) shaping how staff can respond (transference and counter-transference moments).
- Responsiveness to group-think (Janis, 1982) determines how staff will respond to change.
- Presence requires responsiveness to informal ties (for example, nepotism, love affair) that work undercover in the company to lead successfully in times of change.
- Violations of basic principles of social order (Daimler et al., 2008), in particular, the right to belong, years of service, levels of performance, respect for age and hierarchy bind staff's energy, which will impede the effectiveness of change initiatives.
- Social ostracism plays out informally in organizations and can massively hamper change initiatives.

Reflective practice for faceting your leadership presence

I propose the following questions as practice points for leaders to reflect the essence of Integrative Presence in co-creating change and disruption:

I-Sphere:

- What is your logic, repertoire of skills, styles and behaviours to support your responsiveness both in moments of calm and conflict?
- How do you show that you care with fearless feedback?
- What is the value for you in having plans, processes and tools in moments of change?
- What is the value of leader-led connection/commitment through contracting for you?
- Can you find the story in everything?
- What is your visceral response to moments of volatility?
- How do you use 'standing still' to focus on what your body is telling you?

WE-Sphere:

- How can you tell that your staff notice what you care about?
- How does your level of caring impact their capacity to perform?
- How do your staff deal with your level of curiosity about change?
- How do you deal with differences and sameness in interacting with staff?
- How does the way you tell your stories about change influence your staff?
- What is your staff's habitual response to your leadership?
- How do your staff respond to you in moments of volatility?
- How do you notice that you produce working results after each human interaction?
- How can you tell that your staff feel empowered to go with the changes you need to make?

ALL-Sphere:

- How iterative (that is, cyclical and timely, in sprints rather than as a simple step-by-step process) are human interactions, face-to-face conversations and fearless feedback between leaders and staff in your organization? How much are such interactions encouraged to take place?
- How does your organization create knowledge, generate insight and felt experience?
- What is the story your organization can find in your leadership?
- What do those affected by conflict/changes notice about your leadership?
- What happens in your organization concerning your habitual response to conflict/change?
- How many conversations do you begin that the people want to evolve?
- How do you notice that your organization cultivates curiosity?
- What is your peers' level of responsiveness to moments of change?

OMNI-Sphere:

- What is the lens you have on the world?
- How can anyone tell that those you lead build up resilience and autonomy beyond your leadership term or over time?
- What is the history and culture of responding to failure in your organization?
- If I were to take over your leadership role tomorrow, how would the organization 'say hello' to me and 'say goodbye' to you?

Conclusion

This chapter addressed leadership presence as a way to predict change. Change is predictable. Disruption is not unpredictable. Change and disruption are moments of conflict that we constantly co-create, and one that our proximal and distal environments co-create with us in a dynamic dance of responses or the absence of responses to each other.

> I trust that this chapter sets the context for how leaders can best navigate complex adaptive environments (for example, digital transformation and virtual workplaces) and the fundamentals of applying a responsive and spontaneous leadership culture in good times to better cope with bad times.

Forging final reflections

Tünde Erdös and Samer Hassan

Introduction

The major part of the book focuses on the sensorimotor and mental levels of consciousness (Wilber, 2006): the physical and psychological levels of energy. I outline how the physical energy was measured in coaching as well as the impact it is found to have on the psychological energy in the reciprocity of the coach-client relationship. This approach addressed the concept of presence from a rather tangible perspective even if this suggestion might appear counter-intuitive. How is energy tangible? One client even poses the question in his story: 'How can we measure how we are with each other' in coaching?

Measuring energy is not the problem. The problem is that these energies carry duality: in-phase/out-of-phase synchrony, being in-sync and out-of-sync, feeling safe and unsafe. While we addressed how 'the dual self' manifests in the I-Sphere, WE-Sphere and ALL-Sphere, and while we introduced the OMNI-Sphere as the level of energy that is all-encompassing and impacting our presence beyond our mental awareness, I described that I see our 'self' as non-dual energy, which echoes in how we are with each other across all these spheres. It is some cosmic echo over space and time.

The cosmic echo of self – Tünde Erdös

I perceive the integrative spirit of this book as a pulse that appears on the submarine sonar instrument. I do not know how much it will uncover, much the same way as we never know what the echo of coaching uncovers for clients in and beyond the relationship. We have this pulse and we can choose how to reflect the waves.

I addressed how an emerging coaching moment with a client of mine echoed in me and how the research project was born as an emerging blissful moment. What I did not address was that this brief chain reaction of being and experiencing my 'self' as a coach and becoming a coaching scientist had a preceding moment to it, as it has had a consequential moment to it – for instance, this book. So, the question is, 'What happens before and after something happens?'

Flexing muscle memory

To answer this question, in concluding the journey of unfolding the matryoshka of nested dolls, I will invite you to take some time and space for yourself to flex your muscle memory and practise your state of presence. In offering some questions for you to reflect on how your 'self echoes out there', I wish to guide you in noticing how you 'are' and what your 'being' echoes. The questions are not exhaustive. Instead they are intended to be a good starting point for paying attention to your felt experiences. How does presence emerge from the 'back and then' in the 'here and now' and in the 'then and after'? If you do nothing else from this book but implement these reflective practices, you will already be a more effective coach – and you can support the leaders you coach to have higher executive presence. Samer Hassan concludes by offering ways how to flex muscle memory for leaders in coaching as he describes the way in which leaders habitually respond to complexity, conflict and change as a moment of doom and how Somatic Thinking can support leaders in flexing muscle memory towards greater presence.

Being open to the power drive

Imagine you wish to have a great ride in your new Porsche along the beautiful coastline in Croatia on a sunshiny afternoon. You want to have a good time, so you are getting prepared to make it possible. You know you are an excellent driver and have the most technically fit car. You check the weather conditions, and at one point you have the sense that you are ready to enjoy your ride. And then, you are driving … and suddenly some pebbles hit your car. As if it were not enough, a crazy driver hits your car from the side. You lose control. What would it take for you to connect with your 'self' to find peace in the moment, so that the rest can take care of itself?

- What is driving my energies before a critical experience?
- How much am I aware of my meaning-making processes and consciousness states (Mr Control, Exploity and Grandma Wise)?
- What is my awareness of how one 'thing leads to another'?
- To what extent am I caught up in duality: feeling good vs bad, expecting and judging, hoping and despairing, wanting and discarding?
- What is my habitual way of saying 'yes' to something/someone?

I argue that the only energy that binds events and experiences together is openness to the driving power of bliss: do what needs doing in the moment without planning the next steps. Live the present moment by saying 'yes' to the driving power of energies: check in with yourself to see:

- Am I in Grandma Wise state now?
- What are my stimuli to what I am hearing, seeing, sensing and seeing?
- What are my urges and how do I respond to these urges?
- What has happened just now that I see, hear, smell, sense and feel things the way I do?

Seeing and being seen

Sense and see how the person 'over there' will show in your face, in your movements, in your own eyes. There is safety created for them through being seen through your physical responsiveness:

- How brave am I to let you see I am seeing you?
- Do I notice how this recognition changes the course of our interaction?
- Am I confident enough to share the degree to which I feel seen (or not) by you?
- Do I enjoy being a person seeing that I am the channel through which life streams?

Notice how your capacity to sense the person 'over there' and your raising the subject with them might soften your interaction making it more authentic, leading to a more effective exchange more gently and quickly. Your person is the channel through which your life streams – with some of the richest streaming being the other person and environment all around you.

Self-worth and purpose

If it is true that the most basic need in life is 'seeing and being seen', it is quite understandable to feel fear on perceiving that people who are important in our life do not see us. We might say, 'I am not important.' Fear of being alone kicks in as we face the territory of inferiority. We struggle to see others. There is little energy we can source to feel worthy of who we are. Instead we feel unworthy of what we believe we lose.

Do you remember the metaphor of the sea? The sea does not care if it is deep or shallow, or a fountain. It is water. It does not lose its identity in any duality. It does not compare itself to some other forms of water. It has found its purpose: being the sea.

- To what extent am I caught up in the duality of 'if you acknowledge me, I will acknowledge you'?
- When do I notice that my self-worth is not recognized? What happens?
- How often do I put on an image to be seen as I want to be seen?
- How do I feel when my cup of self-worth is filled?

It appears that for us to feel purposeful in any condition, our cup of self-worth needs to be filled. The empty cup of self-worth echoes the doubt of our purpose: we cannot see our purpose. We end up comparing ourselves with all rather than being simply the sea that is dedicated to being the sea.

- What is the echo of my self-worth for my purpose in life? Whose past self-worth is echoed in how I feel worthy or unworthy of my 'self'?
- How often do I feel superior or inferior to someone? What are my physical and psychological energies when I feel superior or inferior to someone?

How do purpose and self-worth relate? We are purposeful whether we feel worthy, or not. Purpose is our essence. It is our bedrock. Our self-worth is therefore not conditioned by any action or non-action. We believe it is. Even if we ceased to exist, this would have a purpose, creating a ripple effect. Our self would have an echo in the cosmos.

Coherence and integration of being and doing

Imagine you are a Muslim man. For you, a woman who is 'not veiled is not the one you want to have for a good wife'. Imagine, you are a liberated woman in the West. For you, a Muslim man puts a woman 'in a golden cage with expectations you cannot easily meet'.

Yet, you are both happy to accept that any person with a religious background that is different to yours can exist. You tolerate. However, the situation changes fast when you speak from a place of being either a man or a woman:

- Can I notice the duality of my energies and how they are coherent with who I truly want to be?
- Can I see a person as a person rather than as a man or woman with any specific bounded energy?
- Am I aware of how my energies are echoed in how I see a man or woman?

We are constantly incoherent in how we are and what we think and how we behave. If we perceive ourselves as individuals, we see a situation differently to how we would see it if we were a specific gender in a specific situation in a specific country.

All that exists – our being – is purposeful without any limitations as we all swim in the same sea of energies. How we act in the world – our doing – is an outward expression of who we want to be and what we value not just as a self-discovery but as it has been passed down to us through our ancestors:

- How does what I do reflect what I care about, who I have become, and how I am and will be in the future?
- To what extent does my doing echo my true 'self'? To what extent does my 'self' echo what I am doing?

- What is the coherent story line of where I come from, where I am, and where I might be going?
- What is my relationship to stillness? How does that relationship influence my physical and psychological energies?

My relationship to the unknown

We do not feel comfortable with the unknown. The unknown about our past and the unknown of what the future brings seem to echo a sense of loneliness in us. A sense of 'death' is imminent. We see it surrounding us everywhere; in social media, in family life, and at work:

- How do I make meaning of my relationship to the unknown?
- What does the unknown about my past and possible future echo in me now?
- How isolated am I in loneliness in my social interconnectedness?

What is beyond the unknown is fearful. To validate our meaning-making of how we are connected to the known, we open ourselves to signs of similarity between 'this and that' as an anchor to stay more grounded and feel less alone. We start looking for proof:

- How do I notice that I am safe with feeling alone?
- How do I respond to my fears of the future as they emerge now?
- How do I want my felt experiences to change me?
- What do I hope humanity will learn from my experiences?

We remind ourselves of the cosmic design of interconnectedness with everything – so we can feel more secure. This drive of seeking connection in the design of interconnectedness is our coping mechanism, which is the same mechanism that has been transmitted to us through belief systems in all cultures for as long as we have existed as humanity. It is this mechanism that stops us from being open to the power drive of purpose.

Coping mechanisms as an echo of self

You may be familiar with the sense of implosion humans sometimes have when they say, 'I have no choice. I have to leave.' Implosion is one example of how we cope to control our sense of safety in relationship to the unknown:

- What is my level of connectedness with the energies out there?
- How do the energies 'out there' echo in how I feel safe?

We may disconnect from anything that feels like the 'unknown' to us while we are still aware – not so much as a denial (for example, when sick, you may experience fear of death) – but more so as a short-term coping mechanism using spiritual and emotional escapism. So, escapism can serve a good purpose and can have a soothing effect. If and where disconnection or detachment is grounded in the perception of 'energy is me' and 'I am energy' and we feel peaceful without needing anything that would connect us to someone or something, we may experience emerging presence. However, if and where detachment is an expression of emotional escapism, we are likely to end up imploding, or exploding. Either way, the results are not likely to help us gain control – a sheer illusion in itself.

Seeing the future of our presence

Physicists have long known that the quantum of light, or photon, will behave like a particle or a wave depending on how physicists observe it (Weizmann Institute of Science, 1998). By observing a particle, physicists mean that they measure its properties. To measure a particle, they need to interact with them. It appears that all interactions will disturb the state of the particle whose properties they want to measure. Hence, we say 'reality is what we make it' and that reality is what we choose it to be:

- What is the legacy I leave behind relating to how I choose to observe and evaluate things?
- How do I choose to see things and people?

We encounter a similar phenomenon in literary arts referred to as foreshadowing. It is a device in which subtle hints are dropped about plot developments that will come later in a story. They function as an advance sign or warning of what is to come in the future. Essentially, when we say, 'Well, history is gonna change' or 'Well, history won't ever change', we may not realize that we are just about to alter the present timeline.

The choices we made to observe presence affected what we found out about it. This is inevitable. By speaking about the 'future flowering of coaching training programmes' (Chapter 9) based on the findings of the research project, I have set a highly responsible act. In foreshadowing the future of coaching by our chosen perspectives for coaching training programmes, we encounter the presence of our future – and the future of our presence:

- How do I cultivate foreshadowing?
- How do I interact with my emotions in foreshadowing?

Emotions like panic, fear and worry first and foremost stem from allowing our own thoughts to get away from us. We focus on the worry and fear of those that we want to rescue from emotional events that they might not experience but which we foreshadow for them and which might not happen if we stopped interacting with them from a place of panic and fear ourselves:

- Can I find the core of my chaos, the eye of the hurricane that never changes through it all?
- What if I stopped foreshadowing?
- What if I landscaped questions that emerge from how I observe something – just like in coaching?

Flexing muscle memory for leadership – Samer Hassan

Imagine that you are a computer. The computer hardware is your inner-world with a processing speed of 1 GHz. The software (operating system and applications) is your outer-world as it was created and re-created for you by others repeatedly (that is, all the stimuli from the outside world). The problem is that while the software is improving, becoming more and more complex and heavy to process with a freakishly accelerated speed that requires more than 2 GHz, you will need at least double the speed that you are comfortable with. You will not necessarily be able to change your 'hardware': you are stuck in your body. We see the hardware becoming obsolete urging us to replace it too. While this might work with a computer, we cannot possibly upgrade our body as human beings to integrate the increasing number of updates we are feeding it with.

Which response would you choose to move forward?

- Do nothing.
- Fight the software progress because it should slow down.
- Upgrade your processing speed.

My claim is that leaders' responsiveness depends on the perspectives they embrace in life as a person. Our role is inseparable from our person. Observing current responses to difficult moments in leadership, I have identified three patterns as coping mechanisms as the most frequently recurring ones among leaders:

1 Denial perspective.
2 Fight perspective.
3 Presence perspective.

Denial perspective – 'Nothing needs to change'

Being exposed to the accelerating moments of change, a leader's inner monologue holding a denial perspective goes something like, 'This is deceiving propaganda of misleading powers, competitors, haters who want to steal our success telling us the world is going to hell, implying it's our fault. NO, it is NOT! We've nothing to do with this now. We only need to focus on how to increase success, stay with our objectives.'

Leaders adopting this perspective are attached to their usual way of doing things. They selectively listen to what will validate their opinion focusing on achieving goals and avoiding confrontation by delegating issues to someone else to evade 'feeling responsible'.

Fight perspective – 'Others need to change'

Leaders adopting this perspective will have the ambitious goal of stopping the present from happening and reversing its flow. They will take it upon themselves to awaken those in 'denial', believing that salvation is in changing others and making others realize how they are about to destroy our world.

Their inner monologue goes something like, 'It's our job to change the world and be of service to people by saving them from themselves. We need to teach them how to be better so we can win the fight against the doom curve.' Leaders adopting the fight perspectives intend to trigger change and respond to change. They have a great 'can-do mentality' with a high sense of justice that feeds on confrontation. They will not shy away from telling others what needs doing to make the necessary changes and stop the doom curve.

Adopting this perspective, leaders have a plan with a clear map of the future and a genuine belief that they will emerge victoriously in the face of adversity. This unshakeable belief bestows upon the 'fight' perspective leaders an appealing charisma that inspires trust, making people want to follow them and trust their plan.

Leaders adopting a fight perspective are great at introducing movements of change to confront destructive social, economic and environmental phenomena spearheading change. However, they do not invest enough in building a self-sustained community of innovators. Once their engine of change stops or is stopped, the change movement dies or deforms into an empty husk of what it once was.

Presence perspective – 'I need to change'

Leaders adopting the presence perspective see the world as a naturally evolving system similar to any other universal system that is bound by the life cycle phases of being born, growing, ageing, dying and being reborn through transformation (Adizes, 2004). They embrace painful change as a natural part of the ageing phase of our cycle of life making our human impact a natural part of the same phase.

Unlike 'fight leaders', 'presence leaders' view a problematic phenomenon as a driving force that will thrive through acceptance, adaptation, and transformation into something different.

They believe that when facing a problematic phenomenon, we need to:

- let go of our biases
- sense what is happening like a radar will do
- interact with the phenomenon to understand its flow and dynamics
- explore the possibility of transforming the energy of a painful phenomenon into an innovative solution

- take an informed action
- start again from step one and refine as we go.

Presence leaders' inner monologue usually goes something like, 'My purpose is to consistently boost my ability to adapt, innovate and share with people to build a community that can continue adapting and innovating with me and long after me.'

Presence leaders are pioneers of innovation in all walks of life:

- transforming trash into building material that can solve housing problems
- turning a well of salty water discovered on agricultural land into a lucrative seawater fish farm, thus solving the declining income issue by diversifying the income of the company
- transforming heterogeneity in a company into an opportunity to expand client reach and innovate
- turning the global warming heat waves and temperature fluctuations into a clean energy power source as a possibility for the future.

Somatic Thinking in leadership presence – Samer Hassan

Mind-based leadership

The human mind is biased to see the world with clarity and certainty making ambiguity and not knowing the most significant challenge we face. So, we weaponize ourselves with knowledge hoping that it will give us the power to defeat our fear of the unknown. Mind-based leaders are like a cartographer who puts all of his and his people's efforts into creating a map of all that there is and needs predicting to control outcomes with certainty. As the unknown is the foremost constant, mind-based leaders predominantly struggle to navigate the unknown.

Presence-based leadership

Somatic Thinking promotes presence as a 'way of being' allowing leaders to become more like a radar without biases. It focuses on sensing what is happening instead of what may happen or once happened and on interacting with, understanding, and responding to what is 'there'. It focuses on speaking and acting in a state of presence instead of preparing and presenting from a place of fear. Coaching and leadership are two sides of the same coin here.

Free the leader's mind

The leader's mind can roam between past, future and present when facing the unpredictability of the unknown. To free the leader's mind, I propose to work with the human behind the leader – practising the Experience Shapers, as follows:

- Expand the leader's awareness of the shapers and train them to pay attention to which shaper dominates their mind when interacting with people and managing situations.
- Train leaders to observe their thoughts and identify which thought belongs to which shaper.
- Activate and optimize leaders' ability to receive more sensory information through the body, which will allow Grandma Wise to be the dominant shaper when interacting with the outer world.

As a result, leaders' ability to free the mind from the clutter of past and future, the attachment to knowing, and controlling the unknown expands significantly removing the main limiter to navigating the unknown effortlessly and with spontaneous responsiveness.

What you may feel inspired to explore in our footsteps – Conclusion

Generally, I call for more advanced and innovative scientific steps to be applied in coaching research (that is, video/audio interaction analysis instruments and sophisticated data analysis tools such as MEA) to look into the processes that emerge in coaching engagements over time if we are to claim credibility for coaching with individual clients and client organizations.

An interesting field to explore next may be the relevance of verbal synchrony in the reciprocal coach-client relationship. What is the essence and function of verbal synchrony? How might it complement the essence of non-verbal synchrony in coaching? What are the qualities of verbal synchrony in Integrative Presence?

Another important field to explore is clients' goal attainment – through the long-lasting beneficial effects of movement synchrony – as a ripple effect of pro-social behaviour in their organizations (Hove and Risen, 2009; Macrae et al., 2008). I believe that this is important as it was found in social sciences (Kokal et al., 2011) that the reward signals experienced through synchrony resulted in interaction partners to be inclined to help others outside that relationship. We need research to understand the ripple effect of reward signals experienced through synchrony in coaching effectiveness.

Further Reading

Albom, M. (1997) *Tuesdays with Morrie: An Old Man, a Young Man, and Life's Greatest Lesson.* New York: Broadway Books.
Almaas, A.H. (2006) *Brilliancy: The Essence of Intelligence.* Boulder, CO: Shambhala Publications.
Barrett, L.F. (2017) *How Emotions Are Made: The Secret Life of the Brain.* Boston, MA: Houghton Mifflin Harcourt.
Bluckert, P. (2006) *Psychological Dimensions of Executive Coaching.* Maidenhead: Open University Press.
Boyatzis, R. and McKee, A. (2005) *Resonant Leadership: Renewing Yourself and Connecting with Others Through Mindfulness, Hope and Compassion.* Boston, MA: Harvard Business School Publishing.
Clark, A. (2008) *Supersizing the Mind: Embodiment, Action, and Cognitive Extension.* Oxford: Oxford University Press.
Coates, J. (2012) *The Hour Between Dog and Wolf: Risk-taking, Gut Feelings and the Biology of Boom and Bust.* London: Fourth Estate.
Damasio, A.R. (1999) *The Feeling of What Happens: Body and Emotion in the Making of Consciousness.* New York: Harcourt Brace.
de Haan, E. (2008) *Relational Coaching: Journeys Towards Mastering One-to-One Coaching.* Chichester: John Wiley & Sons.
Gebser, J. (1985) *The Ever-Present Origin.* Athens, Ohio: Ohio University Press.
Gendlin, E.T. (2003) *Focusing.* London: Random House.
Hamill, P. (2013) *Embodied Leadership: The Somatic Approach to Developing Your Leadership.* London: Kogan Page.
Hawkins, D.R. (1995) *Power vs. Force: The Hidden Determinants of Human Behaviour.* Calsbad, CA: Hay House Inc.
Heckler, R.S. (1993) *The Anatomy of Change: A Way to Move Through Life's Transitions.* Berkeley, CA: North Atlantic Books.
Heller, S. (1991) *The Dance of Becoming – Living Life as a Martial Art.* Berkeley, CA: North Atlantic Books.
Heron, J. (1992) *Feeling and Personhood: Psychology in Another Key.* Newbury Park, CA: SAGE Publications.
Iliffe-Wood, M. (2014) *Coaching Presence: Building Consciousness and Awareness in Coaching Interventions.* London: Kogan Page Ltd.
Johnson, M. (1990) *The Body in the Mind: The Bodily Basis of Meaning, Imagination, and Reason.* 2nd edn. Chicago, IL: University of Chicago Press.
Kabat-Zinn, J. (1991) *Full Catastrophe Living: Using the Wisdom of Your Body and Mind to Face Stress, Pain and Illness.* New York: Dell Publishing.
Kabat-Zinn, J. (2005) *Coming to Our Senses: Healing Ourselves and the World Through Mindfulness.* New York: Hyperion.
Kegan, R. (1982) *The Evolving Self: Problem and Process in Human Development.* Cambridge, MA: Harvard University Press.
Kegan, R. (2003) *In Over our Heads: The Mental Demands of Modern Life.* Cambridge, MA: Harvard University Press.
Lakoff, G. and Johnson, M. (1981) *Metaphors We Live By.* Chicago, IL: University of Chicago Press.

Lakoff, G. and Johnson, M. (1999) *Philosophy in the Flesh: The Embodied Mind and its Challenge to Western Thought*. New York: Basic Books.

Leary-Joyce, J. (2014) *The Fertile Void: Gestalt Coaching at Work*. St Albans: AoEC Press.

Leonard, G. and Murphy, M. (1995) *The Life We Are Given: A Long-Term Program for Realizing the Potential of Body, Mind, Heart and Soul*. Los Angeles. CA: Tarcher/Putnam Inc.

Levine, S. (2002) *Turning Toward the Mystery: A Seeker's Journey*. New York: Harper Collins.

Loehr, J. and Schwartz, T. (2003) *The Power of Full Engagement: Managing Energy, Not Time, Is the Key to High Performance and Personal Renewal*. New York: Free Press.

Merleau-Ponty, M. (2013) *Phenomenology of Perception*. Translated by D.A. Landes. Abingdon: Routledge.

Rogers, C. (1980) *A Way of Being*. Boston: Houghton Mifflin.

Rothschild, B. (2000) *The Body Remembers. The Psychophysiology of Trauma and its Treatment*. New York: WW Norton & Company.

Senge, P., Scharmer, C.O., Jaworski, J. and Flowers, B.S. (2004) *Presence: Human Purpose and the Field of the Future*. Cambridge, MA: Society for Organizational Learning.

Silsbee, D. (2008) *Presence-based Coaching: Cultivating Self-generative Leaders Through Mind, Body, and Heart*. San Francisco: Jossey-Bass.

Solomon, R. and Flores. F. (2001) *Building Trust in Business, Politics, Relationships, and Life*. Oxford: Oxford University Press.

Strozzi-Heckler, D. (2014) *The Art of Somatic Coaching: Embodying Skillful Action, Wisdom, and Compassion*. Berkeley, CA: North Atlantic Books.

Tolle, E. (1999) *The Power of Now: A Guide to Spiritual Enlightenment*. Novato, CA: New World Library.

Wheatley, M.J. (2002) *Turning to One Another: Simple Conversations to Restore Hope to the Future*. Oakland, CA: Berrett-Koehler.

Whitworth, L., Kimsey-House, K., Kimsey-House, H. and Sandahl, P. (2007) *Co-active Coaching: New Skills for Coaching People Toward Success in Work and Life*. Mountain View, CA: Davies-Black Publishing.

Wilber, K. (2006) *Integral Spirituality: A Startling New Role for Religion in the Modern and Postmodern World*. Boulder, CO: Shambhala Publications.

Wilber, K., Patten, T., Morelli, M. and Leonard, A. (2008) *Integral Life Practice: A 21st Century Blueprint for Physical Health, Emotional Balance, Mental Clarity and Spiritual Awakening*. Boulder, CO: Shambhala Publications.

References

Abney, D.H., Paxton, A., Dale, R. and Kello, C.T. (2015) Movement dynamics reflect a functional role for weak coupling and role structure in dyadic problem solving. *Cognitive Processing*, 16: 325–32.

Adizes, I. (2004) *Managing Corporate Lifecycles*. Santa Barbara: Adizes Institute Publications.

Altmann, U., Schoenherr, D. and Paulick, J. et al. (2020) Associations between movement synchrony and outcome in patients with social anxiety disorder: Evidence for treatment specific effects. *Psychotherapy Research*, 30(5): 574–90.

Anshel, A., and Kipper, D.A. (1988) The influence of group singing on trust and cooperation. *Journal of Music Therapy*, 25(3): 145–55.

Athanasopoulou, A. and Dopson, S. (2018) A systematic review of executive coaching outcomes: Is it the journey or the destination that matters the most? *The Leadership Quarterly*, 29(1): 70–88.

Argyris, C., Putnam, R. and Smith, D.M. (1985) *Action Science: Concepts, Methods, and Skills for Research and Intervention*. San Francisco: Jossey-Bass.

Bachkirova, T., Cox, E. and Clutterbuck, D. (2014) Introduction, in E. Cox, T. Bachkirova and D. Clutterbuck (eds) *The Complete Handbook of Coaching*, 2nd edn. London: SAGE Publications, pp. 1–20.

Bachirova, T. and Lawton Smith, C. (2015) From competencies to capabilities in the assessment and accreditation of coaches. *International Journal of Evidence Based Coaching and Mentoring*, 13(2): 123–40.

Bandler, R. and Grinder, J. (1990) *Frogs into Princes: Introduction to Neurolinguistic Programming*. Enfield: Eden Grove Editions.

Barrett, L.F. (2017) *How Emotions Are Made: The Secret Life of the Brain*. Boston: Houghton Mifflin Harcourt.

Bateson, G. (1972) *Steps to an Ecology of Mind: Collected Essays in Anthropology, Psychiatry, Evolution, and Epistemology*. Northvale, New Jersey: Jason Aronson Inc.

Berne, E. (1964) *Games People Play: The Psychology of Human Relationships*. New York: Grove Press.

Biberacher, L., Strack, M., and Braumandl, I. (2010) Ziele erreicht? Beziehung passend? Evaluation einer Coachingausbildung für Studierende [Goals attained? Relationship suitable? Evaluation of a coaching formation for students]. Paper presented at the Conference 8. Kongress für Wirtschaftspsychologie des BDP. Potsdam.

Bishop, S.R., Lau, M. and Shapiro, S. et al. (2004). Mindfulness: A proposed operational definition. *Clinical Psychology: Science and Practice*, 11(3): 230–41.

Bluckert, P. (2006). *Psychological Dimensions of Executive Coaching*. Maidenhead: Open University Press.

Boker, S.M. (2004) Context dependence of interpersonal coordination during social interaction. Paper presented at Learning and Multimodal Communication. Conference. Chicago, Illinois.

Bollas, C. (1992) *Being a Character: Psychoanalysis and Self Experience*. New York: Hill & Wang.

Bordin, E.S. (1979) The generalizability of the psychoanalytic concept of the working alliance. *Psychotherapy: Theory, Research and Practice*, 16(3): 252–60.

Borkovec, T.D. (1994) The nature, functions, and origins of worry, in G.C.L Davey and F. Tallis (eds) *Worrying: Perspectives on Theory, Assessment and Treatment*. Chichester: Wiley & Sons, pp. 5–33.

Bowes, I. and Jones, R.L. (2006) Working at the edge of chaos: Understanding coaching as a complex, interpersonal system. *Sport Psychologist*, 20(2): 235–45.

Bowlby J. (1969) *Attachment. Attachment and Loss*, Vol. 1. New York: Basic Books.

Boyce, L.A., Jackson, R.J. and Neal, L.J. (2010) Building successful leadership coaching relationships: Examining impact of matching criteria in a leadership coaching program. *The Journal of Management Development*, 29(10): 914–31. https://doi.org/10.1108/02621711011084231

Brown-Schmidt, S., Gunlogson, C. and Tanenhaus, M.K. (2008) Addressees distinguish shared from private information when interpreting questions during interactive conversation. *Cognition*, 107(3): 1122–34.

Buber, M. (2008) *Ich und Du*. Stuttgart: Reclam.

Butler, E.A. and Randall, A.K. (2013) Emotional coregulation in close relationships. *Emotion Review*, 5(2): 202–10.

Cacioppo S., Zhou H., Monteleone G. et al. (2014) You are in sync with me: Neural correlates of interpersonal synchrony with a partner. *Neuroscience*, 277: 842–58.

Caramazza, A., Anzellotti, S., Strand, L. and Lingnau, A. (2014) Embodied cognition and mirror neurons: A critical assessment. *Annual Review of Neuroscience*, 37: 1–15.

Carver, C.S. (1998) Generalization, adverse events, and development of depressive symptoms. *Journal of Personality*, 66(4): 607–19.

Cavanagh, M.J. (2013) The coaching engagement in the twenty-first century: New paradigms for complex times, in S. David, D. Clutterbuck and D. Megginson (eds) *Beyond Goals: Effective Strategies in Coaching and Mentoring*. Aldershot: Gower Publishing, pp. 151–83.

Cavanagh, M. and Lane, D. (2012) Coaching psychology coming of age: The challenges we face in the messy world of complexity. *International Coaching Psychology Review*, 7(1): 75–90.

Chartrand, T.L., and Lakin, J.L. (2013) The antecedents and consequences of human behavioural mimicry. *Annual Review of Psychology*, 64: 285–308.

Cockburn, D. (2001) *An Introduction to the Philosophy of Mind*. Basingstoke: Palgrave. Macmillan.

Cotter, S. (1996) Using bioenergetics to develop managers: Ten years of practical application of body-mind psychology with over a thousand managers at Cranfield University. *Journal of Management Development*, 15: 8–16.

Cox, E. (2013) Coaching understood: A pragmatic inquiry into the coaching process. *International Journal of Sports Science and Coaching*, 8(1): 265–70.

Craig, A.D. (2004) Human feelings: Why are some more aware than others? *Trends in Cognitive Sciences*, 8(6): 239–41.

Craig A.D. (2014) *How Do You Feel? An Interoceptive Moment with Your Neurobiological Self*. Princeton, NJ: Princeton University Press.

Cremona, K. (2010) Coaching and emotions: An exploration of how coaches engage and think about emotions. *Coaching: An International Journal of Theory, Research and Practice*, 3(1): 46–59.

Cui, X., Bryant, D.M. and Reiss, A.L. (2012) NIRS-based hyperscanning reveals increased interpersonal coherence in superior frontal cortex during cooperation. *Neuroimage*, 59(3): 2430–37.

Dagley, G.R. and Gaskin, C.J. (2014) Understanding executive presence: Perspectives of business professionals. *Consulting Psychology Journal: Practice and Research*, 66(3): 197–211.

References 145

Daimler, R., Sparrer, I. andVarga, M. (2008) *Basics der systemischen Strukturaufstellungen – Eine Anleitung für Einsteiger und Fortgeschrittene*. München: Kösel-Verlag.
Davidson, R.J. (2000) Affective style, psychopathology, and resilience: Brain mechanisms and plasticity. *American Psychologist*, 55(11): 1196–214.
de Gelder, B. (2006) Towards the neurobiology of emotional body language. *Nature Reviews Neuroscience*, 7(3): 242–49.
de Gelder, B. and Partan, S. (2009) The neural basis of perceiving emotional bodily expressions in monkeys. *NeuroReport: For Rapid Communication of Neuroscience Research*, 20(7): 642–46.
de Haan, E. (2008a) *Relational Coaching: Journeys Towards Mastering One-to-One Coaching*. Chichester: John Wiley & Sons.
de Haan, E. (2008b) I doubt therefore I coach: Critical moments in coaching practice. *Consulting Psychology Journal: Practice and Research*, 60(1): 91–105. https://doi.org/10.1037/1065-9293.60.1.91
de Haan, E. (2011) Back to basics: How the discovery of transference is relevant for coaches and consultants today. *International Coaching Psychology Review*, 6(2): 180–93.
de Haan, E., and Burger, Y. (2005) Person-centred coaching: Facilitating the coachee, in *Coaching with Colleagues*. London: Palgrave Macmillan, pp. 69–74.
de Haan, E., and Duckworth, A. (2013) Signalling a new trend in executive coaching outcome research. *International Coaching Psychology Review*, 8(1): 6–19.
de Haan, E.D., Gray, D.E. and Bonneywell, S. (2019) Executive coaching outcome research in a field setting: A near-randomized controlled trial study in a global healthcare corporation. *Academy of Management Learning and Education*, 18(4): 581–605.
Dewey, J. (1933) *How We Think: A Restatement of the Relation of Reflective Thinking to the Educative Process*. Chicago, IL: Henry Regnery.
Diamond, L.M. and Hicks, A.M. (2005) Attachment style, current relationship security, and negative emotions: The mediating role of physiological regulation. *Journal of Social and Personal Relationships*, 22(4): 499–518.
Dijksterhuis, A. and Bargh, J.A. (2001) The perception-behavior expressway: Automatic effects of social perception on social behaviour, in M.P Zanna (ed.) *Advances in Experimental Social Psychology*, Vol. 33, Cambridge, MA: Academic Press, pp. 1–40.
Divine, L. (2009) A unique view into you: Working with a client's AQAL constellation. *Journal of Integral Theory and Practice*, 4(1): 41–68.
Doyle, N. and McDowall, A. (2015) Is coaching an effective adjustment for dyslexic adults? *Coaching: An International Journal of Theory, Research and Practice*, 8(2),: 154–68.
Drake, D.B. (2009) Evidence is a verb: A relational approach to knowledge and mastery in coaching. *International Journal of Evidence Based Coaching and Mentoring*, 7(1): 1–12.
Eckardstein, von D., Janes, A., Prammer, K. and Wildner, T. (1998) *Muster betrieblicher Kooperation zwischen Management und Betriebsrat – Die Entwicklung von Lohnmodellen im System österreichischer Arbeitsbeziehungen*. München/Mering: Rainer Hampp Verlag.
Erdös, T. (2019a) Our ever-changing moods. *Coaching at Work*, 14(3): 41–4.
Erdös, T. (2019b) Non-verbal synchrony in coaching: The pinnacle of emotion regulation. *Tijdschrift voor Begeleidingskunde*, 8(3): 30–7.
Erdös, T. and Angelis, I. (2020) *The Coaching Science Practitioner Handbook*. Austin, TX: Applied Sciences Publishing.

Erdös, T., de Haan, E. and Heusinkfeld, S. (2020) Coaching: Client factors and contextual dynamics in the change process: A qualitative meta-synthesis. *Coaching: An International Journal of Theory, Research and Practice.*

Erdös, T. and Ramseyer, F. (2020) Change process in coaching: Interplay of movement synchrony, working alliance, self-regulation and goal-attainment. *Frontiers in Psychology*, (in publication).

Farias, M., Wikholm, C. and Delmonte, R. (2016) What is mindfulness-based therapy good for? Evidence, limitations and controversies. *The Lancet Psychiatry*, 3(11): 1012–13.

Feldman, R. (2007) Parent-infant synchrony and the construction of shared timing: Physiological precursors, developmental outcomes, and risk conditions. *Journal of Child Psychology and Psychiatry*, 48(3–4): 329–54.

Feldman, R. (2015) Mutual influences between child emotion regulation and parent–child reciprocity support development across the first 10 years of life: Implications for developmental psychopathology. *Development and Psychopathology*, 27(4): 1007–23.

Feldman, R., Greenbaum, C.W. and Yirmiya, N. (1999) Mother-infant affect synchrony as an antecedent of the emergence of self-control. *Developmental Psychology Journal*, 35(1): 223–31.

Ferrer, E. and Helm, J.L. (2013) Dynamical systems modeling of physiological coregulation in dyadic interactions. *International Journal of Psychophysiology*, 88(3): 296–308.

Fetterman, A.K. and Robinson, M.D. (2014) What can metaphors tell us about personality? *Mind*, 20.

Fowler, C.A., Richardson, M.J., Marsh, K.L. and Shockley, K.D. (2008) Language use, coordination, and the emergence of cooperative action, in A. Fuchs and V.K Jirsa (eds) *Coordination: Neural, Behavioural and Social Dynamics. Understanding Complex Systems*. Heidelberg: Springer, pp. 261–79.

Gardner, W.L., Avolio, B.J. and Walumbwa, F.O. (2005) Authentic leadership development: Emergent themes and future directions, in W.L Gardner, B.J Avolio and F.O Walumbwa (eds) *Authentic Leadership Theory and Practice: Origins, Effects and Development*. Amsterdam: Elsevier, pp. 387–406.

Gendlin, E.T. (1969) Focusing. *Psychotherapy: Theory, Research and Practice*, 6(1): 4–15.

Gendlin, E.T. (2003a) *Focusing*. London: Random House.

Gendlin, E.T. (2003b) Beyond postmodernism: From concepts through experiencing, in R. Frie (ed.) *Understanding Experience: Psychotherapy and Postmodernism*. Abingdon: Routledge, pp. 100–15.

Gessnitzer, S. and Kauffeld, S. (2015) The working alliance in coaching. *The Journal of Applied Behavioural Science*, 51(2): 177–97.

Glaser, J.E. (2014) *Conversational Intelligence: How Great Leaders Build Trust and Get Extraordinary Results*. Brookline, MA: Bibliomotion Inc.

Grant, A.D. and Taylor, A. (2014) Communication essentials for female executives to develop leadership presence: Getting beyond the barriers of understating accomplishment. *Business Horizons*, 57(1): 73–83.

Grant, A.M. (2003) The impact of life coaching on goal attainment, metacognition and mental health. *Social Behavior and Personality*, 31(3): 253–63. https://doi.org/10.2224/sbp.2003.31.3.253

Grant, A.M. (2012) An integrated model of goal-focused coaching: An evidence-based framework for teaching and practice. *International Coaching Psychology Review*, 7(2): 146–65.

Grant, A.M. (2014) The efficacy of executive coaching in times of organisational change. *Journal of Change Management*, 14(2): 258–80.

References

Grant, A.M. (2017) Coaching as evidence-based practice: The view through a multiple perspective model of coaching research, in T. Bachkirova, G. Spence and D. Drake (eds.) *The SAGE Handbook of Coaching*. London: SAGE Publications.

Grassmann, C., Schölmerich, F. and Schermuly, C.C. (2019) The relationship between working alliance and client outcomes in coaching: A meta-analysis. *Human Relations*, 73(1): 35–58.

Greenberg, L.S. and Safran, J. (1989) Emotion in psychotherapy. *American Psychologist*, 44(1): 19–29.

Gregory, J.B., Beck, J.W. and Carr, A.E. (2011) Goals, feedback, and self-regulation: Control theory as a natural framework for executive coaching. *Consulting Psychology Journal: Practice and Research*, 63(1): 26.

Greif, S. (2008) *Coaching und ergebnisorientierte Selbstreflexion*. Göttingen: Hogrefe.

Greif, S. and Berg, C.A. (2011) *Result-oriented Self-reflection – Report on the Construct Validation of Theory-based Scales*. Osnabrück: University of Osnabrück.

Grover, S. and Furnham, A. (2016) Coaching as a developmental intervention in organisations: A systematic review of its effectiveness and the mechanisms underlying it. *PLoS One*, 11(7).

Gyllensten, K. and Palmer, S. (2007) The coaching relationship: An interpretative phenomenological analysis. *International Coaching Psychology Review*, 2: 168–77.

Hamill, P. (2013) *Embodied Leadership: The Somatic Approach to Developing Your Leadership*. London: Kogan Page.

Harding, C. (2006) Using the multiple intelligences as a learning intervention: A model for coaching and mentoring. *International Journal of Evidence Based Coaching and Mentoring*, 4(2): 19–41.

Harding, N., Lee, H., Ford, J. and Learmonth, M. (2011) Leadership and charisma: A desire that cannot speak its name? *Human Relations*, 64: 927–50.

Hatcher, R.L. and Gillaspy, J.A. (2006) Development and validation of a revised short version of the Working Alliance Inventory. *Psychotherapy Research*, 16(1): 12–25.

Hatfield, E., Cacioppo, J. and Rapson, R.L. (1994) *Emotional Contagion*. Cambridge: Cambridge University Press.

Hatfield, E., Bensman, L., Thornton, P.D. and Rapson, R.L. (2014) Emotional mimicry and emotional contagion in social context, in U. Hess and A. Fischer (eds.) *Emotional Mimicry in Social Context*. Cambridge University Press.

Hauser, L. (2017) The science behind powerful questioning: A systemic questioning framework for coach educators and practitioners. *Philosophy of Coaching: An International Journal*, 2(2): 1–5.

Hawkins, P. and Smith, N. (2013) *Coaching, Mentoring and Organizational Consultancy: Supervision, Skills and Development*, 2nd edn. Maidenhead: Open University Press.

Hayes, S.C., Wilson, K.G., Gifford, E.V. et al. (1996) Experimental avoidance and behavioural disorders: A functional dimensional approach to diagnosis and treatment. *Journal of Consulting and Clinical Psychology*, 64(6): 1152–68.

Heidegger, M. (2010) *Being and Time*. Translated by J. Stambaugh. Albany, NY: State University of New York Press.

Hewlett, S.A. (2014) *Executive Presence: The Missing Link Between Merit and Success*. New York: HarperCollins Publishers.

Hove, M.J. and Risen, J.L. (2009) It's all in the timing: Interpersonal synchrony increases affiliation. *Social Cognition*, 27(6): 949–60.

Hunt, J. (2009) Transcending and including our current way of being. *Journal of Integral Thoery and Practice*, 4(1): 1–20.

Hyers, C. (1984) *The Meaning of Creation: Genesis and Modern Science*. Louisville, KY: Westminster John Knox Press.

Ianiro, M.J., Lehmann-Willenbrock, N. and Kauffeld, S. (2015) Coaches and clients and action: A sequential analysis of interpersonal coach and client behaviour. *Journal of Business and Psychology*, 30(3): 435–56.

Ianiro, P.M. and Kauffeld, S. (2014) Take care what you bring with you: How coaches' mood and interpersonal behavior affect coaching success. *Consulting Psychology Journal: Practice and Research*, 66(3): 231–57.

Ianiro, P.M., Schermuly, C.C. and Kauffeld, S. (2013) Why interpersonal affiliation and dominance matter: An interaction analysis of the coach-client relationship. *Coaching: An International Journal of Theory, Research and Practice*, 6: 25–46.

Iliffe-Wood, M. (2014) *Coaching Presence: Building Consciousness and Awareness in Coaching Interventions*. London: Kogan Page.

Iordanou, I. and Williams, P. (2017) Developing ethical capabilities of coaches, in T. Bachkirova, G. Spence and D. Drake (eds) *The SAGE Handbook of Coaching*. London: SAGE Publications, pp. 696–712.

Ireland, M.E. and Pennebaker, J.W. (2010) Language style matching in writing: Synchrony in essays, correspondence, and poetry. *Journal of Personality and Social Psychology*, 99(3): 549–71.

Jackson, P. (2017) Physicality in coaching: Developing an embodied perspective, in T. Bachkirova, G. Spence and D. Drake (eds) *The SAGE Handbook of Coaching*. London: SAGE Publications, pp. 256–71.

Janis, I.L. (1982) *Groupthink*. Boston, MA: Houghton Mifflin.

Jarvis, C. (2012) *Physical Examination and Health Assessment*, 6th edn. St. Louis, MO: Elsevier/Saunders.

Jiang, J.J., Chang, J.Y.T., Chen, H.-G. et al. (2014) Achieving IT program goals with integrative conflict management. *Journal of Management Information Systems*, 31(1): 79–106.

Jones, R.J., Woods, S.A. and Guillaume, Y.R.F. (2016) The effectiveness of workplace coaching: A meta-analysis of learning and performance outcomes from coaching. *Journal of Occupational and Organizational Psychology*, 89(2): 249–77.

Jordan, D.G., Winer, E.S. and Salem, T. (2020) The current status of temporal network analysis for clinical science: Considerations as the paradigm shifts. *Journal of Clinical Psychology*, 76(9): 1591–612.

Kabat-Zinn, J. (2005) *Coming to Our Senses: Healing Ourselves and the World Through Mindfulness*. Westport, CT: Hyperion Press.

Kelso, J.A.S. (1995) *Dynamic Patterns: The Self-organization of Brain and Behaviour*. Cambridge, MA: MIT Press.

Kennedy, D.L. (2013) The impact of development on coaches' use of self as instrument. PhD thesis. Fielding Graduate University.

Kiesler, D.J. (1983) The 1982 interpersonal circle: A taxonomy for complementarity in human transactions. *Psychological Review*, 90: 185–214.

Kleinbub, J.R. (2017) State of the art of interpersonal physiology in psychotherapy: A systematic review. *Frontiers in Psychology*, 8: 2053.

Knoblich, G., Butterfill, S. and Sebanz, N. (2011) Psychological research on joint action: Theory and data, in B.H. Ross (ed.) *The Psychology of Learning and Motivation: Advances in Research and Theory*, Vol. 54. Cambridge, MA: Elsevier Academic Press, pp. 59–101.

Kokal, I., Engel, A., Kirschner, S. and Keysers, C. (2011) Synchronized drumming enhances activity in the caudate and facilitates prosocial commitment – If the rhythm comes easily. *PLoS One*, 6(11): e27272.

Koole, S.L. and Coenen, L.H.M. (2007) Implicit self and affect regulation: Effects of action orientation and subliminal self priming in an affective priming task. *Self and Identity*, 6(2-3): 118–36.

Koole, S.L. and Tschacher, W. (2016) Synchrony in psychotherapy: A review and an integrative framework for the therapeutic alliance. *Frontiers in Psychology*, 7: 862.

Kuhl, J. (2001) *Motivation und Persönlichkeit*. Göttingen: Hogrefe.

Kumar, S.M. (2002) An introduction to Buddhism for the cognitive-behavioural therapist. *Cognitive and Behavioural Practice*, 9(1): 40–3.

Lawley, J. and Tompkins, P. (2000) *Metaphors in Mind: Transformation Through Symbolic Modelling*. London: Developing Company Press.

Lee, G. (2014) The psychodynamic approach to coaching. in E. Cox, T. Bachkirova and D. Clutterbuck (eds) *The Complete Handbook of Coaching*, 2nd edn. London: SAGE Publications, pp. 21–33.

Leonard, G. (2005) *Mastery: The Keys to Success and Long-Term Fulfillment*. New York: Plume.

Levenson, R.W. and Gottman, J.M. (1983) Marital interaction: Physiological linkage and affective exchange. *Journal of Personality and Social Psychology*, 45(3): 587–97.

Linder-Pelz, S. and Hall, M. (2007) The theoretical roots of NLP-based coaching. *The Coaching Psychologist*, 3(1): 12–17.

Lowen, A. (1994) *Bioenergetics: The Revolutionary Therapy that Uses the Language of the Body to Heal the Problems of the Mind*. New York: Arkana.

Lutz, W., Prinz, J.N., Schwarz, B. et al. (2020) Patterns of early change in interpersonal problems and their relationship to nonverbal synchrony and multidimensional outcome. *Journal of Counseling Psychology*, 67(4): 449–461.

Macrae, C.N., Duffy, O.K., Miles, L.K. and Lawrence, J. (2008) A case of hand waving: Action synchrony and person perception. *Cognition*, 109(1): 152–6.

Madison, G. (2012) Let your body be your coach: An experiential-existential perspective on embodied coaching, in E. Van Deurzen and M. Hanaway (eds) *Existential Perspectives on Coaching*. London: Palgrave Macmillan, pp. 117–27.

Mahon, B.Z. and Caramazza, A. (2008) A critical look at the embodied cognition hypothesis and a new proposal for grounding conceptual content. *Journal of Physiology-Paris*, 102(1–3): 59–70.

Marsh, K.L., Richardson, M.J. and Schmidt, R.C. (2009) Social connection through joint action and interpersonal coordination. *Topics in Cognitive Science*, 1(2): 320–39.

McCraty, R. and Rees, A. (2009) The central role of the heart in generating and sustaining positive emotions, in S. Lopez and C.R. Snyder (eds) *Oxford Handbook of Positive Psychology*, 2nd edn. New York: Oxford University Press, pp. 527–36.

McKenna, D.D. and Davis, S.L. (2009) Hidden in plain sight: The active ingredients of executive coaching. *Industrial and Organizational Psychology: Perspectives on Science and Practice*, 2: 244–60.

Merleau-Ponty, M. (2002) *Phenomenology of Perception: An Introduction*. London: Routledge Classics.

Mezirow, J. (1997) Transformative learning: Theory to practice. *New Directions for Adult and Continuing Education*, 1997(74): 5–12.

Molyn, J., de Haan, E., Stride, C. and Gray, D. (2019) A longitudinal randomized controlled trial into coaching effectiveness: The contribution of common factors to coaching effectiveness applying the lessons from psychotherapy outcome research. Paper presented at Harvard Medical School Coaching in Leadership and Healthcare Conference, 28–29 September 2018, Boston, MA, USA.

Molyn, J. and Gray, D.E. (2019) Coaching and students' resilience. Unpublished.

Moreau, P.-A., Toninelli, E., Gregory, T and Padgett, M.J. (2019) Imaging with quantum states of light. *Nature Review Physics*, 1: 367–80.

Nolen-Hoeksema, S. and Morrow, J. (1991) A prospective study of depression and post traumatic stress symptoms after a natural disaster: The 1989 Loma Prieta earthquake. *Journal of Personality and Social Psychology*, 61(1): 115–21.

Nordham, C.A., Tognoli, E., Fuchs, A. and Kelso, J.A.S. (2018) How interpersonal coordination affects individual behaviour (and vice versa): Experimental analysis and adaptive HKB model of social memory. *Ecological Psychology*, 30(3): 224–49.

Oliveira, H. and Melo, L. (2015) Huygens synchronization of two clocks. *Scientific Reports*, 5: 11548.

Orenstein, R.L. (2002) Executive coaching: It's not just about the executive. *Journal of Applied Behavioural Science*, 38(3): 355–74.

Oullier, O., de Guzman, G.C., Jantzen, K.J. et al. (2008) Social coordination dynamics: Measuring human bonding. *Social Neuroscience*, 3(2): 178–92.

Paulick, J., Deisenhofer, A.-K., Ramseyer, F. et al. (2018) Nonverbal synchrony: A new approach to better understand psychotherapeutic processes and drop-out. *Journal of Psychotherapy Integration*, 28(3): 367–84.

Peltier, B. (2010) *The Psychology of Executive Coaching: Theory and Application*, 2nd edn. Abingdon: Routledge.

Peña Ramirez, J., Olvera, L., Nijmeijer, H. and Alvarez, J. (2016) The sympathy of two pendulum clocks: Beyond Huygens' observations. *Scientific Reports*, 6: 1–16.

Pert, C.B. (1997) *Molecules of Emotions: Why You Feel the Way You Feel*. London: Simon and Schuster.

Peterson, D.B. (2006) People are complex and the world is messy: A behaviour-based approach to executive coaching, in D.R. Stober and A.M. Grant (eds) *Evidence-based Coaching Handbook: Putting Best Practices to Work for Your Clients*. Hoboken, NJ: Wiley, pp. 51–76.

Pfeifer, R. and Bongard, J.C. (2007) *How the Body Shapes the Way We Think: A New View of Intelligence*. Cambridge, MA: MIT Press.

Pinel, E.C., Bernecker, S.L. and Rampy, N.M. (2015) I-sharing on the couch: On the clinical implications of shared subjective experience. *Journal of Psychotherapy Integration*, 25(2): 59.

Prochaska, J.O. and Norcross, J.C. (2018) *Systems of Psychotherapy: A Transtheoretical Analysis*. Oxford: Oxford University Press.

Prywes, Y. (2012). Examining the influence of goal attainment scaling on changes in goal attainment in a coaching versus non-coaching context. PhD Thesis. Columbia University.

Ramseyer, F. (2010) Non-verbale Synchronisation in der Psychotherapie. *Systeme*, 24(1): 5–30.

Ramseyer, F.T. (2020a) Motion Energy Analysis (MEA). A primer on the assessment of motion from video. *Journal of Counseling Psychology*, 67(4): 536–50.

Ramseyer, F.T. (2020b) Exploring the evolution of non-verbal synchrony in psychotherapy: The idiographic perspective provides a different picture. *Psychotherapy Research*, 30(5),: 622–34.

Ramseyer, F. and Tschacher, W. (2006) Synchrony: A core concept for a constructivist approach to psychotherapy. *Constructivism in the Human Sciences*, 11(1–2): 150–71.

Ramseyer, F. and Tschacher, W. (2011) Non-verbal synchrony in psychotherapy: Coordinated body-movement reflects relationship quality and outcome. *Journal of Consulting and Clinical Psychology*, 79(3): 284–95.

Ramseyer, F. and Tschacher, W. (2016) Movement coordination in psychotherapy: Synchrony of hand movements is associated with session outcome. A single-case study. *Nonlinear Dynamics, Psychology, and Life Sciences*, 20(2): 145–66.

Reed, R.G., Barnard, K. and Butler, E.A. (2015) Distinguishing emotional coregulation from codysregulation: An investigation of emotional dynamics and body weight in romantic couples. *Emotion*, 15(1): 45–60.

Rees, J. and Manea, A.I. (2016) The use of clean language and metaphor in helping clients overcoming procrastination. *Journal of Experiential Psychotherapy*. 19(3): 30–6.

Reich C.M., Berman J.S., Dale R. and Levitt H.M. (2014) Vocal synchrony in psychotherapy. *Journal of Social Clinical Psychology*, 33(48).

Reich, W. (1972) *Character Analysis*, 3rd edn. New York: Guildford Press.

Riemann, F. (1961) *Grundformen der Angst*. München: Reinhardt.

Röhricht, F., Gallagher, S., Geuter, U. and Hutto, D.D. (2014) Embodied cognition and body psychotherapy: The construction of new psychotherapeutic environments. *Sensoria: A Journal of Mind, Brain, and Culture*, 56(1): 11–20.

Sandler, C. (2011) *Executive Coaching*. Maidenhead: Open University Press.

Scharmer, O. (2008) *Theory U: Leading from the Future as It Emerges*. San Francisco, CA: Berrett-Koehler Publishers.

Schein, E. (2006) *Organisationskultur – The Ed Schein Corporate Culture Survival Guide*. Bergisch Gladbach: EHP.

Schön, D. (1983) *The Reflective Practitioner: How Professionals Think in Action*. New York: Basic Books.

Searle, J.R. (2004) *Mind: A Brief Introduction*. Oxford: Oxford University Press.

Sherrington, C.S. (1906) *The Integrative Action of the Nervous System*. New Haven, CT: Yale University Press.

Sieler, A. (2010) Ontological coaching, in E. Cox, T. Bachkirova and D. Clutterbuck (eds), *The Complete Handbook of Coaching*. London: SAGE Publications, pp. 107–19.

Silsbee, D. (2008) *Presence-based Coaching: Cultivating Self-Generative Leaders Through Mind, Body, and Heart*. Hoboken: NJ: John Wiley & Sons.

Sirois, F.M. (2015) A self-regulation resource model of self-compassion and health behaviour intentions in emerging adults. *Preventive Medicine Reports*, 2: 218–22.

Smith, E.R. (2008) An embodied account of self-other 'overlap' and its effects, in G.R. Semin, and E.R. Smith (eds) *Embodied Grounding: Social, Cognitive, Affective, and Neuroscientific Approaches*. New York: Cambridge University Press, pp. 148–59.

Solomon, R.C. (1972) *From Rationalism to Existentialism: The Existentialists and Their Nineteenth-Century Backgrounds*. Lanham, MD: Littlefield Adams Quality Paperbacks.

Soth, M. (2010) The return of the repressed body: Not a smooth affair. *The Psychotherapist*, 47: 19–21.

Spence, G.B. (2007) GAS powered coaching: Goal Attainment Scaling and its use in coaching research and practice. *International Coaching Psychology Review*, 2: 155–67.

Spence, G.B., Cavanagh, M.J. and Grant, A.M. (2008) The integration of mindfulness training and health coaching: An exploratory study. *Coaching: An International Journal of Theory, Research and Practice*, 1(2): 145–63.

Spence, G.B. and Oades, L.G. (2011) Coaching with self-determination theory in mind: Using theory to advance evidence-based coaching practice. *International Journal of Evidence-Based Coaching and Mentoring*, 9(2): 37–55.

Stacey, R.D. (2011) *Strategic Management and Organisational Dynamics: The Challenge of Complexity*, 6th edn. Harlow: Pearson.

Stephens, G., Silbert, L.J. and Hasson, U. (2010) Speaker–listener neural coupling underlies successful communication. *Proceedings of the National Academy of Sciences*, 107: 14425–30.

Stevens, L. (2009) Understanding how students learn: Preparing students to become professionals. *Perspectives on Issues in Higher Education* 12(1): 16–23.

Stoneham, D. (2009) Changing practices, transforming paradigms: An appreciative approach to developing integral leaders. PhD Thesis. California Institute of Integral Studies.

Strean, W.B. and Strozzi-Heckler, R. (2009) (The) body (of) knowledge: Somatic contributions to the practice of sport psychology. *Journal of Applied Sport Psychology*, 21(1): 91–8.

Strozzi-Heckler, R. (2014) *The Art of Somatic Coaching: Embodying Skillful Action, Wisdom, and Compassion*. California: North Atlantic Books.

Sturt, A., Ali, S., Robertson, W. et al. (2012) Neurolinguistic programming: A systematic review of the effects on health outcomes. *British Journal of General Practice*, 63(604): e757–64.

Tallis, R. (2011) *Aping Mankind: Neuromania, Darwinitis and the Misrepresentation of Humanity*. Durham, UK: Acumen Publishing Ltd.

Theeboom, T., Vianen, A.E.M.V. and Beersma, B. (2017) A temporal map of coaching. *Frontiers in Psychology*, 8: 1352.

Timmons, A.C., Margolin, G. and Saxbe, D.E. (2015) Physiological linkage in couples and its implications for individual and interpersonal functioning: A literature review. *Journal of Family Psychology*, 29(5): 720–31.

Tolle, E. (1999) *The Power of Now*. Novato, California: New World Library.

Tosey, P. and Mathison, J. (2007) Fabulous creatures of HRD: A critical natural history of neuro-linguistic programming. Paper presented at 8th International Conference on Human Resource Development Research and Practice across Europe, Oxford Brookes Business School, 26–28 June 2007.

Tronick, E.Z. (1989) Emotions and emotional communication in infants. *American Psychologist*, 44(2): 112–19.

Tschacher, W., Rees, G.M. and Ramseyer, F. (2014) Non-verbal synchrony and affect in dyadic interactions. *Frontiers in Psychology*, 5: 1323.

Turner, E. (2010) Coaches' views on the relevance of unconscious dynamics to executive coaching. *Coaching: An International Journal of Theory, Research and Practice*, 3(1): 12–29.

Turner, E., and Passmore, J. (2018) Ethical dilemmas and tricky decisions: A global perspective of coaching supervisors' practices in coach ethical decision-making. *International Journal of Evidenced Based Coaching and Mentoring*, 16(1): 126–42.

Vacharkulksemsuk, T. and Fredrickson, B.L. (2013) Looking back and glimpsing forward: The broaden-and-build theory of positive emotions as applied to organizations, in A. B Bakker (ed.) *Advances in Positive Organizational Psychology*, vol 1. Bradford, UK: Emerald Group Publishing, pp. 45–60.

Valdesolo, P., Ouyang, J. and DeSteno, D. (2010) The rhythm of joint action: Synchrony promotes cooperative ability. *Journal of Experimental Social Psychology*, 46(4): 693–95.

van Dijk, H., Schoffelen, J.M., Oostenveld, R. and Jensen, O. (2008) Prestimulus oscillatory activity in the alpha band predicts visual discrimination ability. *Journal of Neuroscience*, 28(8): 1816–23.

Varlet, M., Marin, L., Capdevielle, D. et al. (2014) Difficulty leading interpersonal coordination: Towards an embodied signature of social anxiety disorder. *Frontiers in Behavioral Neuroscience*, 8: 29.

References 153

Waskul, D. and Vannini, P. (2006) *Body/Embodiment: Symbolic Interaction and the Sociology of the Body*. Aldershot: Ashgate Publishing.

Watson, D., Clark, L.A. and Tellegen, A. (1988) Development and validation of brief measures of positive and negative affect: the PANAS scales. *Journal of Personality and Social Psychology*, 54(6): 1063–70.

Watzlawick, P. (1983) *The Situation Is Hopeless But Not Serious. The Pursuit of Unhappiness*. New York: W.W. Norton & Company.

Watzlawick, P., Beavin, J.H. and Jackson, D.D. (1967) *Pragmatics of Human Communication*. New. York: W.W. Norton & Company.

Wegner, D.M., Erber, R. and Zanakos, S. (1993) Ironic processes in the mental control of mood and mood-related thought. *Journal of Personality and Social Psychology*, 65(6): 1093–104.

Weizmann Institute of Science. (1988) Quantum theory demonstrated: observation affects reality. *ScienceDaily*. www.sciencedaily.com/releases/1998/02/980227055013.htm. check

Western, S. (2012) *Coaching and Mentoring: A Critical Text*. London: SAGE Publications.

Wheatley, T., Kang, O., Parkinson, C. and Looser, C.E. (2012) From mind perception to mental connection: Synchrony as a mechanism for social understanding. *Social and Personality Psychology Compass*, 6(8): 589–606.

Whittington, J. (2012) *Systemic Coaching and Constellations: An Introduction to the Principles, Practices and Application*. London: Kogan Page.

Whitworth, L., Kimsey-House, K., Kimsey-House, H. and Sandahl, P. (2007) *Co-active Coaching: New Skills for Coaching People Toward Success in Work and Life*. Mountain View, CA: Davies-Black Publishing.

Wilber, K. (2000) *Integral Psychology: Consciousness, Spirit, Psychology, Therapy*. Boulder, CO: Shambhala Publications.

Wilber, K. (2006) *Integral Spirituality*. Boulder, CO: Shambhala Publications.

Wilber, K. (2007) *A Brief History of Everything*. Boulder, CO: Shambhala Publications.

Wiltshire, T.J., Philipsen, J.S., Trasmundi, S.B. et al. (2020) Interpersonal coordination dynamics in psychotherapy: A systematic review. *Cognitive Therapy and Research*, 44: 752–73.

Wiltshire, T.J., Steffensen, S.V. and Fiore, S.M. (2018) Multiscale movement coordination dynamics in collaborative team problem solving. *Applied Ergonomics*, 79: 143–51.

Yang W.D. (2007) Realizations of turn-taking in conversational interactions. *U.S. China Foreign Language*, 5: 19–30.

Zhan, M. and de Gelder, B. (2019) Unconscious fearful body perception enhances discrimination of conscious anger expressions under continuous flash suppression. *Neuropsychologia*, 128: 325–31.

Index

adaptation 28, 138
  lasting 38
adaptive systems theory 57, 58, 116
affect 20
  balance 37, 38
  negative 37
  positive 37, 50
  regulation, 51
ALL-sphere 60, 63, 65, 67, 117, 121, 122, 126, 129, 131
attachment 29, 94
  knowing 140
  needs 61
  theory 93
attunement 17, 18, 28, 30
authenticity
  being fully present 22
  inauthenticity 22
  leadership 30
  presence, instrument 21
autonomous
  becoming 50, 54, 121, 123
  presence 32
autonomy
  becoming aware 64
  build up 120
  lack of 120
  leadership 130
  mistrust 120
awareness
  building 70, 127
  holistic 74
  in leadership 115, 140
  inner space 24
  intuitive 23
  lack of 25
  mental 24, 78, 81, 131
  of needs 32
  of strengths, weaknesses 101
  social 4, 66
  somatic 16, 20, 40

balance
  accelerating change 63
  daring and caring 95
  needs 98, 110
  Somatic Thinking 79
  synchrony, emotional 38
  tolerate ambiguity 113
being
  connected 59, 92, 135
  in the world 22, 53, 73
  in-sync 88, 131
  present 22, 65, 72
  seen 89, 123
  state of presence 75, 76
  responsive 61
  with clients 44
belong
  right to 128
belonging
  sense of 68, 92
body
  practice 20
body language 17, 23, 98
bonding 31, 42, 48, 49, 50, 53, 54
bored-teenager-effect 50
breathing
  practice 23, 24
Buonarotti
  Michelangelo 113

CAS 57, 116
  alternative perspective 57
  coach-client relationship 58
  complex adaptive systems 57, 116
  complex entities 58
centring 11, 20, 62
change
  affective, cognitive, behavioral 18, 38, 43
  complexity 52, 59, 126, 132, 137
  self-directed 36
change process
  coaching 36, 41, 47, 52,
  dynamic interplay 50, 59, 60,
  leadership 129
  meta-synthesis 42, 52,
  socially constructed 59
clean language 18, 19
client factors 59, 121

Index

coach-client relationship
  interpersonal factor 52
  link, synchrony 20, 30, 42, 44, 49, 61, 132
coaching
  accountability 3, 66
  context-sensitive 59
  definition 14, 15, 60
  development process 14, 17, 32, 36, 45, 60, 62
  echo of 60, 131
  effectiveness 24, 31, 33, 61, 62, 71, 93, 112, 115, 120, 122
  emerging moment 76, 94, 125
  ethical 4, 23, 64
  existential-experiential 20
  integral 17, 18, 19, 59, 61, 67, 125
  leadership 19, 20, 86, 115, 116, 124, 126
  outcomes 42, 52, 53, 87, 99, 100, 121
  presence-based 20, 57, 61
  self-cultivation, 16
  sports 58
  systemic 19, 121
coaching presence
  defining 14, 28, 36, 60
coaching relationship
  bonding, impact 31, 42, 48, 49, 50, 53, 54
  dynamics 20, 21, 31, 32, 68, 72, 120
  goal attainment 44, 48, 49, 93
  here and now 21, 23, 32, 33
  impact, non-verbal responsiveness 11, 31, 32, 52
  self-regulation 37, 38, 42, 50, 52
  use of self 20
co-create
  beyond goals 76
  complexity 125
  conversations 20
  drama 125
  presence, leadership 124, 125, 130
cognition
  embodied 120
cognitive
  system, in presence 23
coherence
  heart 23
  implication 23, 134
  physiological 23
collaboration
  collaborative tasks 49
  interaction 76
  synchrony 77

community
  safe allure 73
  self-sustained 138
complexity
  change conflict 125, 132
  co-created 125
  focus of 59, 125
  navigating 130, 139
  of coaching 59, 92, 125
confidence
  low presence 119, 120
conflict
  change moments 125, 129, 130
  interpersonal, intrapersonal 1, 58
connectedness
  energies 135
  essence of 70
connection
  in the moment 95, 108, 129
coordination
  movements, body 28, 29, 31, 42
  mutual 42
correctional mechanism 48, 49
counter-transference
  coaching research 20
  co-dependency 87
  responsiveness 120, 128
  use of self, self as tool 21
coupling
  as synchrony 20
  inter-brain 42, 43
  measurement 27
  mutual coordination 42
  neural 42
  weak 50
critical moment
  coaching 11
  experience 11, 107, 111
cultivate
  self 24
curiosity
  becoming 25
  change 129
  cultivate 129
  enquire with 25
  experiment with 78, 113
  of coach 91, 92
  presence, openness 25, 36

dancing in the moment 28, 31, 85
Deep Blue 16

156   Index

defence
  mechanism 105
deficits
  information 128
denial 135, 137, 138
  perspective 137
Descarte
  René 16
detachment
  disconnection 136
  emotional 120
  escapism 136
  from lived experience 21
  fully detached 32
  professional 32, 121
development
  cycle, transformation 68
  leadership 115, 116
  six lines of 59
discovery
  journey, transformation 62
disembodied 22
disruption
  co-creating 128, 130
  coping with, coaching 76
  predictability 124, 126, 130
distress 17, 29, 95
  lack of presence 95
duality 132, 133, 134
dynamics
  integrative presence 64, 70
  interpersonal, intrapersonal 38
  of needs 32
  of presence 5, 72
  of reciprocity, 120
  relational 68
  social, human 44, 64
  theory 44
  unconscious 20, 87
dysregulation 38

effortless
  dynamics 30
  physicality 118
  quality, synchrony 30
  responsiveness 118, 140
Einstein
  Albert 14, 62
embodied
  exercises 22, 23, 62
  experience 120, 122
  interaction 22, 62, 126
  metaphors 18
  mind 15, 16, 74, 125
  phenomenology 22, 74
  self 17
  style 116, 125
embodiment 22, 80,
emotional contagion 31, 32, 121
emotions
  alignment 23
  definition 37
  ego 106, 108
  express 37, 79, 104, 106, 136
  in coaching, 54
  negative, stress 23, 29, 37, 79
  sharing 21, 43, 105,
  understanding 95, 96
empathy 26, 28, 110, 120
energy
  analysis 33, 42, 45, 58, 76
  block 17, 120, 121
  bounded 134
  co-created 62
  emergent phenomenon 61
  exchange 70, 71, 72, 110
  integrating all spheres 60, 61, 131
  masculine, feminine 120
  measuring 61, 69, 108, 131
  motion 33, 42, 45, 58, 69, 76, 119
  non-dual 60, 131
  non-verbal 14, 33, 60, 69, 76, 89, 118, 120
  physicality 118
  physics 17, 62
  shift 107, 110
  sourcing 69, 110, 133, 139
  tangible 131
  unfolding 62, 70, 132
enquiry
  reflective 2, 12, 15
environment
  ALL-sphere, 63, 122
  co-create 130
  complex 19, 125, 130
  distal 122
  Integrative Presence 62, 63
  leadership 126, 130
  presence, setting 122
  proximal 121, 130
  WE-sphere 63, 70, 122
escapism 63, 136

Index **157**

eudaimonia 112
evidence base
  presence 3, 4, 7, 14, 15, 18, 23, 27, 52, 57, 64
experience
  somatic 19, 21, 62, 73, 74
  Experience Shapers 78, 79, 80, 81, 82, 139
Exploity 78, 79, 80, 82, 132

factors
  contextual 50, 52, 54, 59, 121
feedback
  fearless 129
  interviews 119, 120
  relational 2, 12, 44, 69, 92
felt experience
  attention to 76, 94, 112, 132
  in organizations 129
  integral coaching 20, 59, 61
  meaning making 37, 73, 76, 132, 135
  self-regulate 33, 36, 39
  sharing 33, 39, 94, 103, 104
fight
  perspective 137, 138
flexibility 66, 67, 118, 121
flow
  emotional, psychological 17
  energy 14, 17, 108
  heart intelligence 23
  interacting with biases 138
  of awareness 23, 24
  of behavior, synchrony 30
  reversing 138
  tensions 17
focusing
  embodied 15
foreshadowing 136, 137
future
  unfolding 70

Gestalt 19, 20, 74
goal attainment
  beyond 49, 53, 76, 115
  completion of coaching 48
  in coaching presence 30, 32, 36, 44, 52, 53, 88, 93
  movement synchrony 30, 36, 38, 44, 45, 48, 49, 52, 53, 140
  self-directed 36, 38, 44, 45, 46, 53
  self-regulation 36, 38, 48, 52, 53
  without relapse 36

goal-reflection
  levels of 50
  presence research 48, 50, 52
Grandma Wise 79, 80, 81, 82, 132, 133, 140
Grove
  David 18

Harvard
  Medical School 29
HeartMath 23, 24
Heidegger
  Martin 22
here and now
  coaching session 17, 18, 32, 33
  experience 16, 18, 21, 32, 33, 36, 78, 79, 132, 136
heritage
  biological 16
HIC
  human interaction cycle 74
human
  being, authentic 21, 22, 32, 71
  being, machine 110
  being, somatic response 21
  being, transpersonal system 17
human being
  role as coach 31, 61, 78, 85, 107
  Somatic Thinking 68, 71, 73, 78, 139
humanity
  authentic human 71
  awareness in coaching 16
  interconectedness 135
Huygens
  Christiaan 27

ICF 21
  definition presence 11, 28
idiographic 48
impact
  of presence 4, 18, 42, 58, 67, 69, 72, 108, 118, 122, 128,
  of responsiveness 10, 33, 67, 69. 118, 128
  systemic 121
in the moment
  dancing 11, 28, 31, 86
  peace 132
  stillness 24, 70
incongruence 10
information
  sensory 73, 74, 75, 80, 81, 82, 140

158 Index

in-sync
  phenomenon 27
In-Sync Model 42, 43, 53
integral theory
  coaching 17, 57, 59, 61, 125
integrate
  presence spheres 60, 121
Integrative Presence pp. 81 - 104
  awareness of dynamics 70
  coaching for 62
  concepts of 117, 123
  defining 60
  leadership 115, 116, 125, 126, 127, 128, 129
  legacy 69, 64, 71
  metaphor 57, 60, 62
  methodology 57, 59, 62, 70
  philosophy 57, 59, 70
  social responsibility 64, 65, 115, 117
  Somatic Thinking 71, 77, 117
  synchrony 61, 71, 140
intelligence
  artificial 16
  conversational 19, 20
  heart 23
  spiritual 25
interaction
  audio/video 140
  body, physicality 74, 118
  dynamic conversations 27, 30
  emergent reciprocal 29, 60, 61
  focused development 14
  interpersonal 29, 60, 61
  leader-led 125, 129
  moment-by-moment 37
  non-verbal 33, 53, 60, 76, 98
  quantum physics 62
  real-time 80
  social 50, 58, 140
  synchrony 29, 30, 37, 50, 53, 61, 62, 140
interconnectedness
  complexity 5, 135
interdependence
  energy 62
  self-regulation 52
interoception 34, 40, 46, 53
interpersonal
  factor 43, 52,
  phenomenon 38, 43
intuition 108, 119

I-sphere
  energy 60, 118,
  Integrative Presence 60, 63, 65, 77, 117, 121, 126, 129
  leadership 126, 129

knowledge
  empirical body of 14

language
  body 17, 23, 98
  verbal 23
leadership
  agile 125
  facting 60, 124, 125, 127, 128
  presence-based 139
  somatic 19, 139
learning
  integral 59
  integrative 36, 117
  process dynamic 49, 50
  transformative 36
legacy
  presence spheres 60, 64
Leonard
  George 112
Little Prince 69
lived experiences 19, 21, 28, 83

mastery
  coaching 9, 24, 25, 26, 55, 83
maturity
  professional 3, 12
MEA 42, 88
meaning making
  embodied experiences 18, 74
  of connectedness 135
  of endings 70
  of identiy 74, 78
  of processes 119, 132
  of unknown 70, 138
  Somatic Thinking 68, 71, 72, 73, 74, 76, 77, 78, 132, 139
memory
  muscle 132, 137
metaphor 18, 60, 62, 107, 133
mime effect 50
mindfulness
  becoming present 25
  meditation 24

mirroring 23
model
  WHO 68
mood
  in the body 17
  measuring 37
  presence 17, 94, 118
  leadership presence 125
  regulate affect 37
movement
  body, presence 20, 23, 28, 29, 30, 31, 38, 53, 61, 63, 67, 68
  coordination of 28, 29, 31
  empathy 28
  random 34, 40, 45, 46
movement synchrony
  authentic responses 30, 32
  balancing emotions 37, 38
  definition 28
  energy 33, 37, 61, 71
  feeling understood 30
  goal attainment 30, 36, 44, 48, 49. 140
  monitoring thoughts 37
  process 34, 36, 38, 40, 46, 54, 140
  ripple effect 53, 62, 140
  self-directed goals 36, 38, 44, 45, 46, 53
  self-regulation 35, 36, 37, 38, 41, 42, 43, 47, 48, 50, 52, 53
  working alliance 42, 43, 48, 49, 50, 51, 52, 53, 54
Mr Control 78, 79, 80, 82, 132
Multple Perspective Model 121

needs
  acknowledge 61
  attached to meeting 61
  awareness of 32, 88
  basic 26, 68, 93
  faceting 124
  emerging 39
  impact on responsiveness 32, 33, 118
  in leadership 116, 126
  meeting 32
  missing 76, 97
  priority 102
  responsiveness 32, 33, 39, 61, 63, 69, 94, 118, 119, 120
  role of 61
  sharing 43, 86, 88, 94, 119, 121
  tease apart 31

network analysis 48, 50, 52
Newton
  Isaac 71, 72
NLP 23, 97
noise
  cognitive bias 122
nomothetic 48
non-verbal
  interact, effort 29, 30, 140
  response 14, 28, 31, 32, 99, 120
  signals 61, 140
not knowing 70, 119, 139

OMNI-sphere
  biological nature 67
  dynamics 64, 68, 70
  ethics 64, 65
  Integrative Presence 60, 63, 64, 65, 67, 69, 70, 121, 126
  leadership 126, 130
  psychological nature 64, 68
  social, human 64, 65, 67
  spiritual nature 64, 69
open heart 25, 104
open mind 25, 104
open will 25
outcomes
  unexpected 4, 52
over-confidence
  low presence 119, 120

Pasteur
  Louis 109
patterns
  habitual 19
perception
  body shapes 16
  differences of 127
  emotion 16, 59, 106, 108
  heart as organ 26
  in synchrony 30, 77, 81
  interaction link 30
  meaning making 75, 76, 78, 100
  motor movement 30
  sensation, cognition 59
  somatosensory 77
  visual 24
perceptiveness
  level of 111
  somatosensory 40

Index

perspectives
  temporal 78
power
  of negative thinking 123
practice
  evidence-based 1
  fundamentalist 3
  future coaching 115, 118
  integral presence 19, 20, 59, 67
  memory muscle 132, 137
practice points 128
presence
  adaptation 28, 38, 138
  purposeful 60, 72, 73
  coach-focused 44
  coaching, effectiveness 7, 31, 61, 62, 71, 76, 116, 119, 120, 122, 123, 128, 140
  concepts of 3, 5, 14, 26, 69, 117, 123
  core competence 4, 7, 11
  cultivating self 24
  dancing 11, 28, 85
  direction in research 52, 109
  dynamics of 5, 31, 64, 72, 108, 138
  embodying 63, 77
  emerging 2, 36, 58, 76, 125, 131
  essence of 11, 24, 26, 60, 69, 70, 89, 115, 116, 122, 128, 140
  four-step process 77
  future of 115, 118, 123
  impact of 3, 4, 7, 17, 18, 37, 58, 65, 69, 72, 118
  investigate 18, 23, 30, 62, 110, 111
  lack of 33, 61, 69, 75, 87, 98, 113, 118, 121, 128
  landscape of 14, 15, 21
  leadership 115, 124, 125, 126, 127, 130, 139
  mastery 24, 25
  meaning making 14, 20, 37, 55, 57, 70, 74, 75, 76, 83, 119, 132
  model 55
  myths 13, 14, 15, 21, 26, 72
  partnering process 3, 31
  practice methods 20
  realities 14, 15, 26, 72
  role for effectiveness 31, 61, 115
  skills 83, 120
  socially constructed 59
  somatic nature 59, 62, 76
  spiritual nature 24, 26, 59, 64, 69
  spontaneous capacity 39, 53, 63, 69, 86, 118
  transformation 67, 92, 138
  two-party realities 128
presencing 25
professional proximity 95, 96, 121
psychotherapy
  emotion regulation 42, 43, 53
  influence 20, 43
  research, synchrony 29, 42, 43, 49, 53
  working alliance 42, 43, 49, 53

quantum entanglement 62
questioning
  deep listening 25, 26
  judgement 26, 98, 110
  powerful 25, 26

reactivity 29
reciprocity
  coach-client relationship 29, 31, 120, 131
  coordination 29, 31
  dynamics, of 120
  emotional contagion 31, 121
  impact, of 131
  presence 30, 31, 120
  responsiveness 29, 30, 31
  synchrony 29, 30, 31, 131
receptivity
  environmental 29
reflection-in action 36
reflection-on-action 36
refocusing 36
rehearsing 19, 22
relational
  field 21
  pattern 61, 68
  presence 2, 21, 31, 36, 44, 57, 60, 68, 69, 92
  sharing 21, 121
relationship
  coach-client, needs 20, 31, 32, 61, 68, 70, 86, 110, 118, 120
  coach-client, outcomes 41, 42, 52, 53
  coach-client, partnering 31, 68
  coach-client, quality 30, 31, 41, 49, 53, 103, 118

coach-client, reciprocal 31, 61, 140
coach-client, research 2, 21, 30, 31, 32, 52, 58, 59, 60, 61, 67, 68
non-verbal 11, 20, 30, 53
research
  developmental 29, 38
  feedback-driven 3
resilience
  build up 130
response
  absence of 130
  habitual 19
  needs, sensitive 29
responses
  authentic 21, 30
  emotional 19, 38, 42, 53
  physical 10, 21, 33, 58, 118, 120
  visceral 126
responsiveness
  leaders 125, 126, 128, 129, 137, 140
  non-verbal 10, 11, 12, 28, 29, 30, 31, 33, 35, 52, 61, 67, 69, 86, 98, 118
  perceiving 128, 133
  presence, spontaneous 11, 28, 30, 31, 39, 52, 61, 63, 69, 86, 94, 118, 125, 126, 140
  to what, whom 31
  trusted source 29
ripple effect 11, 38, 53, 61, 62, 121, 134, 140
risk-taking 93, 121, 122

safe
  psychologically 30, 68, 69
  unsafe 33, 61, 98, 131
safety
  establishing 63
Saint-Exupéry
  Antoine 69
self
  dual 60
  echo of 60, 131, 135
  embodied 16, 17, 22, 122
  inner 24, 108, 110
  non-dual 60, 97, 131
  non-quantum reality 60
  spirit 69
  unspoken 10, 27, 118
  whole 16, 60

self-acceptance 110
self-as-tool 21
self-awareness 24, 113
self-cultivation 16
self-directed 36, 38, 44, 45, 46, 50, 53
self-enquiry 15, 92
self-knowledge 25
self-other 29
self-reflection
  measuring 37
  result-oriented 36
self-reflective
  mastery 25
self-regulation
  affective 36, 38, 43
  capacity 36, 37, 38, 42, 53, 95
  cognitive 36, 37, 48, 50, 51, 54
  co-regulation 38
  emotional 36, 37, 38, 42, 48, 50, 52, 53, 54, 95
  integrating in presence 36
self-regulatory
  cycle 36
  resources 38, 53
  theory 43, 52
self-respect 66
self-worth 63, 68, 133, 134
  conditioned 134
  doubt 134
  echo of 134
  perception 107
  purpose 133
  source 63, 68, 133
sensations
  express 79, 88
  meaning making 20, 57, 78
  unfolding 91
sense
  globally 76, 122
sensing
  disruption of 76
  interoception 34
  quality, receptivity 121
  sharing, coaching 33, 39, 52, 99, 119, 121
  Theory U 25
  WHO model 68
serendipity 109, 111, 112, 113
Sherrington
  Charles 34

skills
  self-regulation 38
  sensory motor 16
Snow-White Phenomenon 2, 119
somatic
  origin 73
Somatic Thinking 4, 68, 71, 72, 73, 74, 76, 77, 78, 117, 132, 139
spirituality
  science of 4, 67
spontaneous responsiveness
  confidence levels 118
  impact of needs 32, 33, 69, 94, 118
  interoception 53
  I-sphere 63, 118, 126, 129
  measuring 28
  thinking, impact 86
  unknown 140
SRRM 37
states
  emotional, psychological 17
stillness
  enforced 24
  inner 24, 69, 70
stimuli
  Exploity 78, 70, 80
  external 63, 78
  Integrative Presence 62, 63, 77
  internal, body 63
  perceiving 73, 78, 79, 80
  physical 63, 73, 78, 79, 80, 81, 133
stress 17, 23, 24, 29, 94, 95, 97
success
  relational 20, 69, 128
symbolic modelling 18, 19
synchrony
  anti-phase 27, 28
  goal attainment 30, 32, 36, 38, 44, 45, 48, 49, 51, 52, 53, 140
  in-phase 27, 28, 131
  working alliance 42, 43, 48, 49, 50, 51, 52, 53, 54

task agreement 31
task setting 42, 49, 50, 51, 53, 54
The Matryoshka 5, 55, 69, 132
transactional analysis
  TA 68
transformation
  biological 67
  cycle of life 138
  physical 67
Tronick
  Ted 29
trust
  ALL-sphere 63
  bonding 29, 31, 53
  coach-client relationship 30, 31, 32, 52, 53, 63, 104, 120
  conversational intelligence 19, 20
  inner knowing 120
  leadership 30, 115, 125, 130
  pre-frontal cortex 19
  safety, connectedness 32
  time lag 10, 99

uncertainty
  attain presence 95
  Mr Control 78
  normality 95
unconscious
  needs 32, 87
unknown
  controlling 140
  denial 135
  future echo 135
  related ideology 70
  relaxing into 25
  sense of loneliness 135
  unfolding future 70
unpredictability 59, 72, 126, 139
unspoken 2, 10, 11, 27, 118
use of self 20, 65

vulnerability
  client impact 52
  presence 93
  value 93

WBECS 1
Weizmann
  Institute of Science 136
well-being 23, 36, 62, 97
WE-sphere
  Integrative Presence 60, 63, 65, 117, 121, 126, 129, 131
  leadership 126, 129
will power 24
wisdom
  experiential 3, 12, 83, 117
world
  inner and outer 74, 76, 81, 137